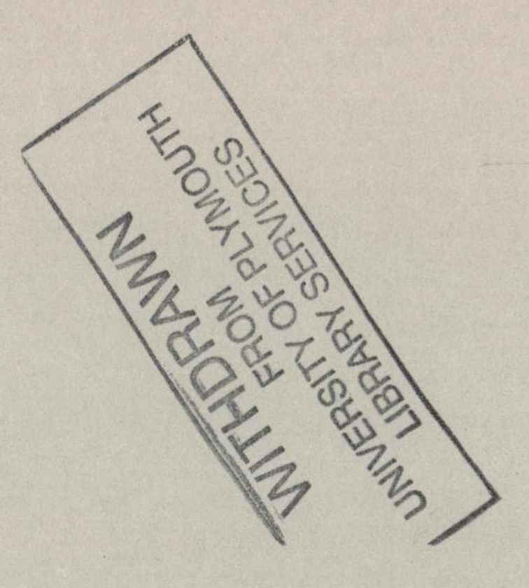
WITHDRAWN
FROM
UNIVERSITY OF PLYMOUTH
LIBRARY SERVICES

KW-468-010

Flexible Production

FLEXIBLE PRODUCTION

Restructuring of the International Automobile Industry

Rebecca Morales

Polity Press

First published in 1994 by Polity Press
in association with Blackwell Publishers

Editorial Office:
Polity Press
65 Bridge Street
Cambridge CB2 1UR, UK

Marketing and production:
Blackwell Publishers
108 Cowley Road
Oxford OX4 1JF, UK

238 Main Street
Cambridge, MA 02142, USA

ISBN 0 7456 0752 7

A CIP catalogue record for this book is available from the British Library and the Library of Congress.

Typeset in 10 on 12pt Palatino
by TecSet Ltd, Wallington, Surrey
Printed in Great Britain by TJ Press (Padstow) Ltd, Cornwall.

This book is printed on acid-free paper.

Contents

Preface

The longer I studied the automobile industry, the more I wondered why my observations did not conform with the traditional literature. This book is an effort to reconcile my reality with theory. It is an exploration into the future of the international political economy through an examination of several recurring themes in which the automobile industry is held constant: the nature of the state in the international political economy; technological innovation as a catalyst for promoting regionalism; and changing North–South relations.

In the past, liberals and neo-Marxists have argued that political intervention in the economy has slowed growth and deterred investment. Since Adam Smith first condemned mercantilist intervention in eighteenth-century Britain, followers of what is now called the neo-classical tradition have held that competitive markets are the best form of exchange. Review of flexible production challenges these neo-classical arguments. The shortening of the product life cycle mandates firms to work in conjunction with the public sector to promote innovation, intra-regional production, and global trade.

Along similar lines, conventional notions of regionalization have tended to focus either on macro-level economic or on political explanations. This study takes us one step further and looks at the techno-industrial foundation of regionalization. And although studies of regionalization have generally overlooked the future of developing nations, this analysis brings the prospects of developing nations into the fore by exploring the basis of technology and intra-regional trade.

It is from this perspective that the book is written. The international automobile industry is studied for the purpose of developing insight into how states and firms are redefining competitiveness. Thus, at one level, this volume can be understood as essentially a case study; on another, it is also a foundation for constructing theory.

Support for this work came from many sources. The National Science Foundation provided a grant for the majority of the fieldwork, for which I am very grateful. Additional support for fieldwork, data collection, analysis, writing, and editing came from the Claremont Graduate School; the University of California at San Diego Center for US–Mexican Studies; the University of California at Los Angeles Academic Senate; the Wissenschaftszentrum Berlin für Sozialforschung; and the Volvo Corporation. I would also like to thank Zoltan Acs, Dave Andrea, Mimi Constantinou, and Carlos Quandt for their insightful observations, along with the many industry personnel, colleagues, friends, and family members whose ideas and good cheer have contributed to this manuscript.

Rebecca Morales
Claremont, California
May 6, 1993

1

Flexibility in an Interdependent World Economy

Signs of Change

Japan's rise to market leader in the international automobile industry within two decades sent multiple signals throughout the world. One was the realization that this extraordinary growth marked the decline of US hegemony and the beginning of a new world order in which Japan occupied a more central position. The second was a more subtle message – that behind this transference of power lay a fundamental shift in the basis to competition. In contrast to the postwar period of US economic hegemony when market dominance could be determined by price, the economic instability of the 1970s and 1980s favored other factors. Sustained market uncertainty forced firms to respond rapidly to changes, while severely disadvantaging those lacking the necessary corporate strategies and organizational structures to behave similarly. Under these conditions, Japanese firms had proven highly responsive to change in contrast to US or European manufacturers. Perhaps even more importantly, the economic conditions also penalized those nations lacking the institutional means to promote economic stability. Japan, with its dense institutional structure, could relatively effectively distribute and minimize the market risks that were endemic to this period. Despite the recessionary setback of the 1990s that stifled worldwide growth, their mechanisms for adjustment remained essentially intact. Thus Japan's emergence as a major economic contender signalled a fundamental change in the way firms and nations could shape economic outcomes.

In the USA this understanding was slow to materialize. Initially, Japan's competitiveness in the automobile industry was thought to lie solely in methods of "lean" production characterized by low inventories; open communication among workers, suppliers, and distributors; and continuous improvement.[1] Numerous studies had shown that US and European auto makers suffered from wasteful and chaotic practices in the design, manufacture, and distribution of automobiles. Yet their efforts to emulate Japanese production practices merely perpetuated a game of constant catch-up. With each market setback, it became increasingly clear that improved manufacturing alone could not transform the underlying conditions giving rise to "best practice".

The limits to a purely manufacturing strategy were perhaps most dramatically revealed in the USA during the 1980s. US auto makers invested $6 billion in the development, engineering, plants, and equipment for mini-vans between 1980 and 1990, and $3 billion in mid-sized cars. Further, they adopted methods of perceived best practice. Despite this extraordinary level of investment, they suffered not only a 45 per cent drop in overall profits between 1988 and 1990, but severe erosion of the mid-sized car market. Although mini-vans continued to produce a positive cash flow, it was feared that the market lead could still be lost. Successful penetration of the luxury car line had already proven devastingly effective when Honda introduced the Acura, to be followed by Toyota (Lexus), Nissan (Infiniti), and Mitsubishi (Diamante). The inability of American firms to stem the slide of the mid-sized car market after years of new investment and reorganization suggested that the core of the problem extended well beyond methods of manufacturing.[2]

This impression was revealed in the Structural Impediments Initiative (SII), discussions held during the early 1990s aimed at resolving the huge US–Japanese trade imbalance that was due largely to imported autos and parts. An expressed concern was that the domestic structure of Japanese industry, in itself, created an "unfair" advantage. It was argued that the problem lay in financially linked groups of companies known as *keiretsus* that allegedly violated US antitrust law. These industrial alliance groups, by definition, gave priority to member firms identified through cross-sharing ownership and purchasing arrangements. The structure encourages the sharing of knowledge and risks among firms and governmental entities. Though consistent with Japanese law and custom, such alliances were illegal in the USA. During the SII discussions, when US trade negotiators had hoped to change the *keiretsu* structure, they instead learned how committed Japan was to this system for organizing industrial production that had proven successful worldwide. Masaru Yoshitomi, director of the Japanese government's Economic Research Center, was reported to have said: "your large companies bring diseconomies of scale, while Japan's *keiretsus* allow flexibility and long-range investment ... you Americans should not be closed to Japanese ideas or you risk fading competitively, as the Europeans faded before American prowess early this century."[3] Through such exchanges it became clear that significant, if not irresolvable, differences lay in their interpretations of industrial organization. It further appeared that underlying the success of Japanese manufacturers and their eclipse of US and European producers in world markets was an ideological break in concepts fundamental to defining markets. It was these deeper issues that lay at the core of the SII conflict.

The realization that the basis to competitiveness in the international economy had changed spawned a generation of studies on industry structure and strategy on the one hand, and on the rationale underlying industrial policies in various countries on the other. Drawing on these two windows into the problem, this study focusses on how the automobile industry grew, thrived, and met the international challenge and, further, how it was supported within advanced industrialized and industrializing nations. The present research combines analysis of both the firm and the state from the perspective that their mutual interaction defines competitiveness. As such, this is a comparative international study of firms and nations, holding the automobile industry constant.

The automobile industry provides particular insight into issues of changing industry structure and appropriate industry policy because it remains central to the economic welfare of most advanced industrialized nations and key industrializing countries. Though clearly mature, the automobile industry has recently begun to experience changes in both product and process brought on by demands for greater fuel efficiency, decreased pollution, and increased affordability. Alternative fuel vehicles, such as electric cars, and other transportation advances that represent a radical departure from existing petroleum-based auto design and manufacture are gaining attention in the industry.[4] Thus, poised on a new technological frontier, and forced to introduce new methods into the existing product, the automobile industry actually shares much in common with advanced technology industries.

Several models of industrialization will be analyzed here, based on the premise that within market economies the institutions supporting industrialization and the basis of competition are themselves uniquely defined and critical to determining economic success. These models focus on the "free market" legacy apparent in the USA[5] and the UK, the "controlled market" of Japan[6] or South Korea, and the "structured market" of corporatist European countries.[7] Within the logic of these systems, states and firms maneuver to establish economic advantage. There are three dominant industrial structures that constitute the focus of this analysis of the automobile industry: the integrated firm; the quasi-integrated firm; and the quasi-market structure. Integrated firms, exemplified by the large-volume producers of the USA and Europe, are characterized by predominantly internal transactions and limited governmental interaction. The quasi-integrated firm, typical of Japan, is characterized by extensive external transactions with supplier firms that are controlled by or subordinated to the assembler, and by extensive external support. In the quasi-market structure evident to varying extents in Europe, the principal economic activities are externalized and linked through interdependent networks, often with government participation. The logic of these structures embraces both cause and consequence of the nature of state support. Whereas the integrated firm structure is most compatible with a free market economy, the quasi-integrated and quasi-market structures are most compatible with governed market economies. The way in which firms and society are linked in the development, manufacture, and distribution of goods constitutes a *production system.* It is argued here that a critical element to understanding competitiveness lies in the *flexibility of a production system.*

From this line of reasoning, success of the Japanese system can be attributed to the effectiveness of specific governmental interventions combined with corporate strategies. Industrial targeting sheltered the industry during its formative years, while the dense network of inter-firm, inter-agency relations of the *keiretsus* gave it the necessary level of security and stability to compete internationally. Individual firms did not need to realize success by maximizing profits for any given product, but could seek competitive advantage by upgrading production and through the flexibility derived from process innovation and organization. Only much later was the industrial sheltering replaced by Japanese marketing and production skills. The nation's institutional structure promoted by government policies made Japanese firms especially suited to adopt flexible responses to the increasingly competitive climate of the world market. Although these relationships have changed over time, the system remains fundamentally resilient.

At the heart of the issue is how to conceptualize the economy when chronic uncertainty is the norm, how to situate the role of industry relative to government, and how to devise policies for supporting industrialization without stifling competition. This requires a redefinition of market mechanisms especially with respect to the transmission and generation of risk and innovation, and a re-creation of the basis to competition through appropriate institutions. It is unnecessary for the institutions of nations to become clones of the Japanese system to be effective.[8] In fact, Japan provides only one of several successful examples.

The Era of Flexibility

Flexibility became particularly critical issue as markets became congested and unpredictable. Under these conditions, being competitive required that firms provide the most value at the lowest cost and in the shortest period of time.[9] Production had to incorporate product differentiation without sacrificing advantages of scale. As some economists have noted, this required the establishment of "a complex production system, substituting differentiated goods for homogeneous output, a flexible process for rigid assembly lines, and global markets for price competition in a restricted market. Flexibility became the way to reduce the risk of generating 'wrong' capacities."[10] Production flexibility began to take on special meaning.

Up to this point, flexibility had referred to the efficient manufacture of cars made according to a fixed relation between given inputs and expected outputs. Automobile manufacture was largely a rigid, linear process designed to produce standardized products for price-competitive markets. Any changes in the final product required massive changes in the rigid process. Lags between a steady and expected demand and the discontinuous availability of supply created "frictional" excess capacity.[11] Flexibility in the system came from the management of frictional excess capacity through control over daily operating costs and by cutting expenditures.

However, as markets became increasingly uncertain, productive flexibility depended on an intrinsic ability to adapt to change – a concept that was more structural than frictional in nature. This was the essence of the pioneering notion of "flexible specialization" which Michael Piore and Charles Sabel introduced in the mid-1980s to mean "a strategy of permanent innovation: accommodation to ceaseless change, rather than an effort to control it."[12] The idea extends beyond the micro-economics of the firm and includes systems of economic adjustment. Flexibility emphasizes the interface between industries and governments in sustaining innovation and is linked with the way market uncertainty is perceived and distributed within an economy and society in the effort to sustain long-term capacity for change. In this context, *flexible production* refers to the structuring of production and markets through the joint actions of governments and private enterprise for the purpose of encouraging innovation and minimizing risk.

Why would firms and governments want to combine their efforts? The answer lies in their survival strategies as economic actors. Many firms have faced a reduced return on investments because of flat market demand, a decline in market share, and an increase in fixed costs. Market uncertainty has required that they increase expenditures in product design and production at the same time that they shorten the product life cycle. With fewer opportunities for capturing returns on investments, they have begun to externalize activities to the supplier base, smaller firms, or public institutions so as to spread the costs and risks of investment. Similarly, they have begun to adopt international marketing and production strategies to keep abreast of fast-breaking trends in different markets. Together these strategies allow them to capture wider economies of scale while achieving product differentiation. Through the externalization and internationalization of production, economic activity shifts from the firm to the a group of firms and to society – that is, to the "production system."

These strategies coincide with government efforts to balance international policy objectives with domestically oriented economic development. The constraints on sovereign states attempting to take independent economic actions in an interdependent world combined with the high uncertainty governing economic markets has generated a search for multilateral regional mechanisms for stabilizing conditions. Nations with shared market and trade interests are joining forces. This is evident in the unification of Europe through the European Economic Community, the North American Free Trade Agreement, trade arrangements between Brazil and Argentina, and trade agreements among China, South Korea, and Taiwan, and among the Association of South East Asian Nations (ASEAN). These state initiatives creating *de facto* regional trading blocs complement the international decentralization of corporate activities.

At the sub-state regional level, as manufacturers attempt to capture market share through product differentiation, local policies aimed at expanding the supplier base, training personnel, making finance capital available, enhancing research, and assisting in technology transfer often hold the key to their success. This is particularly important as the distribution of entrepreneurial costs are increasingly borne outside the firm. Countries that invest in an educated labor force, scientific competence, and the acquisition of technical knowledge - factors critical to sharing risk and encouraging innovation - provide clear directives for managing economic adjustments.

Thus flexible production implies a convergence of interests between firms and governments in creating competitiveness. At the core lie flexible responses for redistributing risks, re-creating stability, and stimulating innovation. Often this requires lowering the cost of production while increasing efficiency and product variability. For corporations to achieve these objectives often leads to actions that coincide with governments' developmental goals, and vice versa.

What happened to make flexibility so critical? The answer lies in increased trade and investment flows; decreased monetary, supply, and financial predictability; heightened technological change; and shifting patterns of consumption. Their interaction created a climate of prolonged economic uncertainty.

Sources of Change

Trade and Investment Flows In part, instability is a function of successful policies directed at encouraging trade. During the postwar period, as Europe and Japan engaged in economic reconstruction, and the developing nations of Latin America and Asia adopted programs directed at building industrial capacity, manufacturing output became the engine of the world economy. Throughout the 1960s, annual manufacturing output growth rates as high as 5.8 per cent and 6.4 per cent were common in developed and developing countries, respectively.[13] Entering the 1970s, the engine of growth began to show signs of exhaustion in industrialized countries, though it continued to surge in an emerging group of newly industrialized nations: respective manufacturing output growth rates of 3.4 per cent versus 7.5 per cent attest to the strength of the latter.[14] The severe worldwide recession of the early 1980s presented a further setback for manufacturing production worldwide that later rebounded to 5.6 per cent in developed nations and 6.8 per cent in developing nations by the end of the decade.[15]

The average growth rate of world trade between 1961 and 1966 of 9.0 per cent jumped to 21.4 per cent by 1970 to 1975.[16] Despite the global recession of the early 1980s, when trade in manufactures came to a near halt (1.3 per cent), by 1987 this had revived to 21.4 per cent. By far the largest increase in the annual growth rate of trade came from developing market economies. During the mid-1980s the annual growth rate of trade of manufactures from developing market economies to the world was an extraordinary 33.8 per cent.

One incentive to international trade came from progressive dismantling of trade barriers, beginning in the late 1950s with the creation of the General Agreement on Tariffs and Trade (GATT). Once set in motion, international trade as a whole expanded nearly 70 per cent faster than the growth rate of world GNP from the 1960s to the end of the 1980s.[17] This was particularly evident in certain growth-related industries such as automobiles, which saw its share of exports in world car production rise from 18 per cent in 1960 to 38 per cent in 1980.[18]

The expanding role of developing countries in the world economy constituted a significant portion of the increased trade. During the decade of the 1970s, the value of annual exports from developing countries grew from $9.5 billion to over $100 billion, representing a rise in share of world exports of manufactures from 5.0 per cent to 9.2 per cent. However, the mid-1970s marked a pivotal point in trade relations, as developing nations were becoming clearly differentiated in their export performance of industrial products. An important sub-group of nations out-performing others as export contenders consisted of Brazil, Hong Kong, India, Mexico, Taiwan, and South Korea, while the rest of the industrializing aspirants made only sporadic contributions.[19] Of this group, Brazil and Mexico representing "early" industrializers, and South Korea, a "late" industrializer, surfaced as major automobile and auto parts designers, manufacturers, consumers, and exporters.

As these nations industrialized, the nature of traded products emanating from developing countries shifted from final goods (finished products) to intermediate goods (items going toward making finished products), and again to capital goods (machinery for manufacture of products). From 1970 to 1981, in contrast with the modest growth evident in developed market economies, the export of capital goods more than doubled in developing countries,[20] This corresponded with the rise of developing countries as exporters of increasingly sophisticated products. Further, while much of the trade was between discrete firms, or *inter-firm* in nature, a growing percentage of intermediate goods traded also reflected *intra-firm* trade within multinational corporations (MNCs) engaged in international sourcing. This was particularly evident in developed countries with open economies and signficant transnationalization such as the USA, the UK, and Sweden, where approximately 20 to 30 per cent of international trade consisted of intra-firm trade.[21]

The change in the nature of trade and investment came in approximately four waves. The first began immediately after World War II and consisted of direct foreign investment by MNCs primarily to developing countries. The second emerged with the abundance of Euro-dollars throughout the 1970s, when easily available finance capital made credit to domestic or branch plant operations a preferred form of investment.[22] The third followed from the chronic and widespread balance of payments disequilibria of the 1980s. The necessity to export gave rise to technical agreements, joint ventures, alliances, and other types of indirect investments in which risks and responsibilities were spread across firms and with governments. The fourth trend was toward direct foreign investment within developed economies. In the USA, the value of all foreign direct investment from 1986 to 1987 grew by 62 per cent, and in the automobile industry by approximately 32 per cent.[23] In the European Community, the value of inward investment increased by 90 per cent from 1987 to 1988.[24] Through increased trade and investment, the structure of manufacturing output within developed and developing nations began to approximate each other.[25]

Thus, throughout this period, the structure of the international economy and the nature of global interdependence took on several dimensions: one was a shift in the economic balance among countries due to the regenerative powers of Japan and Europe combined with a growing presence from an emerging group of developing countries; another was a shift in the composition of industrial production worldwide as developing countries successfully made the transition from consumer goods manufacture to capital and intermediate goods manufacture; while a third consisted of a shift in the patterns of international trade and investment from inter-industry to intra-industry trade, followed by a rise of new forms of indirect and direct foreign investment.

These changes were reflected in the role the state maintained in determining terms of trade and investment. Throughout the protectionist era of the 1930s, and continuing through periods of import-substitution industrialization and then later during the national reconstruction efforts following World War II, nation states defined the primary market. Boundaries of national sovereignty *coincided* with market boundaries. For the most part, multinational operations were highly fragmented, nationally oriented, and lacking in unified global coordination. This changed as corporations relied on intra-industry trade as a form of lowest-cost sourcing to address international competition. The scope of corporate production and marketing strategies turned from discrete national markets to international markets, and, as such, corporate and state interests *diverged*. Another shift occurred with the *reconvergence* of state and corporate interests and the rise of new investment mechanisms necessitating processes of mutual adjustment.

With reconvergence, the possibilities for insertion by developing nations into the world economy broadened. Initially, foreign investment in developing countries aimed at domestic markets had been characterized by the transference of older technology and labor intensive methods of production, or, if for export, confined to low value-added products. But with the growth of internal markets and, later, increase in export markets, a number of nations began to encourage production based on technological and scientific competence. This developed into an even more critical issue as exports became requisite to rectifying the balance of payments crises. From 1970 to 1985 the market share of high- and medium-intensity research and development export products from developing to developed market economies essentially tripled.[26] Brazil, Mexico, South Korea, India, Argentina, Yugoslavia, and Taiwan, among others, emerged as competitors in such industries as steel, machine tools, automobiles, petrochemicals, weapons, and aeronautics.[27] However, the outcome of greater world trade, investment, and competition among developed and developing nations was bidding wars and rising protectionist sentiments that unsettled the climate for international trade and investment.

Monetary, Supply, and Financial Conditions Another source of global instability emanated from the uncertain supplies of energy resources and finance capital. The issue surfaced in 1971 when the gold standard was abandoned, followed in 1973 by the devaluation of the US dollar and the creation of the OPEC oil cartel. World exchange and financial markets grew highly unpredictable and volatile, while commodity prices rose sharply. In the absence of fixed exchange rates, trade and commodity prices fluctuated with changes in exchange rates. This, in turn, amplified the costs of international investing and trading. For countries with high and unpredictable inflation rates, the penalties were even greater. Economist Laura D'Andrea Tyson offered the following insight into the situation:

> Oil price increases encouraged a reallocation of resources to energy development, resulted in major changes in the profitability of different industries, producers, and countries, fueled the inflationary surge of the 1970s, generated stagflationary conditions in the developed economies, and produced the oil surpluses that financed the ill-fated growth of commercial bank lending to developing countries.[28]

A search for managed currency exchanges was slow to materialize because of the extraordinary international policy coordination required. The climate of financial unpredictability paved the way for the creation of regional trading blocs as a means of stabilizing commodity flows, as it simultaneously undermined the viability of the General Agreement on Tariffs and Trade as an institution for achieving multilateral consensus.

The necessity to minimize foreign exchange risks became a motivating factor behind the drive by multinationals to establish global operations. In some mature industries, such as steel and automobiles, which saw market inroads by new competitors with favorable exchange rates, the destabilizing effect of fluctuating exchange rates intensified the dispersion of production to international sites. This fueled the dual problems of expanding competition and excess capacity.

The creation of the OPEC oil cartel had other unsettling effects. In the USA it spawned a 45 per cent increase in the price of transportation fuel, a 65 per cent increase in fuel for production, and a 73 per cent increase in fuel for home heating. The extraordinary price increases triggered runaway inflation with wages chasing prices. The windfall oil revenues also stimulated a massive transference of income from petroleum-importing to petroleum-producing countries.

Of the $49 billion in petrodollars deposited in international banks between 1974 and 1976, a significant portion went toward investment in developing countries, with multinational firms using external sources, rather than such internal funds as retained earnings or intra-firm loans to finance subsidiary expansion and other activities.[29] As a consequence, financial investment in Latin America throughout the 1970s surpassed the extent of foreign direct investment. In contrast to the 1960s, when foreign direct investment comprised 30 per cent of external financial support in Latin America while bank loans and bonds accounted for 10 per cent, by the 1970s these figures were 20 per cent and 57 per cent, respectively.[30] Within developing countries, the largest share of borrowing came from private sources, particularly banks participating in the Euro-currency market, whose financial reserves went to a select group of nations. The five countries of Mexico, Brazil, Venezuela, South Korea, and Algeria accounted for one half of all publicly announced Euro-currency bank credits to developing countries between 1976 and 1979, resulting in impressive economic growth, especially in the production of consumer goods.[31]

However, indebted industrialization also tied these countries and their lending institutions to recessionary tendencies created by rising oil prices. During the second round of oil price increases in 1978-9, heavily indebted rapidly industrializing countries were forced to export in order to service their debt. Often exports consisted of products that directly competed with goods made in industrialized nations, which only compounded the already growing competition. The surge of oil prices forced contractionary demand policies within industrializing countries and precipitated the most severe world recession since the Great Depression of the 1930s. Higher real interest rates in developed economies coupled with liberalization of capital controls stimulated a dramatic shift in financial flows away from beleaguered indebted nations. Capital flows began to outpace trade flows such that the annual value of transactions on the London Euro-dollar market reached $15 trillion in 1985, at least twenty-five times the value of world trade.[32] So urgent was the situation that the United Nations *World Economic Survey* of 1989 reported: "In 1988, for the sixth consecutive year, there was a net transfer of financial resources from poor to rich countries, reaching a new record of $33 billion."[33] The hyper-capital activity created enormous distortions in monetary exchange rates evident in the continued appreciation of the US dollar relative to European and Japanese currencies during the first half of the 1980s.[34]

Energy costs also destabilized markets of such energy-dependent industries as automobiles. Following the oil embargoes of 1972 and 1979, Japanese fuel-efficient cars quickly penetrated the US market. This fortuitous timing propelled Japanese manufacturers into a position of global competitors. The growing competition also required that auto-makers invest in research into new products and processes despite plummeting revenues.

The unstable macro-economy further motivated firms to shorten investment-time horizons by entering into alliances with other firms, parastatal organizations, or governmental agencies. To minimize their capital outlay and market risks, foreign investors often preferred to hold minority interests in equity participation through joint ventures, technical arrangements, licensing agreements, franchising, product contracts, management contracts, turnkey contracts, and international subcontracting.[35] The popularity of risk-minimizing alliances by firms found a natural complement in national policies designed to control external investment. Within developing countries, governmental controls had become requisite for meeting mounting debts. The types of non-tariff barriers to trade they began to adopt included foreign investment review boards, local content and export performance requirements, import quotas, "voluntary" export restraints, marketing arrangements, limits on profit remittances, discretionary licensing and state trading, and restrictions of foreign investment by sectors, foreign takeovers, and foreign equity.[36] Though clearly interventions, they also created a climate of stability.

Technological Change The pressures of competition and unstable markets forced heavy investments by firms at a time of decreasing revenues. Technological innovation and acceleration of the product life cycle became essential to maintaining competitiveness. The growing centrality of research and development took the form of increased research and technical personnel, and greater research and development expenditures.

In some instances, companies improved production through enhanced information flow and more highly coordinated operations by using programmable automation, such as computer-aided design, robotics, numerically controlled machine tools, flexible manufacturing systems, and computer-integrated manufacturing. However, instead of setting new standards, the expanding range of technological possibilities often led to a proliferation of choice in the technological configuration, organization, and management of production that far exceeded the ability of organizations to adapt.[37]

The profusion of technological choice and escalating research costs prompted changes in industrial organization. During the Industrial Revolution, scientific activities were often independent of enterprise. But by the late nineteenth and twentieth centuries they had become proprietary, especially within industries where significant profits could be derived from technological rents and economies of scale. Internal control of research and development over the years created barriers to entry and led to industry concentration and the centralization of research, generally near headquarters. Later, global competition precipitated changes that moved industrial organization toward joint ventures in design and development of new products and processes and the decentralization of research and design functions. Through joint ventures, firms could share research and development costs, yet continue to compete in the production, marketing, and servicing of products. Through the decentralization and internationalization of knowledge-based activites, firms could also increase their market penetration.

Inter-firm and university collaborative efforts intensified, such as the Japanese joint program between MITI (Ministry of International Trade and Industry) and the Agency for Industrial Science and Technology fostering long-term basic research in private industry, or the US government's effort through the National Science Foundation to establish university and industry cooperative research centers. The nature of research capability and technology began to extend beyond the firm and beyond national boundaries, and were becoming less rigid, more fluid, and more central to the development of regions.[38] This lowered the cost of manufacture as it regionalized production. The choice was not confined to industrialized nations, but included developing countries with strong scientific and engineering capacity.[39] With regionalization, firms could more accurately target the demands of diverse markets.

Consumption A fourth major change that took place during the postwar era was that consumer goods markets became saturated as they matured. This was most evident in the USA where, by 1970, 99 per cent of households had televisions, refrigerators, radios, and electric irons, and, by 1979, there was one car for every two residents.[40]

In addition, markets became more fragmented due, in part, to a growth of income inequality worldwide. Income disparity began to grow in the mid-1970s in the USA[41] Between 1973 and 1985, real weekly wage in manufacturing dropped by 4.3 per cent and real family income declined by approximately 5 per cent, while the proportion of low-income families earning less than $20,000 increased from 30.6 per cent to 34.0 per cent.[42] The growing stratification of society diminished the purchasing power of a historically stable middle class and fragmented the market. A similar bifurcation was evident elsewhere. For example, when the promise of growth in Mexico, Brazil, and other rapidly industrializing nations during the 1960s and 1970s collapsed with the 1980s recession, income patterns also began to skew. Worldwide, saturation and fragmentation suggested that auto markets were becoming highly congested and less homogeneous.

These trends placed a heavy emphasis on correctly identifying and targeting market segments through product differentiation. As it became more difficult for firms to sustain large-scale production within single markets, many looked abroad as a way of expanding the market base. This had the effect of increasing international trade. They also encouraged the introduction of specialized products and niche production and a reduction of the number of cars made per model, as well as a lowering of the time required to bring a product to market. And as changes in the demand structure accelerated, it triggered a massive restructuring in the industry.

Context of Uncertainty

Thus, when taken together, the overall effect of the multiple destabilizing tendencies in trade, technology, supply, and demand on the international automobile industry was that it made flexible production the operative strategy for design, development, and manufacture. The outcome was a convergence of industry and government interests in the process of economic adjustment, a new set of industry leaders, a vastly redefined automobile industry, and a new focus on the role of government in determining industrial competitiveness.

Restructuring of the International Automobile Industry

Since its inception, the auto industry has evolved through several phases. The first, beginning in the 1890s and continuing to the 1920s, consisted of the craft era. Initially, the scale of manufacture and structure of markets favored European producers. The second, lasting from the 1920s to the end of the 1970s, came with the rise and decline of mass production. As markets broadened and large-scale manufacture predominated, US firms took the lead. The third and current period is characterized by international competition and flexible responses. After two decades of macro-economic instability, the balance of industrial powers has become more equalized among the USA, Europe, and Japan, though Japan is clearly the driving force (see table 1.1).

Three general trends characterize the recent period:

1 a growth in the diversity and sophistication of vehicles;
2 a consolidation of regional markets coupled with increased trade;
3 a restructuring of methods of production from conception to manufacture to meet cost, quality, and time-based requirements.

A Growth in the Diversity and Sophistication of Vehicles The legacy of automobile development was decidedly different in the major auto-

Table 1.1 *Total motor vehicle production in selected countries, 1900-90*

	1900	*1925*	*1950*	*1975*	*1990*[1]
North America					
United States	4,192	4,265,830	8,005,859	8,986,513	9,888,036
Mexico	0	0	21,575	360,678	820,558
Western Europe					
(W) Germany	2,312	62,753	306,064	3,186,208	4,660,657
Italy	0	49,400	127,847	1,458,629	1,874,672
United Kingdom	0	167,000	783,672	1,648,399	1,295,611
Sweden	0	–	17,553	366,753	335,853
Asia-Pacific					
Japan	0	–	31,597	6,941,591	13,486,796
South Korea	0	0	0	36,264	1,321,630
Eastern Europe					
Yugoslavia	0	0	0	205,567	342,727[2]
South America					
Brazil	0	0	0	930,235	914,576
World	9,504	4,900,730	10,577,426	32,998,363	44,165,033

[1] Automotive News, *1991 Market Data Book*.
[2] 1989 data, MVMA, *World Motor Vehicle Data* (1991).

Source: Motor Vehicle Manufacturers Association, *World Motor Vehicle Data* (1991).

producing regions. From the 1920s to the 1970s, the USA was the world leader in the manufacture of consumer durable goods. During the 1950s, it produced nearly one-half of all manufactured goods and 75 per cent of the world's cars. It was also the largest unified consumer base. With access to large and growing markets, the US automobile industry was unparalleled in high-volume manufacture. Annual quantities of 250,000 to 500,000 cars per model were common for US producers, though rare among foreign car makers facing narrower market segments.

European car makers, on the other hand, confronted extremely fragmented markets and historically lower income levels. Until the creation of the EEC in 1954, trade barriers limited market accessibility, as did driving customs, which varied across countries and made designing for multiple markets costly. High sales, license, and gasoline taxes also favored fuel-efficient designs. Together these factors reinforced differentiated tastes and standards. In many instances, manufacturers produced for limited segments, at low volumes, and with little interchangeability of components by "family" groups. Long product runs were often necessary to secure economic returns at low volumes.

In contrast to the USA and Europe, Japan was a late developer. With the help of public policies, the automobile industry propelled the nation's development through a concerted export program. The auto industry emerged from other existing industries and gradually expanded from entry-level to mid-range vehicles, and then to upper-segment vehicles with progressive penetration of foreign markets.

Other countries followed diverse paths of development. Among early industrializers, particularly those in Latin America, the automobile industry commonly evolved through stages of final product importation, later up-graded to the assembly of semi-knock-down and complete knock-down cars, then the development of a parts industry, and lastly manufacture of complete vehicles, initially for the domestic market and later for export markets. The failure of this industry to provide the engine for industrialization, particularly through import substitution industrialization, left a legacy of foreign manufacturers dominating the industry, usually operating in fragmented segments. Among late industrializers, such as South Korea, the path of development more frequently followed the Japanese experience.

In each instance, the segment structure reflected their history of development. In general, cars are categorized into three main segments. The largest is the mass-market mid-range and is comprised of medium-sized cars. The second consists of entry-level models, or small and inexpensive cars directed at first-time buyers and multiple-vehicle owners. These cars are generally made in large volume. The third group consists of specialty cars, such as luxury, and some four-wheel drive vehicles, which are often made in small lots. Ideally, manufacturers differentiate between products sold on value and price – or those in the first two categories – and products sold on technology and styling – or those in the third category. In reality, the distinctions may not be so sharply drawn.

Examination of the segment structure in the USA, Europe, and Japan reveals significant changes associated with the maturity, consolidation,

Figure 1.1 *US automobile production by segment, 1973–88*

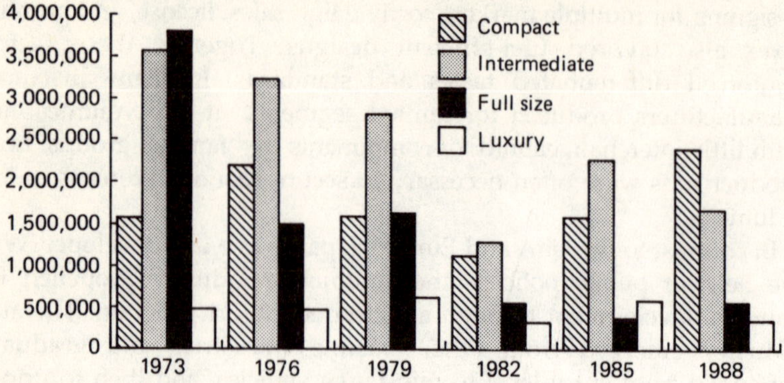

Source: Ward's Automotive Yearbook (1991).

and expansion, respectively, of these markets. As illustrated in figure 1.1, from 1966 to 1986 new car registrations in the USA showed a decided downshift. In Europe, the trend from 1974 to 1980 was from small and luxury segments to mid-range segments (see tables 1.2 and 1.3). By contrast, Japanese data suggest a decided up-grading from 1980 to 1988 (see table 1.4).

Within these markets, variation increased. US, Italian, German, and Japanese car manufacturers expanded the number of models, bodies, and engines from the 1970s to the 1980s (see tables 1.5, 1.6, 1.7, and 1.8). Only for the USA did this translate into fewer units per model on average. The USA also experienced a decrease in the average lot size of production (see table 1.9). This indicated a tendency toward under-utilized capacity (see figure 1.2).[43] On the whole, vehicles displayed more options and more configurations using basic components.

A Consolidation of Regional Markets and Increase of Trade For the most part, growth of the world automobile market has been accompanied by a decline in the number of domestic producers operating within national markets, an increase of foreign offerings, and a regional delineation of markets. Production of passenger vehicles from 1960 to 1990 remained steady in North America, grew in Western Europe and Asia-Pacific, and stalled in Eastern Europe and South America (see table 1.10). Within the three major trade areas, industrializing nations have become an integral part of the regional markets. In North America, there has been a growing presence of Mexico; in Western Europe, Spain is

Table 1.2 *European automobile production by segment, 1974*

	A	*B*	*C*	*D*	*E*	*F+G*	*Total*
Fiat	260,855	368,157	305,945	128,509	74,402	1,854	1,139,722
Lancia[1]	–	108,314	–	14,894	28,669	–	151,877
Alfa Romeo	–	–	100,030	44,655	44,142	–	188,827
Volkswagen	–	–	189,890	432,503	348,573	–	970,966
Audi-NSU	–	–	22,146	171,399	93,735	1,286	288,566
Ford	–	–	217,560	466,499	52,443	28,978	765,480
GM	–	–	354,636	119,358	166,509	26,144	666,647
Daimler-Benz	–	–	–	–	–	328,917	328,917
BMW	–	–	–	–	57,353	121,894	179,247
Renault	241,039	302,182	137,279	325,111	126,591	–	1,132,202
Peugeot	–	137,982	193,625	488,23	213,680	–	594,110
Citroën	270,817	56,894	150,490	–	–	40,039	518,240
Leyland[2]	–	173,964	122,926	184,138	81,226	46,457	608,711
Chrysler	–	77,460	216,794	66,071	22,546	–	382,871
Total	772,711	1,224,953	2,011,321	2,001,960	1,309,869	595,569	7,916,383
% total	9.8	15.5	25.4	25.9	16.5	7.6	

[1] Lancia and Autobianchi.
[2] Austin, Jaguar, Rover, and Triumph.

Segments:
A = small specialty
B = small
C = lower middle
D = upper middle
E = mid-specialty
F = luxury
G = luxury specialty

Sources: Associazione Nazionale fra Industrie Automobilistiche (ANFIA); Comité des Constructeurs Français d'Automobiles (CCFA); Motor Vehicle Manufacturers Association of the US (MVMA); Verband der Automobilindustrie EV (VDA).

outpacing the UK in the production of cars; and in Asia-Pacific, South Korea has become a world competitive new entrant. Within the two key remaining trade areas of Eastern Europe and South America, the situation is currently one of stagnation, though historically Russia and Brazil have been regional market leaders.

The issue of emerging blocs remains a point of contention. Aggregate trends show only modest increases. From 1980 to 1989, US trade with countries in the Western hemisphere ranged between 33 per cent and 34 per cent, while Japan's trade with countries in the Pacific increased slightly from 30 per cent to 32 per cent, and Western European trade with other Western European countries increased from 48 per cent to

Table 1.3 *European automobile production by segment, 1983*

	A	*B*	*C*	*D*	*E*	*F+G*	*Total*
Fiat	184,466	408,475	262,767	90,182	24,999	–	970,889
Lancia[1]	–	80,149	33,934	59,812	10,472	–	184,367
Alfa Romeo[2]	–	–	44,659	112,035	34,507	2,027	193,228
Volkswagen	–	166,246	591,259	218,649	–	–	976,154
Audi	–	–	–	193,208	146,570	6,160	345,938
Ford	–	356,551	505,761	378,900	33,791	–	1,257,003
GM	–	246,300	459,834	377,694	146,876	20,032	1,250,736
Daimler-Benz	–	–	–	–	109,837	340,305	450,142
BMW	–	–	–	–	245,875	152,790	389,665
Renault	170,928	423,111	807,687	227,016	51,954	–	1,680,697
Peugeot	44,928	154,995	–	189,434	212,739	3,470	605,566
Citroen	101,537	144,719	59,653	181,643	–	56,729	544,281
Talbot	87,052	85,300	112,702	46,392	1,302	–	332,766
Leyland[3]	49,100	175,200	101,800	50,000	33,700	28,000	437,800
Total	638,011	2,241,046	2,980,067	2,124,965	1,052,640	609,511	9,646,232
% total	6.6	23.2	30.9	22.0	10.9	6.4	

[1] Lancia and Autobianchi.
[2] Alfa Romeo and Alfa Nissan.
[3] Austin, Jaguar, Rover, and Triumph.

Segments:

A = small specialty
B = small
C = lower middle
D = upper middle
E = mid-specialty
F = luxury
G = luxury specialty

Sources: Associazione Nazionale fra Industrie Automobilistiche (ANFIA); Comité des Constructeurs Français d'Automobiles (CCFA); American Automobile Manufacturers Association (AAMA); Verband der Automobilindustrie EV (VDA).

Figure 1.2 US industrial capacity usage motor vehicle and parts manufacturers, 1971–87

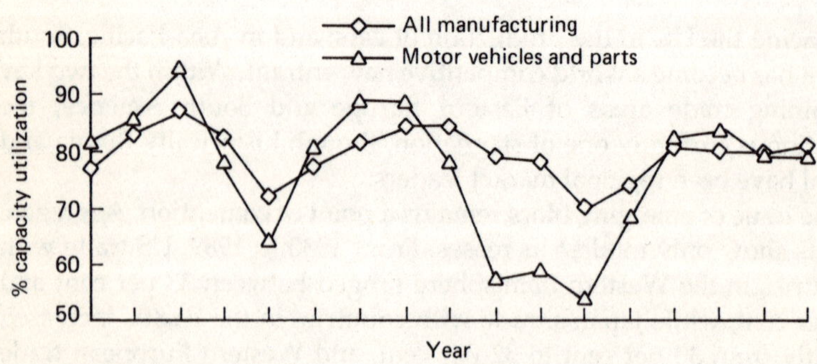

Source: AAMA, *Market Data Book* (May 25, 1988), p. 86.

Table 1.4 *Japanese automobile production by segment, 1980, 1985, 1988*

	1980	*1985*	*1988*
Standard cars			
Domestics	247,519	461,482	586,327
Fuji	0	0	698
Honda	0	0	11,404
Mitsubishi	5,141	4,879	7,948
Nissan	124,609	171,881	197,580
Mazda	730	357	768
Toyota	116,994	284,330	367,900
Others	45	35	29
Imports	185,976	216,558	273,292
Segment total	433,495	678,040	859,619
% segment total	1.9	2.5	2.9
Small Cars			
Domestics	19,901,776	24,052,913	26,573,044
Daihatsu	365,723	494,015	465,134
Fuji	354,146	386,916	467,183
Honda	1,087,641	1,719,120	2,186,186
Isuzu	273,714	458,200	511,969
Mitsubishi	1,342,876	1,716 540	1,625,018
Nissan	6,781,724	7,373,970	7,568,488
Suzuki	97	23,524	92,397
Mazda	1,252,268	1,694,058	1,873,355
Toyota	8,439,380	10,185,962	11,782,785
Others	4,180	608	529
Imports	223,902	296,288	392,070
Segment total	20,125,678	24,349,201	26,965,114
% segment total	90.2	90.1	91.1
Midget Cars			
Daihatsu	409,821	373,255	369,166
Mazda	70,493	29,795	11,298
Mitsubishi	392,886	394,422	404,048
Subaru	382,710	393,905	324,170
Honda	418,309	207,711	98,370
Suzuki	518,413	607,278	565,378
Others	1,045	13	25
Segment total	2,193,678	2,006,379	1,772,455
% Segment total	9.8	7.4	6.0
Total cars	22,319,356	27,033,620	29,597,188

Source: Japan Automobile Manufacturers Association.

55 per cent.[44] Yet sector specific data suggest extensive regional trade. For example, US trade data reveal that from 1982 to 1986 the volume of trade (imports and exports) in auto parts between Canada and the USA was approximately four times that between the USA and Japan, while the volume of trade with Mexico approximated that with Japan.[45] The active trade of auto parts within the region reflects the high level of integration of these three nations in the manufacture of motor vehicles.

A pattern of regionalization is even more apparent when examining firm specific trade and investment preferences. General Motors, Volkswagen, and Toyota displayed distinct tendencies toward consolidation of regional activities and regional markets from 1977 to 1987.[46] General Motors, the most international of these three firms, maintained core functions consisting of design, manufacture, and assembly facilities in the USA and Germany, and through Isuzu and Suzuki in Japan; it established second-tier manufacture and assembly (i.e., not design) in Mexico, Brazil, Britain, Spain, and Australia; and it operated third-tier assembly facilities (knock-down) in a number of sites. The decade from 1977 to 1987 represented a period of simplification and consolidation of its production strategy. Volkswagen and Toyota, on the other hand, being less international, retained core functions in the headquarter locations of Germany and Japan while maintaining second- and third-tier activities within key regions. Volkswagen began retreating from critical markets, in particular the USA, in contrast to Toyota, which was expanding primarily into Southeast Asia, North America, and South America.

Despite tendencies toward regionalization, trends toward internationalization continue. The result has been greater import penetration and increased trade even in countries with lingering protective barriers, combined with a growing trade deficit attibuted to vehicles and parts (see tables 1.11 and 1.12). Another measure of globalization is the rise in strategic alliances, joint ventures, and similar arrangements that provide alternatives to direct foreign investment (see figures 1.3 and 1.4).

Restructuring of Production to Meet Cost, Quality, and Time Requirements Perhaps the most significant change to occur in auto production as a result of the larger competitive field of players has been a compression of the time required to bring products to market. The transcendence of time over cost or quality, and the cumulative effect of all three have set new criteria for competitiveness. With the shortening of product life cycles, companies can no longer rely on economies of scale, or even of quality, to retain and enlarge their market segments –

Table 1.5 *Aggregate product diversity of US auto makers*

		M	*B*	*E*	*Production*	*P/M*
1975	General Motors	25	–	11	3,511,958	
	Ford	17	–	8	1,819,267	
	Chrysler	8	–	5	975,448	
	American Motors	4	–	4	244,941	
	Total	54	–	28	6,551,614	121,326
1980	General Motors	28	61	15	4,483,575	
	Ford	15	31	6	1,475,835	
	Chrysler	9	21	4	640,207	
	American Motors	4	9	2	199,613	
	Total	56	122	27	6,799,230	121,415
1985	General Motors	40	77	16	4,738,143	
	Ford	16	29	8	2,084,727	
	Chrysler	15	27	4	1,152,922	
	American Motors	3	7	3	166,379	
	Total	74	140	31	8,142,171	110,029
1986	General Motors	37	78	14	5,956,170	
	Ford	17	33	8	2,063,684	
	Chrysler	17	28	4	1,077,075	
	American Motors	3	7	3	95,436	
	Total	74	146	29	8,292,365	112,059
1987	General Motors	40	79	12	4,084,606	
	Ford	14	28	9	1,922,479	
	Chrysler	17	27	3	1,047,222	
	American Motors	2	7	4	41,539	
	Total	73	141	28	7,095,846	97,203
1988	General Motors	38	67	14	3,620,790	
	Ford	13	23	8	2,143,535	
	Chrysler	19	29	7	1,033,549	
	Total	70	119	29	6,797,874	97,112

M = number of models.
B = number of bodies.
E = number of engines, measured by size of displacement.
P = volume of production, in units.

Source: Ward's Automotive Yearbook, 1978-89.

Table 1.6 *Aggregate product diversity of Italian auto makers*

		M	*B*	*E*	*V*	*Production*	*P/M*
1975	Alfa Romeo	7	12	6	15	189,682	
	Autobianchi	2	2	3	4	71,347	
	De Tomaso	3	3	1	3	235	
	Ferrari	3	3	2	3	1,337	
	Fiat	8	14	8	25	1,006,660	
	Innocenti	2	5	3	6	33,061	
	Lamborghini	4	4	6	4	276	
	Maserati	4	4	3	4	201	
	Total	33	47	30	66	1,302,799	39,479
1980	Alfa Romeo	7	11	9	22	219,571	
	Autobianchi	1	3	4	3	76,585	
	De Tomaso	3	3	1	1	84	
	Ferrari	5	5	4	8	2,381	
	Fiat	9	13	10	47	995,455	
	Innocenti	1	3	2	5	39,770	
	Lamborghini	1	1	1	1	64	
	Lancia	8	8	6	18	110,756	
	Maserati	4	4	4	7	555	
	Total	39	51	40	116	1,445,221	37,057
1985	Alfa Romeo	9	23	10	34	157,625	
	Autobianchi	2	4	3	4	99,896	
	Bertone	2	3	3	3	5,806	
	De Tomaso	3	3	1	4	56	
	Ferrari	4	7	3	8	3,125	
	Fiat	8	15	18	53	972,687	
	Innocenti	4	2	2	10	15,218	
	Lamborghini	2	2	2	2	249	
	Lancia	3	3	7	13	127,322	
	Maserati	2	4	3	6	5,668	
	Total	39	137	52	66	1,387,652	35,581
1987	Alfa Romeo	7	12	13	32	192,024	
	Autobianchi	1	2	5	2	109,619	
	Bertone	1	1	1	1	1,557	
	De Tomaso	3	3	1	4	48	
	Ferrari	5	4	3	8	3,902	
	Fiat	7	11	15	61	1,226,722	
	Innocenti	3	3	3	10	10,443	
	Lamborghini	2	2	2	2	313	
	Lancia	4	6	9	23	164,567	
	Maserati	1	3	2	8	3,658	
	Rayton Fissore	1	1	3	4	447	
	Total	35	158	54	48	1,713,300	48,951

M = number of models.
B = number of bodies.
E = number of engines, measured by size of displacement.
V = number of versions, i.e., model/body/engine recombinations.
P = volume of production, in units.

Source: Prezzi delle automobili, various issues, 1975-87.

Table 1.7 *Aggregate product diversity of German auto makers*

		M	*E*	*V*	*Production*	*P/M*
1975	Audi	3	7	14	196,246	
	BMW	16	8	16	217,458	
	Daimler-Benz	10	12	17	350,098	
	Opel	7	11	19	593,270	
	Porsche	3	4	10	9,424	
	Volkswagen	11	12	25	934,786	
	Total	50	54	101	2,301,282	46,026
1980	Audi	7	7	20	285,052	
	BMW	18	8	18	330,087	
	Daimler-Benz	11	13	20	401,848	
	Opel	8	12	33	699,640	
	Porsche	3	4	5	28,622	
	Volkswagen	11	12	43	1,094,629	
	Total	58	56	139	2,839,878	48,963
1985	Audi	6	10	34	358,612	
	BMW	17	12	21	431,085	
	Daimler-Benz	10	11	34	510,479	
	Opel	6	9	24	797,786	
	Porsche	4	6	7	54,458	
	Volkswagen	12	11	41	1,236,872	
	Total	55	59	161	3,389,292	61,623
1987	Audi	6	12	45	417,234	
	BMW	17	14	31	442,760	
	Daimler-Benz	10	11	39	556,906	
	Opel	6	10	21	793,848	
	Porsche	4	5	6	48,520	
	Volkswagen	11	11	43	1,237,829	
	Total	54	63	185	3,497,097	64,761

M = number of models.
E = number of engines, measured by size of displacement.
V = number of versions, i.e., model/body/engine recombinations.
P = volume of production, in units.

Source: Verband der Automobilindustrie EV, *Tatsachen und Zahlen, 43 (1979), 46 (1982), 52 (1988).*

Table 1.8 *Aggregate product diversity of Japanese auto makers*

		M	*B*	*E*	*Production*	*P/M*
1975	Daihatsu	4	19	5	92,123	
	Honda	3	21	4	328,107	
	Isuzu	3	13	2	64,735	
	Mazda	6	76	6	387,145	
	Mitsubishi	5	39	8	288,846	
	Nissan	9	97	12	1,532,731	
	Fuji	2	23	3	108,663	
	Suzuki	3	18	2	50,668	
	Toyota	10	145	10	1,714,836	
	Total	45	451	52	4,567,854	101,508
1980	Daihatsu	5	38	7	155,604	
	Honda	3	23	3	845,514	
	Isuzu	3	38	5	107,057	
	Mazda	7	56	7	736,544	
	Mitsubishi	8	64	8	659,622	
	Nissan	11	219	13	1,940,615	
	Fuji	2	28	4	202,038	
	Suzuki	4	15	4	87,830	
	Toyota	12	234	15	2,303,284	
	Total	55	715	66	7,038,108	127,966

M = number of models.
B = number of bodies.
E = number of engines, measured by size of displacement.
P = volume of production, in units.

Source: Japan Automobile Manufacturers Association.

they must innovate constantly to anticipate the changing demands of customers. This new criterion has affected the nature of manufacture among both large-volume and niche producers.

Technological solutions optimizing both economies of scale (quantity) and scope (variety) among cars made in large volumes have had as their primary objective retention of surface-level product differentiation combined with greater standardization of structural components. Scale economies are derived from the interchangeability of major parts and the replication of core technology. Illustrations

Table 1.9 *Total models[1] produced by lot size for US auto makers[2]*

Lot size	*Year* 71	72	73	74	75	76	77	78	79	80	81	82	83	84	85	86	87	88	91
0-50	14	13	9	12	14	17	17	13	14	16	15	22	22	25	21	26	31	27	32
50-100	5	7	11	11	15	14	13	13	15	11	12	11	19	12	18	13	15	15	16
100-150	8	5	2	6	8	9	5	6	8	9	7	13	8	14	14	13	11	14	14
150-200	6	4	5	3	4	5	4	5	8	7	8	5	6	5	7	8	5	4	5
200-250	2	3	5	6	6	5	3	6	3	4	2	2	2	5	5	6	3	3	5
250-300	5	3	3	1	3	2	3	4	7	1	2	1	1	3	2	2	1	0	1
300-350	3	3	4	2	2	5	3	5	2	0	1	1	1	2	0	0	2	0	0
350-400	0	4	3	5	1	0	6	2	2	1	1	0	0	1	2	1	1	2	3
400+	2	3	5	1	0	2	2	2	3	3	3	0	0	1	0	1	1	2	2
Total	45	45	47	47	53	59	56	56	62	52	51	55	59	68	69	70	70	67	78

[1] Definition of model: 1) Classified by year of production, not model year; 2) differentiated by name, front wheel drive vs. rear wheel drive, not by engine type or size; 3) Sportsvan, Club Wagon, Voyager and Sportsman were counted as trucks from 1980, but as passenger cars before that date. 1991 is an estimate derived by linear extrapolation based on the annual average growth rate in each lot-size category for years 1983 to 1988.
[2] These figures are for Ford, General Motors, and Chrysler.

Source: *Ward's Automotive Yearbook*, 1988, 1987, 1986, 1980.

include the modular construction of engines and built-up components, stamping procedures that use quick die change, and flexible manufacturing systems that facilitate changes in the type and sequence of different designs within a part family during the assembly process. These methods allow companies to streamline product offerings while simultaneously increasing market penetration.

A different strategy applies to small-scale or niche production. These products by definition have distinct body styles and engines, and are made in small volumes. The main difference between small- and large-volume production lies in the assembly process, which tends to be more labor intensive, and in the lower volume of components and core technology used, although these are also often interchangeable. The strategy here is to emphasize economies of scope aimed at precise targeting of changing market segments, combined, where possible, with economies of scale.

Both large-scale and small-volume manufacturers are attempting to alter the sequence of design, development, and production to reduce the time involved, improve quality, and lower cost. The traditional sequence of car manufacture is a flow that progresses from (1) raw

Table 1.10 *Production of passenger vehicles by country, 1960-90*

	1960	*1965*	*1970*	*1975*	*1980*	*1985*	*1990*[1]
North America							
United States	6,703	9,335	6,550	6,717	6,376	8,185	6,069
Canada	323	709	923	1,058	847	1,077	1,072
Mexico	133	237	286	242	346		
Total	7,026	10,044	7,606	8,012	7,509	9,504	7,487
Western Europe							
(W) Germany	1,817	2,734	3,528	2,908	3,521	4,167	4,661
France	1,175	1,423	2,458	2,546	2,939	2,632	3,295
Italy	596	1,104	1,720	1,349	1,445	1,389	1,874
United Kingdom	1,353	1,722	1,641	1,267	959	1,048	1,296
Spain	40	159	450	696	1,029	1,230	1,679
Sweden	110	182	279	316	235	401	336
Others	223	213		926	958		531
Total	5,314	7,555		10,008	11,086		13,672
Asia-Pacific							
Japan	165	696	3,179	4,568	7,038	7,647	9,948
South Korea	14	18	57	264	987		
Australia	125	304		283	317		361
Others							495
Total							11,791
Eastern Europe							
USSR	139	201	350	1,201	1,327	1,332	900
Yugoslavia	10	36	112	183	255	218	290
Others					914	707	584
Total					2,442	2,257	1,774
South America							
Brazil	82	103	250	524	983	777	731
Others	51	102		799	434		19
Total	133	205		1,323	1,417		750
World	12,999	19,103	22,494	25,856	29,191	32,292	35,475

[1] Based on first eleven months.

Sources: Long Term Outlook for the World Automobile Industry (Paris: OECD, 1983), p. 8; Motor Vehicle Manufacturers Association, *World Motor Vehicle Data* (1991); *Ward's Automotive Yearbook* (1991).

material processing, to (2) raw material, parts, and components fabrication, (3) body component stamping and fabrication and metal casting, (4) engine, transmission, and other systems and sub-systems assembly and sub-assembly, and, lastly, to (5) final assembly, with testing and evaluation taking place at each step. Preceding this process are stages of conceptualization, prototype design, and marketing and feasibility studies. Following production are measures required to bring completed vehicles to market and, ultimately, maintain the

Table 1.11 *Value of trade in automobiles and parts ($m. current)*

Origin	*Years*	*Destination* *AME*	*DME*	*CPE*	*World*
AME	1961	1,980	630	5	2,630
	1966	4,690	860	25	5,580
	1970	10,024	1,078	48	11,160
	1975	23,570	3,331	72	26,983
	1980	54,770	8,615	151	63,547
	1985	77,477	6,529	764	84,783
	1987	117,481	7,639	315	125,418
DME	1961	3	22	–	26
	1966	3	24	–	26
	1970	15	43	–	62
	1975	61	325	2	392
	1980	320	986	5	1,322
	1985	1,174	829	93	2,103
	1987	5,070	948	64	6,104
CPE	1961	37	15	110	165
	1966	39	21	320	380
	1970	69	45	277	391
	1975	231	72	675	981
	1980	661	216	1,077	1,954
	1985	211	170	819	1,199
	1987	406	259	996	1,662
World	1961	2,020	670	115	2,820
	1966	4,750	910	345	5,990
	1970	10,108	1,166	325	11,613
	1975	23,862	3,728	748	28,355
	1980	55,751	9,818	1,233	66,824
	1985	78,862	7,528	1,676	88,085
	1987	122,937	8,847	1,376	133,184

Notes: based on SITC [Standard Industrial Trade Classification], passenger road vehicles and their parts.

AME = Advanced market economies.
DME = Developing market economies.
CPE = Centrally planned market economies.

Source: United Nations, *Monthly Bulletin of Statistics*, various issues (May 1967–May 1989).

products.

Market responsiveness has required that product planning and development become more integrated with manufacturing. Both the internal and external configuration of manufacturing reveal efforts to overlap design, development, and production so as to reduce the time

Table 1.12 *Annual growth rate of trade in automobiles and parts (%)*

		Destination			
Origin	*Years*	*AME*	*DME*	*CPE*	*World*
AME	1962-6	18.8	6.4	38.0	16.2
	1967-70	20.9	5.8	17.7	18.9
	1971-75	18.6	25.3	8.4	19.3
	1976-80	18.4	20.9	16.0	18.7
	1981-5	7.2	(5.4)	38.3	5.9
	1986-7	23.1	8.2	(35.8)	21.6
DME	1962-6	0.0	1.8	–	0.0
	1967-70	49.5	15.7	–	24.3
	1971-5	32.4	49.9	–	44.6
	976-80	39.3	24.9	20.1	27.5
	1981-5	29.7	(3.4)	79.4	9.7
	1986-7	107.8	6.9	(17.0)	70.4
CPE	1962-6	1.1	7.0	23.8	18.2
	1967-70	15.3	21.0	(3.5)	0.7
	1971-5	27.3	9.9	19.5	20.2
	1976-80	23.4	24.6	9.8	14.8
	1981-5	(20.4)	(4.7)	(5.3)	(9.3)
	1986-7	38.7	23.4	10.3	17.7
World	1962-6	18.7	6.3	24.6	16.3
	1967-70	20.8	6.4	(1.5)	18.0
	1971-5	18.7	26.2	18.1	19.5
	1976-80	18.5	21.4	10.5	18.7
	1981-5	7.2	(5.2)	6.3	5.7
	1986-7	24.9	8.4	(9.4)	23.0

Notes: based on Table 1.11; negative values in parenthesis.

AME = Advanced market economies.
DME = Developing market economies.
CPE = Centrally planned market economies.

Source: United Nations, *Monthly Bulletin of Statistics,* various issues (May 1967–May, 1989).

Figure 1.3 *Interrelationships among the world's major auto makers (developed country firms), 1987–90*

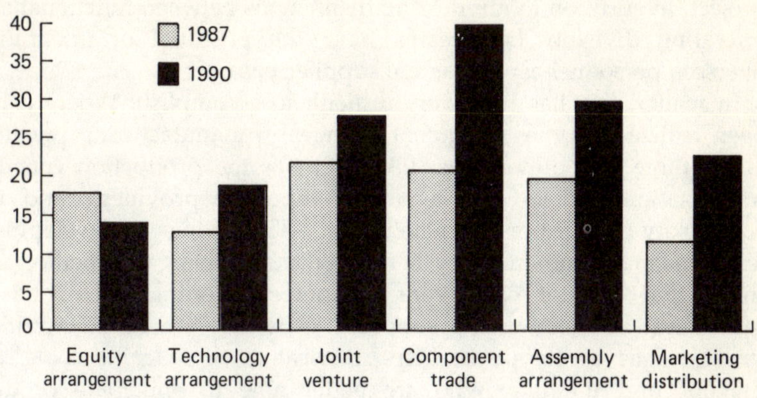

Source: Ward's Automotive International

Figure 1.4 *Interrelationships among the world's major auto makers (developed and developing country firms), 1987–90*

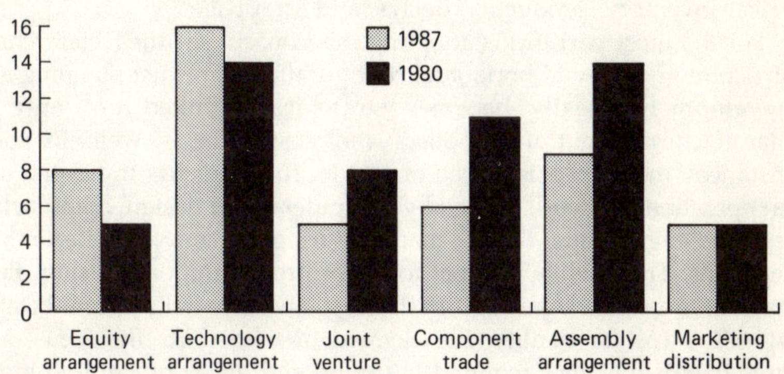

Source: Ward's Automotive Yearbook

between conception and production, variously described as simultaneous or concurrent engineering, or integrated manufacturing. In some instances, staffs are redeployed such that product designers work more closely with manufacturing process designers, and supplier managers with production logisticians and quality controllers, to make decisions as close as possible to the operating level.[47] This may be accomplished by formation of project or product development teams for the purpose of replacing the rigid structure of functionally segregated, vertically defined organizations. Ad hoc teams comprised of managers and technicians from different parts of a firm, along with representatives of vendors and even customers, may be assembled for the duration of the project. In addition to minimizing distinctions between functional and operating divisions, the teams have the potential of integrating overseas personnel as well as the supplier base.

In reality, this has been very difficult to accomplish. Where it has been realized, studies document changes in manufacturing practices along three key dimensions: the length of the production run; the organization and involvement of component providers; and the complexity of logistics and scheduling.[48] The savings in development lead time in the auto industry between firms applying this method and those that do not can average nineteen months.[49] This has a multiplicative effect among suppliers, especially among such critical providers as prototype builders, fabricators of machine tools, die makers, and the like, who are better able to anticipate product requirements in advance when they are part of the design and development team. The complex interaction involved leads to higher quality output as a result of the incremental and constant nature of improvements and innovation coupled with cost savings derived from lower inventory, production delays, and scrappage.[50]

For the most part, firms adopting this concept see their hierarchical structure give way to horizontal configurations. Product planning and development ideally becomes strategically linked not only to manufacturing, but to suppliers and customers as well. In some instances, the emphasis placed on service functions has translated into an operations network unified by computer-aided design, manufacturing, and engineering, flexible manufacturing systems, and telecommunications. Thus, while efficient forms of production on the shop floor have been proven significant in the past, and especially when dictated by either cost or quality, the element of time shifts the focus onto fundamental changes required in design and development within the firm, among suppliers, and with respect to manufacturing, and, hence, the concept of the firm itself.

The Role of the State

The most important political factor contributing to the transition of the auto industry has been the role of the state in structuring markets. Whereas previous models of industrial success rested on industry-led systems of economic adjustment in which the state was a supporting actor, current market leaders depend on either a government-led or a negotiated mechanism between governments and firms for economic guidance.[51] The concept as it is now evolving is one of active participation by governments in determining market outcomes.

Analysts of successful new market economies in East Asia lend insight into the emerging role of governments. Compelling arguments have been made for understanding the ascendence of these countries as the result of governed market structures, as opposed to that of either a free-market or a simulated free-market approach.[52] The most dynamic auto companies can be understood as the product of countries with these state structures. And as argued here, this structure is increasingly appropriate for developed countries because of the growing mutuality of interests corporations hold with political bodies, in both advanced industrialized and industrializing countries.

The difference today from prior years lies in the element of risk and the centrality of innovation in assuring competitiveness that exceeds the adjustment mechanisms of most firms. The economic uncertainty necessitates a strong state presence if the state is to provide a suitable environment for enterprise. This is different from either replacing market signals, as attempted by failed command economies, or, at the other extreme, providing incentives to simulate the relative prices and factors of a free market. Rather, it presumes a type of "market guidance... effected by augmenting the supply of investible resources, spreading or 'socializing' the risks attached to long-term investment, and steering the allocation of investment by methods which combine government and entrepreneurial preferences."[53] There are many instruments that a state has at its disposal for exercising this leverage. Those selected indicate the nature of national objectives for guiding the economy and industrial growth. This is reflected in the structure of the auto industry.

A Framework for Analysis

It is argued here that a critical element to understanding how firms are achieving flexibility is the examination of their underlying industrial structure within the context of a production system. As noted earlier, a production system refers to the way firms and society are linked in the development, manufacture, and distribution of goods. There are three dominant industrial structures that constitute the focus of this analysis of the industry: the integrated firm; the quasi-integrated firm; and the quasi-market structure. The logic of these structures are reflected in the nature of state support. The integrated-firm structure is the counterpart of a free-market economy, while quasi-integrated and quasi-market structures are associated with governed market economies. The purpose of this study is to illustrate how these systems define competitiveness.

With this as background, the remainder of the book is as follows. Chapter 2 links changes in the industry to theories of firm structure, state policies, and economic development. Chapter 3 focusses on the USA, the rise of the large-volume producers, and the basis for their vulnerability and necessity for change. The USA provides the clearest example of integrated-firm industrialization developed within a free-market economy. In Chapter 4 the industrial systems of Japan and Europe are examined. The UK sets the context for understanding early free-market industrialization. In Japan, industrialization developed along a quasi-integrated logic within a governed market economy. By contrast, German producers emerged out of an economic environment which permitted both quasi-market and integrated-firm structures supported by a corporatist environment. This is followed in Chapter 5 by an analysis of auto production in developing countries in which a distinction is made between those nations that industrialized during the prominent years of mass production versus more recent entrants into the international economy. Whereas countries following the Anglo-American tradition patterned themselves around the integrated-firm model, later entrants, particularly in East Asia, displayed more of the characteristics of the other two structures. The countries of Brazil, Mexico, South Korea, and the former Yugoslavia are the primary focus here. Chapter 6 is a synthesis of the main ideas discussed in terms of the politics of production as they apply to the auto industry and with respect to regional development. The implications of this analysis for understanding the emerging regionalism are presented here.

2

Industrial Production, Regional Development, and Public Policy

The Economic Challenge

An important distinction between the current period and that of the postwar era is the high uncertainty which raises the costs and risks of trade and investment. In their efforts to restore economic stability, firms and governments have begun to change with respect to industrial organization and the nature of institutions that support industrial activity. This reformulation of firms as productive entities and of states in their capacity to provide economic guidance challenges conventional concepts of firms, markets, and industrial institutions. The new concepts and configurations also lie at the core of the on-going transformation of the international automobile industry. With this in mind, this section focusses on the theoretical foundations of the emerging industrial structures and approaches toward organizing markets to provide a framework for understanding trends in the automobile industry.

The analysis draws on several literatures, including theories of the firm, regional development, international trade and production, innovation, and the state. Economist John Dunning once argued that an eclectic approach is necessary to understand the choices open to multinational corporations operating across national boundaries because internationalization magnifies the variables affecting key decisions.[1] Similarly, this analysis draws on several lines of thought in recognition that the current period of internationalization and uncertainty introduces additional dimensions to the process of creating competitiveness.

The discussion begins with an examination of the firm, since this is central to the recent transformations. The key concepts introduced here concern the internal structure of the firm and their external relations with other firms and the state. The primary idea is that the boundaries of the firm have begun to change as activities that were once internalized are increasingly borne by others, and as the relationship with these external actors is defined by dual attempts to minimize risk while encouraging innovation. In the auto industry, this has led to massive changes in some of the world's most influential firms.

Changing Boundaries of the Firm

According to traditional micro-economic theory, firms and industries in different national economies behave the same and are similarly organized. Firms are defined in terms of a "production function" where production is a function of various combinations of capital, labor, and other inputs. The logic is that firms will utilize capital, labor and other factors of production according to their marginal productivity, and in accordance with the greatest profit-maximizing combination of factors. If factors of production are substitutable and independent, then what matters is finding the right combination. This simple but powerful concept has pervaded neo-classical thinking, and has become the convention accepted by other disciplines.

In reality, however, firms are far more complex. Drawing on the experience of the manufacturing giants of the most powerful countries, economic historian Alfred Chandler, among others, argued that, because large firms created internal economies, they represented the most efficient units for coordinating and allocating, resources in an economy. Their structure reflected a certain synergy with the whole being more than the sum of the parts. In contrast to the market, which Adam Smith referred to as the "invisible hand," Chandler called the management system of large businesses the "visible hand" and the institution, particularly as displayed in the USA, "managerial capitalism." The internal organization of large complex businesses was viewed as offering distinct advantages over the market mechanisms which governed smaller enterprises. Specifically, the administrative coordination characteristic of modern multi-business enterprise is said to replace small traditional enterprise when administrative coordination permits greater productivity, lower costs, and higher profits than coordination by market mechanism.[2]

The description provided by Chandler – in reference to the formative period of modern capitalism in the USA (1850s to 1920s) when large multi-unit businesses exerted considerable power in the market over small, single-unit entrepreneurs – was premised in transaction cost analysis. Transactions refer to the transference of a good or service from one economic entity to another. An underlying tenet is that firms and markets are alternative methods for coordinating resource allocation. What was retained in the firm was argued by economist Ronald Coase to be governed by the following axiom: "a firm will tend to expand until the costs of organizing an extra transaction within the firm become equal to the costs of carrying out the same transaction by means of an exchange on the open market."[3]

Contained in this statement are three critical elements. One is that a firm consists of internalized transactions managed as a coordinated whole through its own governance structure. Second is that the external environment is governed by the traditional market place through price mechanisms. Third is that the size of the firm and extent of internal activities can shift with changes in either the internal or external environment – that is, they represent a particular trade-off or set of choices reflective of conditions at one point in time. Thus, the large firms described by Chandler operated in an economic environment where financial, research and development, labor training and deployment, and other service functions were more efficiently carried out internally rather than externally, as were key stages in the transformation of products. Such was the case for large, and in particular US, auto makers.

The Internal Environment of the Firm

The internal organization of any firm reflects its strategy for entering the market. There are many configurations which vary by national custom, although certain forms have tended to predominate. Historically, the primary model for the organization of large firms was along either functional lines or operational divisions and structured according to a hierarchy.[4] For years, this structure was argued to display the greatest efficiency of industrial organization.[5] Through managerial hierarchies, jobs became specialized and staffed by individuals with unique sets of expert skills combined with deskilled blue-collar workers. Within the hierarchical governance system, tasks were allocated to functional divisions with the consequence that administrative decisions replaced price signals and market mechanisms.[6] This extraordinary division of labor and governance structure resulted in significant internal economies. The apparent success of hierarchical configurations led analysts to conclude that peer groups and other non-hierarchical means of internal organization were far less efficient for making and implementing decisions.[7]

By undertaking multiple tasks, large firms could enjoy economies of scale, access to information, and control over research and development which jointly helped to assure market dominance. In addition, control over innovation and technology secured "technological rents," or profits derived from technological monopolies.[8] The internalization of different steps of production, or vertical integration, further assured control over the timing, quality, and cost of inputs, choice of product or process technology, and command of product innovation.[9] Vertical integration reduced the transaction costs from uncertain inputs. This might be caused by the inability of a supplier to obtain the equipment needed to manufacture a product, for example, or for other reasons attributed to market failure. Excessive integration, on the other hand, created unnecessary costs – a lesson learned by the Ford Motor Company when it integrated all stages of auto manufacture from steel processing to assembly at its River Rouge plant during the 1920s.

Despite hypothetical advantages, the rise of large firms could occur only with access to large markets that afforded the extensive returns on investment required to make administrative coordination cost effective. In a somewhat circular manner, when product and process innovation were oriented towards capturing economies of scale, enterprises could realize substantial growth. And as noted by Chandler, "conversely in those sectors and industries where technology did not bring a sharp increase in output and where the market remained small and specialized, administrative coordination was rarely more profitable than market coordination."[10]

Access to large markets reinforced the oligopolistic control by large, multi-unit firms. They could compete for market share and profits, a combination attained through their internal organization of entrepreneurial functions and corporate planning, and through adoption of product differentiation and marketing strategies. This efficient system of managerial capitalism spread with great rapidity, particularly in the USA, and, as it did, it defined the firm, relations among firms, and the market:

> What the new enterprise did... was take over from the market the coordination and integration of the flow of goods and services from the production of the raw materials through the several processes of production to the sale to the ultimate consumer. Where they did so, the production and distribution came to be concentrated in the hands of a few large enterprises. At first this occurred in only a few sectors or industries where technological innovation and market growth created high-speed and high-volume throughput. As technology became more sophisticated and as markets expanded, administrative coordination replaced market coordination in an increasingly larger portion of the economy. By the middle of the Twentieth Century the salaried managers and large mass transporting enterprises coordinated current flows of goods through the process of production and distribution in major sectors of the American economy. By then the managerial revolution in American business had been carried out.[11]

The success of this system extended across countries. Multinational enterprises, with their concentrated buying and selling power, easily penetrated less developed market economies. By internalizing proprietary knowledge, they could retain technological rents. The asymmetry created with host countries generated market imperfections that invariably worked to the advantage of multinationals structured to capture economies of scale.[12]

The hierarchical internal organization combined with vertical integration proved to be a successful model when markets were large and stable, but it was rigid and inflexible when markets became fragmented and unstable. The short-run advantage of "economizing on scarce decision-making capabilities" by appropriating knowledge through narrowly defined expert skills or by utilizing deskilled blue-collar workers, both organized according to a hierarchy, sacrificed adaptability for productive efficiency.[13] Vertical integration added another constraint by requiring a fixed commitment to a cost structure that could not be easily changed when the market became increasingly unpredictable.

The persistence of market instability required more than minor adjustments by firms; it required complete reorganization. Firms with non-hierarchical forms of intra-organizational coordination that were discretionary or participatory in structure were more responsive to changes in demand because of their adaptive capability. Based on an entirely different system of rewards, rents here were derived from the processing of complex information attained by maximizing communication within the organization. This focussed attention on the collective unit, rather than the skills of individuals or other unique factors, and it favored individuals with broad skills engaged in interdisciplinary tasks.[14] Instead of displaying a vertical configuration, these firms were horizontal, project oriented, and fluid in their internal structure. These attributes permitted the firms to become extremely competitive as economic instability prevailed.

The strength of this system lay in the way economies could emanate from continuous innovation and rapid adjustment.[15] Since interaction among firms increased the diffusion of new technologies, cooperative arrangements based on information sharing were encouraged. With emphasis now on the clustering and coordination of firms, the productive unit shifted from the firm to the way firms were linked, and gave new significance to the external environment of the firm.

The External Environment of the Firm

Just as theories of the internal environment of the firm evolved from neo-classical notions of undifferentiated production functions, through concepts of hierarchical management in which positive returns are created from scale and functional organization, to horizontal firm systems distinguished by strategic structures and returns generated from informational rents, so theories of the external environment have similarly evolved. According to conventional economics – premised in perfect information, constant returns to factors, and other ideal conditions – the external environment is argued to be governed solely by market transactions. Only in instances of market failure caused by the high costs of defining and enforcing property rights or in administering transactions, and the like, is public intervention justified. The sharing of information among firms is argued to distort rather than improve market interactions. Yet these unrealistic underlying assumptions have made it impossible to account adequately for diminishing or alternatively increasing returns to such critical factors as innovation that may result from external interactions. As noted by economist Michael Best, "the transactions costs framework is tautological unless the distinctive costs of market and firm coordination are explained."[16]

Understanding how innovation is created is critical to this issue. The importance of innovation is evident as escalating research and development costs are created by a shortening of the product life cycle. The ability to be constantly innovative is imperative when new products must come to market at an accelerating pace. In integrated firms with a low norm of risk, innovations are internalized and introduced periodically as major breakthroughs.[17] Within horizontal structures, however, innovations are more likely to be introduced in iterative and incremental steps. Economist Alfred Marshall, when writing during the turn of the century, noted that the opportunity for innovation increases when small firms act as coordinated economic units cooperating in production, as opposed to when they act as singular entities competing in the market.[18] These coordinated units created by a complex web of interactions in the process of production, essentially function as alternatives to integrated firms. Within these systems, the generation and diffusion of innovation occurs incrementally due to the high level of firm interaction. External economies are created by a shared resource base, accumulated skills, and access to specialized activities – which would otherwise be appropriated by integrated firms as internal economies.[19] The economies generated are argued to exceed the advantages of integrated firms when markets are segmented and highly differentiated because of the ability of the overall structure to adapt to change.[20]

Although firms can hypothetically create such a coordinated system spontaneously, in fact this rarely happens. They are more often trapped in a "prisoners' dilemma" where all participants must act collectively for the group as a whole to benefit. Usually there must be some impetus encouraging cooperation, such as cartel legislation, or the presence of an organizing body. The organizing function may be undertaken by large firms through their relationship with smaller firms, or by the state or member driven service organizations. These organizing agents provide services that would otherwise be undertaken internally by large integrated firms having far more massive resources at hand relative to smaller firms.[21] The array of services include production, distribution, management, research and development, finance, and labor training and deployment.

Alternative Models of Industrialization

If viewed in the abstract, three distinct models of industries emerge: those with a vertical structure; those with a horizontal structure; and those with a combination of the two. They are further distinguished as: (1) integrated; (2) quasi-market; and (3) quasi-integrated. "Vertically integrated" refers to the integrated firm organized by hierarchies as reflected by the large US firms of the postwar period. These firms have recently begun to take a more horizontal configuration. The quasi-market structure, sometimes referred to as the "network" system, is characterized by the externalization of economic functions based on a horizontal configuration comprised primarily of small firms as illustrated by certain European industrial districts. The quasi-integrated system is also characterized by substantial externalization of economic functions and interaction among small firms, but with organizational control retained by one or more large or core firms, as illustrated by Japanese *keiretsus*. These firms can be either vertical or horizontal in organization.

Though distinct in their structure, these models are actually fluid, and tend to evolve. As argued by Charles Sabel, both large and small firms are attempting to benefit from each other's attributes – i.e., to capture economies of scale and to produce flexibly – through a process of "double convergence." He writes:

> As large firms reorganize, they try to recreate among their specialized units the collaboration characteristic of relations among firms in the flexible-specialization economies. As these latter expand, they create centralized laboratories, marketing agencies, and technology consultancies inspired by large-firm models. And as this reciprocal borrowing proceeds, flexible large firms and their smaller counterparts enter into direct alliances. One form such alliances take is a long-term subcontracting relation between the newly consolidated operating unit of a multinational and a nearby network of flexible subcontracts. Another is the formation within one or several areas of flexible specialization of an industrial group composed of a large firm with expertise in marketing and finance and smaller firms with expertise in production. Either way, the fabric of the local economy is reinforced at the same time that local firms are more directly tied into international markets.[22]

Despite tendencies toward convergence, distinctions remain in the nature of transactional activities associated with these structures. Relations between integrated firms and their suppliers consist of an unequal principal/agent arrangement where core firms control transactions with suppliers. These transactions result in a transfer of property rights and are defined in contractual terms. Among network firms, or those which operate within a quasi-market structure, providers and purchasers of goods function as both principals and agents and the relationship is equalized. It is therefore essential that firms in quasi-market systems adopt cooperative behavior. Within quasi-integrated systems, transactions exhibit a semi-hierarchical, semi-cooperative relationship. Thus the nature of the external environment associated with the integrated firm structure versus that of the quasi-market or quasi-integrated firms spans the range from pure market to controlled market forces. And as activities are shifted out of the integrated firm, the significance of the region as a site of production increases.

Further, in contrast to vertically organized firms which are designed to maximize economies of scale (i.e., economies derived from increased output per input), horizontally organized firms and firm structures based on extensive external linkages are designed to maximize economies of scope (i.e., economies derived from increased variation in output per input). That is, and borrowing from the perspective that the structure of a firm reflects its strategy, the structure of a firm must change to capture different economies.[23] Thus, within a horizontally configured firm, economies of scope may result either from research and development exchanges between divisions of different products for the purpose of generating product innovation, or from research and development exchanges between the design and manufacturing phases of the same product for the purpose of generating process innovation. Attempts by horizontally configured firms to capture economies of scope through these means represent alternatives to network structures in which economies of scope in product or process innovation are derived through external relations. Figures 2.1 and 2.2 illustrate the different firm configurations based on integrated, quasi-integrated, quasi-market examples, and according to vertical or horizontal structures.

As illustrated in these figures, within vertically integrated structures, research and development is concentrated in core firms, and their relationship with suppliers is on an individual basis. Within horizontally integrated firms, feedback loops integrate internal activities. Inter-connections with first-tier suppliers also require that they have some research and development, and perhaps sub-assembly, capability. Within quasi-integrated firms, first tier suppliers have both research and development and sub-assembly capability. As they become more horizontal, this capability increases to the point that suppliers may become quite strong relative to core firms. Since the quasi-market configuration does not differentiate between core and supplier firms, the notion of a vertical versus horizontal configuration does not apply. The process of double convergence, or attempts by smaller supplier and larger core firms to approximate each other through mutually beneficial relationships, leads toward quasi-integrated configurations.

Figure 2.1 *Vertical configurations*

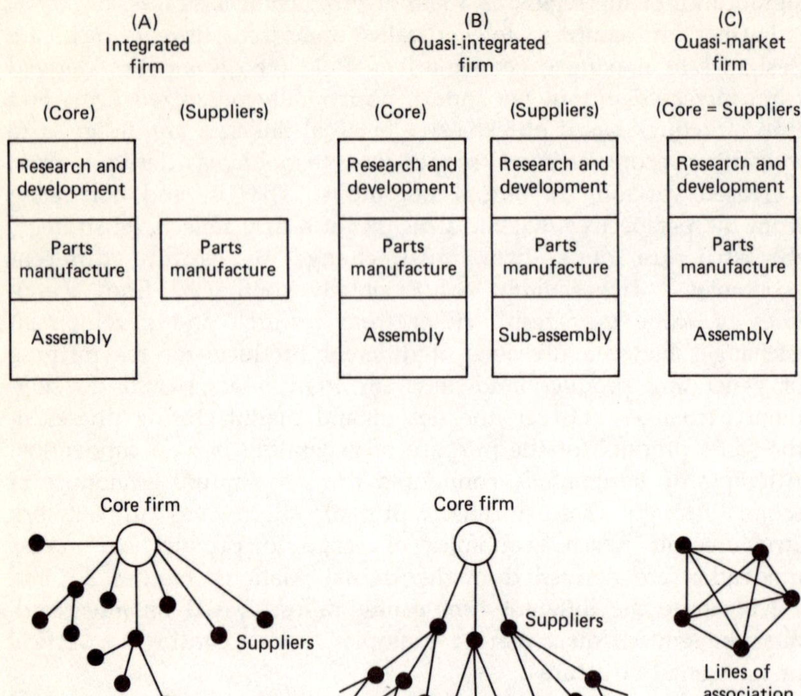

[1] This can have any distribution of activities – even having one or two, and not all three.

Industrialization and Regional Development

Within vertically integrated firms, functional activities are essentially discrete, so headquarter activities, research and development, component manufacture, and assembly may all take place in different locations to capture the greatest cost advantage of labor, transportation, and other inputs. Within horizontal structures that require interaction among functions, proximity is at a premium, and a cost advantage is sought from agglomeration economies. Here, access to a common labor pool, shared information and infrastructure, and the creation of a coherent market all provide positive returns to the

Figure 2.2 *Horizontal configurations*

(A)
Integrated
firm

(Core) Feedback loops

Research and development | Parts manufacture | Assembly

(Suppliers)

Research and development | Parts manufacture | Sub-assembly

Core firm

Suppliers

(B)
Quasi-integrated
firm

(Core)

Research and development | Parts manufacture | Sub assembly

(Suppliers)

Research and development | Parts manufacture | Sub-assembly

Core firm

Suppliers

(C)
Quasi-market
firm

(Core = Suppliers)

Research and development
Parts manufacture
Assembly

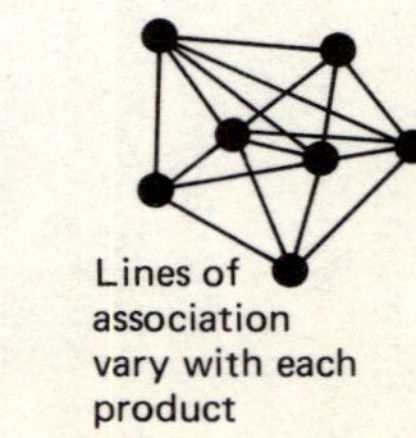

participants. They also create spillovers in the region, where spillovers resulting from increased research and development, or shortened product life cycles, result in innovation rents.

Economists have identified three complementary knowledge bases from which innovation spillovers may arise: formal knowledge contained in universities and research and development centers of private enterprise; tacit knowledge contained in the skilled labor and technology employed within an industry; and knowledge used in marketing innovation contained in business services.[24] These represent aspects of basic research, applied research, and the capacity to commercialize knowledge.

As firms agglomerate, they take advantage of knowledge contained in basic, applied, and informational sources in the region. By the act of concentrating productive activity, they further have the effect of fostering innovations.[25] That is, the ability to interact is reinforced by local institutions and resources. Since small firms appropriate fewer innovative functions relative to large firms, they have been shown through empirical studies to benefit more from knowledge-based spillovers in a region.[26]

These spillovers are most apparent in research and development, marketing, labor training, and access to capital. Each can be made available by one or more large firms, by groups of firms, or by the public or quasi-public sector. For example, basic research can be provided by major corporations, by public or private laboratories, or by universities. Studies indicate that innovative small firms make greater use of university research than do larger firms, reconfirming the importance of state policies to this group.[27] Similarly, while applied knowledge, or the ability to commercialize basic research and development, labor training, and capital availability can be controlled by large firms, they can also be provided by industry interest groups, public educational systems, or public investment funds. Studies also show that reliance on external debt is more critical to small firms than to large firms.[28] Reliance on large firms by smaller firms for innovative functions results in the former acting as the organizing agent. As previously noted, this role can also be performed by the state or by consortia of small firms. The more externally oriented the production system, the more the spatial configuration of production is defined by the region and the more the need for proximity to undertake transactions. As this occurs, the system of governance necessary to guide productive activity shifts from the firm to the region.

International Trade and Investment

The emergence of regions as the creators of economic wealth changes patterns of international development. Theories of international trade have traditionally been the product, and have explained the experiences, of relatively autonomous firms choosing among autonomous nations. They were initially derived from classical models which conceived of the world in terms of national markets distinguished by differences in factor endowments. The genesis of this idea lay in the work of Adam Smith who argued in *The Wealth of Nations* that the key to economic power was economic growth, and further that growth was a function of the division of labor.[29] An elaboration of this concept was provided by David Ricardo in the law of comparative advantage.[30] The argument was that, when countries specialize in the production of those goods in which they enjoy the lowest comparative costs, all participants benefit from international exchange over the long term. Thus international firms sought basic resource inputs from less developed regions, which they then transformed in developed nations and returned as final goods to international markets. This relationship characterized by sectoral differentation – that is, some regions specialized in resource extraction, others in manufacture, and so on – became known as the *classical* international division of labor.

As domestic markets within developing regions grew, and the capacity for manufacture along with consumption became feasible, multinational corporations looked to overseas sites as locations for extending the life of older technology or for establishing low-cost production. They further began to address world markets by assigning to a single division either the manufacture of a single product line worldwide, or the responsibility for servicing one geographic area with several products. Through internal transfer pricing, these firms gained a competitive edge over domestic competitors, a practice that contributed to dependency by host countries. This cost advantage led multinationals to integrate developing countries into their production strategies, with the result that headquarter functions were located in industrialized nations while routinized manufacturing activities were located in industrializing nations. The consequent functional differentiation of regions became known as the *new* international division of labor. (NIDL)[31]

This new configuration introduced into economics the importance of the mobility of factors of production, the cost of transportation, and increasing returns to scale. Further, the concept of relative factor endowment was expanded to include "human capital" and "opportunity costs," where human attributes and the potential for alternative investments influenced trade and investment choices. These ideas were combined with the concepts of marginal utility and general equilibrium theory that were central to neo-classical economics to show that a nation's comparative advantage was determined not only by its natural resources, but also by the relative abundance and most profitable combination of factors, including capital, labor, management, and technology. These were defined as a nation's created advantage and were expressed in the well-known Heckscher–Ohlin–Samuelson model.[32]

These ideas were further augmented by the notion that firms displayed changes in their structure and locational requirements associated with the "product cycle." During different stages of a product's development, from innovation to maturity, the production function changes, as do locational preferences. The changing technology and economies of scale of a firm over time introduce a dynamic element to the notion of comparative advantage.[33] During its early years, a firm seeks locations close to innovations and incipient markets but, as it matures, low-cost inputs dominate the locational decision for routinized activities.

Although theories of comparative advantage and product life cycle theory led one to expect a certain functional specialization of regions (i.e., the NIDL), experience showed that trade between countries increased rather than decreased as countries grew similar in industrial structure and levels of per capital income. This suggested that, instead of becoming differentiated by functional activities, areas were becoming differentiated by international trade regimes. One indication was a rise in the proportion of manufacturing subject to non-tariff restrictions within major industrialized countries.[34] The increase in non-traditional policy mechanisms such as voluntary export restraints and discretionary licensing by states suggested that economic rents were shifting from foreign corporations to the state, or to domestic corporations.[35] It also indicated that developing countries recognized the necessity of producing their own capital goods and technologies rather than to risk continued dependence on both transnational corporations and other countries for innovations.[36]

With the ability to accrue rents, particularly technological rents, becoming highly unpredictable, firms needed to share the costs and risks of research and development. This supported an increase in international alliances with host governments or national producers, and was indicative of a new "assertive pragmatism" between firms and governments.[37] Uncertainty provided the incentive for industries to spread research and development costs as widely as possible, and encouraged states to share in the investment. It resulted not only in a change in the distribution of profits derived from innovation, but also in a change in the structure of world trade. Rather than the configuration described by the NIDL, forms of *regional collaborative competition* began to emerge.[38]

Innovation Theory and Practice

The tendency towards the regionalization of production leaves open the question as to what this means for developing countries. Are developed nations invariably favored over developing nations as innovation becomes an important element for determining competitiveness? Innovation theory provides insight into the rationale for innovative activity to take place in industrializing countries. According to theories of comparative advantage, research and development should occur in developed nations possessing an educated work force, advanced research facilities, and other requirements for high-technology growth, including finance and infrastructure. By extension of this reasoning, countries not in the technological forefront should fall further behind. Bound by unilaterally defined relationships, advanced semi-industrialized nations would be expected to acquire only second-tier technologies for mature products using standardized technology and practices.

However, this approach has led to an oversight of certain fundamental dimensions of a country's capacity for technological development. Among most developing countries, learning by doing and learning by using have been the primary means of acquiring technological mastery. These processes underlie much of the productivity increase observed among industrializing countries.[39] A nucleus of knowledge frequently emerges from supposedly low-technology industries which is then upgraded by the progressive appropriation of skills. Expertise arises from the adaptation, improvement, and creation of capital goods in labor-intensive industries, with textiles being a prime example, that is then transferred to other industries.[40]

The oversight results because conventional economic theory based on production functions assumes that technological innovation is an exogenous factor. As a consequence, it is inadequate for understanding technological change. The production function assumes an unambiguous relationship between inputs and outputs. Factor substitution in response to changes in factor prices leads to movements along the production surface between two known methods. Technological change, therefore, involves breakthroughs that shift the production function itself. Alternative techniques are depicted as a series of isoquants (or combinations of capital and labor which produce a given level of output, and which are typically mapped as a set of curves), each representing a different technology.

Yet experience shows that, instead of choice of technique, the innovative process is best described as one of the search for and learning of new techniques.[41] Before production begins, knowledge as to method must be acquired. However, neo-classical theory underplays product and process innovation and overplays factor saving. This tendency makes neo-classical formulations weak in explaining either productivity growth or increasing returns to scale. A neo-classical approach would reject adoption of inferior techniques just because cheap inputs exist or because of their developmental potential, although this is the choice in many capital-intensive industries of Third World countries.

"Evolutionary theories" of innovation address these issues by attempting to reconcile the endogenous nature of technical change in production processes with the structural forces behind those processes and techniques.[42] It is argued that any knowledge base contains specific search and learning procedures for the development of new products and methods of production. These sets of perceived possibilities are embedded within technological paradigms[43] or technological regimes.[44] Since search procedures and knowledge bases are specific to an industry and to the technological paradigm, innovation tends to be produced from a limited set of techniques which are available to a firm or a region. These, in turn, are enhanced by the spatial consolidation of capital, skills, components, markets, and enabling institutions.[45] The geographical convergence of these factors accentuates the rate and direction of innovation. Therefore the technological proficiency and, consequently, differences in the competitive position of regions emerge from mutually reinforcing processes involving the interaction of producers, suppliers, and governments.

Within developing countries, indigenous knowledge acquisition through learning by doing and learning by using can be reinforced and improved upon by corporate strategies that decentralize research functions. Studies indicate that multinationals are beginning to establish advanced research and development facilities in developing countries where they can take advantage of a wider knowledge base and at a lower cost.[46] These possibilities for sharing in the innovative process broaden the extent to which national and local governments can become active in determining the nature of development. They also bring new elements into the process of regionalization, since developing countries have significant potential for sharing in the trends.

The State and the Market

With changes in firm strategy and structure, states have greater opportunities to be active participants in the economy. In contrast to the silent partner of "free-market" economics, a proactive position requires assertion by a strong state. Political scientist John Hall defines "strong" as "the extent to which the state can actually penetrate and tax society, and hence organize it and provide it with services, from education to justice."[47] This is distinguished from the appropriation of power through despotic means or, alternatively, by the relinquishing of power to market forces. The minimum a strong state can do is provide infrastructure, though increasingly it must also stabilize the conditions underlying investment and production. Certain sectors are particularly responsive to state guidance. These include high-technology or knowledge-intensive industries whose social gains in the form of spillovers exceed the private returns captured by firms. By attracting industries yielding high returns, states can create positive external economies. With control over technology and rapid technological change being key determinants of market position, and in recognition that the generation of knowledge may be imperfectly appropriated, support for knowledge-intensive activities is becoming a priority for many governments.

State support is most necessary at the outset of the development of a technology. Technological development may require significant fluidity initially, but once market positions are determined technology tends to freeze. As noted in previous studies:

> When a technology is in its infancy, and still fluid, the line of its technological evolution is inherently uncertain... The pace and direction of development are matters of decision. This depends partly on circumstances and partly on individual choices... After positions freeze, a radically new technology will not be developed unless it is so attractive that producers and users are willing to walk away from their investments in earlier technologies.[48]

Thus the window of opportunity for when a state may support technological development is limited. State action must be both timely and appropriate for establishing complementary assets necessary to firms.

Public support of innovative activities varies according to underlying notions of efficiency. Economists identify three kinds of efficiency: Ricardian efficiency, which refers to the allocation of resources according to their effects on current economic conditions; growth efficiency, which refers to the allocation of resources according to their effects on economic growth (e.g., "infant industry argument"); and Schumpeterian efficiency, which refers to the allocation of resources according to their effects on the pace and direction of technological change.[49] Ricardian efficiency operates under the assumptions of traditional economics – price competition, exogenously derived technological change, constant returns to factors, and trade based on comparative advantage. According to a "free-market" logic, government actions in the market distort market signals and promote inefficiency. However, as previously noted, through the geographic concentration of productive activities and processes that result in dynamic learning, it is possible to achieve increasing returns factors. Thus, according to growth or a Schumpeterian logic, it is reasonable to promote these outcomes through policy intervention, particularly if market signals may not yield desired results. Under conditions of imperfect competition and rapid technological change, a targeting strategy based on a combination of growth and Schumpeterian efficiency is argued to generate higher levels of economic welfare over time than a market strategy based on Ricardian efficiency.[50]

From this perspective, governmental actions that guide development and assure constant technological innovation are both appropriate and necessary to promote competitiveness. Public policies can provide support for research and development, finance, labor training, and other activities which may be internalized in large firms but which network firms may find cost prohibitive, and therefore are externalized but not to the market. In return, states capture rents from higher wages or profits that translate into higher tax receipts. The spillovers generated by industrialization are retained in the region, with the combined effects of increased social infrastructure, enhanced industrial linkages, and high levels of innovation resulting in the spread of beneficial externalities across firms and industries. The outcome of such intervention is increased competitive advantage of the region. Since extensive research and development costs can create barriers to entry in an industry, and a lack of continuous research and development support can result in loss of "first-mover advantage" in a market, there is strong incentive for governments or other institutions to intervene in research and development on behalf of industries in which they have a vested interest. Similar arguments can be made about finance capital, labor training, and other functions in which private firms find limitations to their ability to recapture investments through profits.

Thus regional policy can encourage innovation, spread beneficial externalities, and capture first-mover advantage. In this capacity, regions are instrumental in redefining the concept of firm and the nature of competition. Pro active involvement of public entities in establishing complementary assets to the private sector can facilitate regional collaborative competition. By their participation, firms signify that they find it preferable to adjust to costs resulting from governmental rules where risks can be assessed than to operate under conditions where risks are unpredictable. Thus both firms and governments make adjustments as they evolve toward regional solutions.

National Variation

The nature of public support for enterprise varies extensively across countries, and reflects the logic behind competition. For example, interventions in the USA and the UK are generally designed to organize markets through macro-economic adjustments, such as import or export policies. In contrast, industrial policies in Germany, Italy, and Japan are designed to organize market structures through long-term finance capital, marketing assistance, access to supplier networks, labor training, and research and development investments, thereby minimizing the risks that their firms confront. The primary distinctions among countries lie in their process of economic adjustment – that is, who takes the initiative, what mechanisms are available, and, even more fundamentally, the structure of markets and institutions that express the logic of the economy. Two critical markets are those for labor and capital.

The extent to which these markets lend themselves to the adjustment process lies in the nature of external versus internal mobility. A market for labor consists of the allocation and supply of labor which is determined by the means of entry into employment and nature of mobility. The model of labor utilization that has evolved in *laissez-faire* economies depends upon a mobile market of autonomous individuals with undeterred access to employment.

Alternatively, in models from controlled market economies, barriers to entry and mobility are used to organize the labor market. This is revealed in the nature of the internal and external labor markets of the USA and Japan.

In the USA, which descended from the liberal legacy, the external labor market is highly mobile and the internal labor market is relatively inflexible. In Japan, just the opposite is the case. Here, most hiring takes place at graduation, through a centralized personnel department of a firm. By contrast, in the USA, hiring takes place at any time in the career trajectory of an individual, and is extremely decentralized. Job changes across firms are both more frequent and more casual in the USA. On the other hand, once inside a firm, a Japanese worker can more easily change job categories, while for an American this is far more difficult. Further, in core firms Japanese workers often encounter life-time employment and pay based on senority rather than job classification, whereas in the USA workers are paid according to skill and job category and to a lesser extent according to seniority. (In neither Japan nor the USA is the job security of core firms replicated in peripheral firms, though the distribution of power is arguably more unequal in Japan.[51]) The differences are captured in the following observation:

> In the United States, labor allocation and reallocation occurs by workers crossing the firm-market boundary more often, but occupational boundaries less often, than in Japan. In Japan, workers tend to stay within the firm-market boundary but cross occupational boundaries more frequently than in the United States.[52]

These differences reflect the way risk is allocated within society. During periods of economic stress, market uncertainties are externalized into the labor market in the USA. On the other hand, in Japan they are expressed as changes in either occupational patterns or use of peripherialized labor. While in the USA this creates direct pressures to lower wages and diminish welfare claims, such is less apparent among the economically franchised segments of the labor force in Japan. Whereas Japanese firms have considerable discretion in the reallocation of labor within firms, this is less common among US companies.

Capital markets in these countries, on the other hand, operate in just the opposite manner. In contrast to labor markets, capital markets provide considerable discretion for firms in the USA but to a far lesser extent in Japan. Internal financing is more prevalent in the USA than in Japan, where there is a greater reliance on bank loans. Based on return on investment analysis, US firms allocate capital among divisions according to specified criteria. Within Japan, capital allocation more frequently requires coordination between the divisions and banks, and is therefore less accessible for reallocation to other divisions. The bank–firm relationship is strengthened by the fact that banks in Japan can hold an equity position in firms, and further because, equity and corporate bond markets are less well developed, alternative options for funding are limited.

Thus, in times of financial stress, US firms with their restricted internal labor markets, and in search of the best return on investment, will relocate to low-wage sites, diversify into unrelated but lucrative product lines, and vertically disintegrate. Japanese firms, with strong ties to external financial sources and more flexible internal labor markets, will more likely search for a solvent business partner through the bank, diversify into related product lines, reallocate labor within the firm, and vertically disintegrate.[53]

The opportunities for state intervention are clearly distinct in these two systems. Levers for intervention are weak in the USA but stronger in Japan. And, as political scientist John Zysman argued: "the financial structure constrains government choices so sharply that it can influence the shape of the political process of adjustment."[54] A parallel argument can be made for labor markets. As a framework for analysis, Zysman offers three distinct models of adjustment: state-led; company-led; and negotiated. Within this framework, Japan displays a credit-based financial system with administered prices and a state-led model of adjustment; the USA has a capital market financial system with competitive prices and a company-led model of adjustment; and Germany consists of a credit-based financial system with price formation dominated by banks and a negotiated model of adjustment. The Japanese situation can be argued to be brokered or state-led.[55] In either case, it offers more opportunity for state direction than is apparent in the USA. Both negotiated and state-led systems provide greater opportunity for state action than in a company-led environment. Thus the governed-market approach to development that has proven highly successful in developing countries has strong parallels in developed nations.[56] Whether states tend to adopt either a free-market approach to market adjustments, or some form of governed-market approach, what they take up is complemented by industry strategy and structure. This is revealed in the competitive postures of both firms and states.

Context for Understanding the International Automobile Industry

The analysis that follows presents automobile industry firms according to the distinctions previously identified: integrated, quasi-market, and quasi-integrated, and as to vertical or horizontal configuration. The nature of the internal and external environment of auto firms is developed to show how various structures require or are supported by state policies and institutions. This is presented within the dynamic framework of industrial convergence.

In turn, states are examined with respect to their free-market or governed-market ideology. The position explored here is that, owing to the risks created by economic instability, a governed-market approach presents a more successful model for making adjustments in the automobile industry than does a free-market approach. This is examined by studying the basis to competitiveness in the automobile industry within different nations.

Further, on the assumption that regionalization represents a strategy for establishing stability and hence competitiveness, the issue of how regionalization is manifested is pursued by studying the strategies of firms and the responses of states. The question explored is how North–South integration is occurring in light of *de facto* industrial regionalization. The argument presented is that developing nations which increase their technological capacity are not necessarily subordinated to the technological trajectories of industrialized nations. These issues are studied by examining patterns of design, development, and manufacture in the auto industry across nations.

Lastly, and based on the above, policies for supporting innovation and competitiveness are assessed in light of the pressures on firms and states to share market risks. This comes from the conviction that the value of these ideas put to practice determines their ultimate worth.

3

Automobile Production and the Industrial Legacy of the USA

Transformation of the US Automobile Industry

The US auto industry is at a crossroads. In fifteen years between 1974 and 1991, the US share of North American automotive sales dropped from 85 per cent to 56 per cent, triggering a record post-World War II loss of $6.7 billion.[1] The drop in sales forced hundreds of plant closures and lay-offs. In just two years, from 1978 to 1980, some 200,000 jobs were lost. The restructuring that began in the 1970s and continues in the 1990s has induced a massive transformation of the US automobile industry. In the assessment of MIT industry analyst Martin Anderson, "the profound changes made [in the US auto industry] ... between 1976 and 1982 [may have] constituted the largest shift in technological, human and capital resources in US industrial history."[2] Pressures continue to mount for even more change. Initially, adjustments in the industry were designed to promote greater efficiency through cost minimization, but by the early 1980s they began to accentuate productivity increases through innovation. The industry is still in flux, and could evolve in a number of directions. However, it has already forced a number of institutional changes that make possible entirely new forms of industrialization. This is an examination of the nature of industrial change, institutional responses, and implications for future developments.

Past as Prologue

The history of the US auto industry captures the essence of this nation's industrial development during its fifty years of global economic dominance. From the 1920s to the 1970s, Keynesian policies of demand-led growth stimulated the mass production and mass consumption of consumer durable goods. Assured of a large consumer base, car makers easily sustained models in annual quantities of 250,000 to 500,000. Model differentiation based on marketing, styling, and price, a notion introduced by former GM President Alfred Sloan, generated a continual demand for new cars. With emphasis on superficial restyling, control over advertising and dealership networks became a critical means of managing production. Production itself consisted of large-scale operations using flow methods of manufacture and dedicated equipment housed in specialized plants. Engine production, assembly, and other steps of manufacture which were designed to achieve economies of scale tolerated only marginal changes in the design of the fundamental body structure or powertrain of the car. It became standard practice for body variations and common parts to be used by a limited number of platforms (or base models), which were further distinguished by "family" type. The entire system was driven by cost minimization and output maximization that proved to be very efficient during the periods of economic stability, but not very resilient to change.

To understand how this formula for success lost its efficacy, the analysis traces the development of the industry as it passed through several distinct stages: (1) the era of craft production; (2) the rise of mass production; (3) crisis; (4) internationalization; and (5) regionalization. During each phase, the underlying basis to productivity and profitability changed, which was revealed in the corporate strategies, the nature of industrial organization, and the location of productive activity. Despite apparent evolution, the transition from craft manufacture to mass production did not represent a natural progression. It was the result of economic pressure and institutional bias. Only much later did small-scale manufacture re-emerge as a critical element for sustaining competitiveness.

The birth of the industry in the USA took place in 1894, when the first car was made with the intent of commercial manufacture and sale. Within a few years, numerous small manufacturers were scattered across the nation making finely crafted machines that were unique in design and fueled by many different substances from steam to gasoline.

They operated on a small scale, making their product by hand through the creative application of multiple skills. For two decades, these small manufacturers flourished. But mass production quickly dominated the national market when, in 1914, the Ford Motor Company adopted the moving assembly-line and applied the concept of interchangeable parts to standardize the product, and when General Motors introduced the notion of annual model changes, popularized in the 1920s. A wave of consolidation swept the country as small craft manufacturers and less competitive mass producers succumbed to mergers, acquisitions, and bankruptcy. Whereas approximately 88 assemblers operated nationwide during 1921, by 1933 only ten major firms remained. Just the remnants of a small craft tradition survived through the production of racing and other specialty vehicles, though these retained links to mass production through innovations and parts used in common.

The demise of craft producers was not inevitable, since it did not necessarily occur in other nations: in fact, it was more common for both traditions to develop side by side. Rather, in the USA, this was the result of a large, unified consumer market and public policies that favored large-scale manufacture. Neither was it necessary that large manufacturers follow the path of standardized manufacturing. Initially it appeared that GM might have introduced flexible mass production since, in contrast to Ford's strict adherence to standardization it championed a policy of model differentiation. However, GM suffered a series of product design setbacks in the 1930s which made it wary of flexibility at a time when Ford was particularly successful, through standardization, in reducing the cost of car ownership.[3] For lack of other incentives, the industry was pushed in the direction of the archetypical mass production that came to characterize American manufacture.

Once the market for street vehicles was dominated by a handful of firms, the industry concentrated around Detroit and the Midwest. As early as 1914, 63 per cent of the value of all autos and parts made in the USA was coming out of Michigan, in some measure owing to the availability of parts suppliers serving the bicycle and related industries. With a relatively small investment, car makers could establish an assembly plant and maintain operations capitalized on the one hand by customers who paid cash on delivery, and on the other by parts producers who provided credit for their components.[4] As of 1909, Michigan was producing cars 25 per cent cheaper than elsewhere in the nation.[5] While access to parts and capital gave Michigan an initial advantage for investment, the logic of locating assembly operations close to markets soon became evident.

By way of illustration, as the demand for cars grew, the Ford Motor Company responded in two ways. One was to increase vertical integration, most notably in 1916 at the River Rouge plant, which combined everything from steel processing to final assembly. The other was to decentralize assembly in order to lower transportation costs, maintain better supervision over dealers, and circumvent tariff barriers. The second strategy proved more successful in the long run. The first Ford branch plant in the USA was established in 1910. By 1914 there were seven regional assembly plants, including one in Los Angeles and another in San Franciso. During the 1920s, when Ford accounted for between 40 and 50 per cent of autos made in the country, this number expanded to 32. Foreign operations followed a similar logic (Canada, 1904; England, 1911; Japan, 1924; Germany, 1939; and France, 1934), resulting in a large international network within a few decades.

Throughout this period the USA became a more open economy. Tariffs on automobiles dropped from 45 per cent in 1914 to 10 per cent by 1934. But this had a negligible effect on market share because the domestic manufacturers were already quite strong. By contrast, erection of high tariff walls elsewhere encouraged US firms to take over foreign production or invest abroad to overcome trade-related cost penalties. These world-competitive mass producers easily penetrated major global markets, and by 1937 US auto makers accounted for 76 per cent of the world output of cars, a level they maintained until the 1950s.[6]

As the industry matured, the nature of both process and product innovations evolved from major breakthroughs to minor adjustments.[7] The most efficient new technologies quickly diffused throughout the industry and determined the nature of the product and, consequently, production. Within a short period of time, a dominant design emerged using gasoline-powered internal combustion engines. The basic car was similar in structure across manufacturers, as was the method of manufacture, and radical innovation was replaced by incremental changes in styles or comfort. The most efficient level of production for capturing scale economies was in lots of 250,000 to 500,000 units, although popular models could reach as many as 1.5 million units.

Car production consisted of design and development, component fabrication, the assembly process, and distribution. Initially, each branch plant assembled the full model range, thus requiring that the entire system shut down with every model change. After World War II, when the demand for autos was at an unprecedented high, plants were converted to capture economies of scale through the production of one or two models. At the outset, engine plants were situated close to assembly sites and manufactured the full range of engine models. Eventually, they too began to specialize, thereby diminishing the need for proximity to any particular assembly plant.[8] Over time, the assembly process and manufacture of major parts became specialized and spatially separated.

The assembly function occurred at branch plants located close to consumer markets, as did the manufacture of minor mechanical parts used in both the original equipment and aftermarkets. Production of engines, stampings, and other major parts was located primarily in the Midwest, where these were central to national markets. Management and research and development were headquartered near Detroit. Within an assembly site, parts would arrive in disassembled batches and be held in inventory until time for incorporation into the final product. As a result, branch plant sites consisted of large, single-story buildings for undertaking assembly and sub-assembly, surrounded by expansive lots for holding inventory.[9]

Car manufacturers attained oligopolistic control over their extensive, and highly competitive, supplier base through sourcing policies. The car makers concentrated on the assembly of final vehicles and the manufacture of major mechanical parts, body stampings, and other key components, though some of the parts were also sourced externally. Thousands of less strategic parts were provided by suppliers. Assemblers used competitive bidding and multiple sourcing to force independent suppliers and subsidiaries to compete by lowering costs. In addition, parallel parts production gave them the latitude they needed to shift orders whenever costs became too high at any one site.[10] Both manufacturing and engineering capabilities were duplicated internally and externally to maintain leverage. Despite a tendency to duplicate material, technical and design decisions remained within the domain of the core firms. The competitive relationship with suppliers and subsidiaries was efficient so long as production runs were long and predictable and parts requirements were standardized. However, this was not the case once cooperation was required for product and process innovation, as in the development of modular systems or built-up parts.

Selective vertical integration also provided a certain element of control over suppliers, although it subjected the subsidiaries to core-firm union agreements, which rigidified costs. Through vertical integration, formerly independent parts suppliers became captive to particular assemblers. By removing parts suppliers from the market, this policy became an effective strategy for squeezing out competition. The extent of vertical integration varied by company and over time.

Initially, firms combined "design flexibility and shallow vertical integration . . . when the rate of technological change in the product was rapid. As product designs stabilized after the war, however, other factors, like the strength of dealerships and customer service, became more important."[11] After the war, vertical integration increased as auto makers attempted to control key inputs. In 1980, GM made nearly half of its parts, Ford approximately 40 per cent, Chrysler 39 per cent, and American Motors 20 per cent.[12] That is, GM, being a full model manufacturer, attempted to maintain considerable control over critical inputs and hence was more integrated; for Ford, with its policy of cost reduction and standardization, less integration was consistent since this was more cost effective; while Chrysler and American Motors, from their relatively weaker positions, maintained less control over their inputs.

Despite the fact that forward linkages were less integrated, auto makers could control the quantity and stock of cars delivered to dealers through exclusive franchising. In this way, they passed along the risks associated with holding inventories of completed vehicles to dealers.[13] When Sloan's concept of product differentiation based on annual model changes became standard practice, distributors were forced to market and display a variety of options, so they turned to large car lots as a means of maintaining inventories.

The low-cost principle governing relations with suppliers was replicated in the relationship car makers forged with workers. Since contract agreements between car makers and suppliers could be broken during market downturns, workers played the part of economic shock absorbers, and seasonal lay-offs and speed-up became standard means for adjusting costs. Primary-sector workers could generally negotiate compensation for market fluctuations; however, this was usually beyond the reach of secondary-labor-market workers. Cost-minimizing pressures translated into a high level of economic insecurity for both suppliers and secondary sector-workers.

As mass production replaced artisanship, the composition of the labor force changed. Skilled craft persons declined in number and were replaced by narrowly skilled production workers who gained security through unionization.[14] The United Auto Workers sit-down strike at GM in Flint, Michigan, led to the first national contract for any union (1937) and triggered a wave of national recognition strikes. Initial negotiations were preceded by combative confrontations, strikes, and lay-offs. After years of annual or biennial strikes and employment instability, in 1948 GM and the UAW entered into a historic agreement that became a model for other industries. The agreement achieved relative employment stability sought by both workers and employers by linking wage increases to productivity gains and cost of living increases. With the incentive to strike diminished, workers sought rewards based on wage increments, job retention, seniority, and job titles. They came to focus on compensation rather than broader social or economic issues. Unionized core-firm workers became distinguished from non-unionized workers by pay differentials, benefits, and job security.[15] These employment security provisions and wage gains tied to productivity increases transformed blue-collar workers into middle-income consumers who ultimately drove the engine of the economy.

The Institutional Context for Mass Production

The form of industrialization based on mass production/mass consumption, which Antonio Gramsci referred to as "Fordism," was extremely effective during the postwar economic expansion.[16] After World War II, automobile manufacture and consumption became so integral to national prosperity that one out of every six jobs was directly or indirectly related to automobile production. Even though by 1960 there was one car for every three Americans, the USA remained the most important market in the world. It was not only the largest market for cars, it was the largest market for *large* cars. Despite labor costs that could be 30 per cent more for a large car than for a compact vehicle, selling prices could differ by 174 per cent, making large cars far more profitable to produce and therefore the segment of choice.[17] Car makers profited by making large cars in quantity distinguished by superficial changes; core workers benefited from the relatively stable employment and access to a comfortable middle-class life style; and the economy expanded.

The observation that what was good for General Motors was good for the nation had an element of truth, since this was an industry-led economy.[18] Government policies assured growth and perpetuation of mass-production industrialization by remaining invisible. The prevailing ideology of "free-market" economics restricted the government to protecting competition and arbitrating conflicts. As noted by the Harvard Business School Project on the Auto Industry and the American Economy, this logic translated into two dominant policy themes:

> ... first, that macro-economics is the only appropriate role for the federal government in the economy and in the competitive performance of the

> industry; and second, consistent with the first theme, that government should only respond to the demands placed on it and should not attempt to formulate or execute a specfic competitive strategy. Together, these two principles frame a classical definition of American economic-political theory: laissez-faire economics responding to the dictates of the marketplace, and demand-responsive government, balancing competing claims.[19]

At one level were explicit macro-economic policies that defined the rules governing competition in product markets, such as antitrust, trade, tax policy, and regulation. At another were imbedded policies that structured labor and capital markets. Implicit policies directed at factor markets and explicit macro-economic policies were equally important in shaping industrialization, and both favored the rise of standardized production over more flexible means of manufacture.

Perhaps no other policy captured the essence of US market ideology than that of antitrust, which is unique in its application in the USA compared with other countries. The purpose of antitrust is to ensure economic efficiency by prohibiting restraints on trade and the creation of monopolies. Over the years, interpretations of "economic efficiency" have led to ambiguity in the enforcement and explicit purpose of this legislation. One constant is that court rulings have established that neither size alone nor monopoly, *per se*, violate antitrust legislation if they are the result of superior management or products. On the other hand, the extent of vertical and conglomerate mergers were limited if the case involved a leading firm operating in a concentrated market and a potential new entrant.[20] During the 1950s and 1960s, the prevailing opinion was that market power, *per se*, is harmful. In the 1970s, as the pendulum swung, just the opposite was upheld – namely that the artificial barriers and exclusionary behavior, previously argued as inhibiting competition, in fact created efficiency through scale economies.[21] Over time, public policy became increasingly less interventionist, and more favorable to large firms, and it consistently upheld basic notions of competition in the market among firms, and between firms and the government. As noted by economist David Audretsch, "whereas cooperation has been the cornerstone of public policy in Europe and Japan, antitrust is the epitome of the adversarial relationship between government and private business in the United States."[22] This view shaped the structure of the US automobile industry during the period of its greatest domestic and international influence.

Trade policy, tax policy, and regulation supported this concept of the economy. Principles of free trade were adhered to even when trading partners did not correspond. Corporate tax rates were consistently low, although they offered few credit incentives. And until the 1960s the auto industry faced few restrictive regulations. At the local level, public policies focussed on industry promotion through tax incentives as a way of luring jobs into a particular locale, which was the least interventionist form of economic development.

The means for shaping product–market interactions by the government occurred through the labor and capital markets. Mobility in the exernal labor market, defined primarily by education and wage and employment policies, set the parameters to labor-market transactions. The labor market external to firms was highly fluid, but it was restricted internally, since labor unions could negotiate a myriad of narrowly defined blue-collar positions, complemented by management, engineers, and other skilled persons focussed on equally narrowly skilled positions. Job tasks became specifically defined and highly differentiated, and involved little interaction. In their discussion of the automobile industry, the authors of the MIT Commission on Industry Productivity site this phenomenon in Detroit. Accordingly, a "Taylorist" process was acknowledged on the factory floor and beyond. Engineering and management were Taylorized as well, resulting in skilled and professional workers with deep but very narrow skills.[23] On the one side, US industrial relations supported the narrowly focussed "compensation orientation" of unions and management,[24] while on the other the educational system performed a similar function for engineers and managers by its method of "specialist" training.[25] Jobs were discrete, highly monitored (the role of the industrial engineer performed an important gatekeeper function), and highly differentiated by levels of pay. Despite a wide variation in remuneration, pay levels were restricted by the potential for people to be replaced given the extraordinarily mobile external labor market.

Government influence over capital markets was even more tangential, although it was significant among firms. Capital markets functioned according to an entirely different logic from that of labor markets. Large car makers could maintain considerable discretion in their ability to allocate capital among divisions. Access to capital depended on bond ratings and stock values which responded well to projects that promised a high return on investment in the near term, rather than risky projects, or those with a focus on long-term market penetration, or where returns were not easily assessed. Neither debt nor equity capital were readily available to small manufacturers. Given this bias, capital markets, complemented the needs of mass car makers operating in large, stable markets.

Crisis and Transition

These mutually reinforcing policies of industry and government were so successful up through World War II that the nation was oblivious to indications of potential weakness. Yet signs of growing international competition had already begun to surface as early as the 1950s. First England (1950) and then Germany (1956) took the lead away from the USA in the world export of new cars through export-promotion programs. Aided by the formation of the European Economic Community (EEC) in 1957, European auto makers began in the 1960s to adopt standardized and interchangeable parts, which broadened the European consumer market. They also entered the US market relatively easily as a result of low US tariffs (5.5 per cent) and a lack of domestic content requirements – despite the signing by the USA and Canada of the Canadian Automobile Agreement (1965) aimed at removing tariffs and expanding the domestic market base. In 1968 the EEC instituted a policy of free internal trade coupled with a 17.6 per cent external tariff, which further consolidated the regional market. As the strength of foreign firms grew, by 1970 the share of world auto production attributed to domestically based US firms had slipped to 30 per cent.

To improve trade relations and investment conditions in the USA, in 1971 the gold standard was dropped and the dollar was allowed to devalue. This was still insufficient to counteract the 1973 and 1979 OPEC (Organization of Petroleum Exporting Countries) oil shocks, which raised the price of oil fourfold and plunged the USA into a series of deep recessions. As an energy-saving measure, the USA adopted the Energy Policy and Conservation Act of 1975. This established the average annual miles-per-gallon, or corporate average fuel economy (CAFE), standard each auto maker had to achieve. But it was a crisis response with no overall strategic plan for recovery, and the legislation compounded the auto industry's problems. Oil scarcity and high gasoline prices made small cars the choice for over half of new car buyers, and, as a premier small-car maker, Japan climbed by 1975 to the position of second to the USA in the production of autos and first in passenger-car exports.

The heightened competition precipitated a wave of plant closures and capital flight. From 1979 to 1980, 20 plants closed or announced closure, directly affecting the employment of more than 50,000 workers and indirectly affecting another 350,000 to 650,000. The number of employees working in auto assembly dropped from nearly 470,000 in 1978 to 317,000 in 1982. Unemployment among workers in motor vehicles and parts production rose from 3.9 per cent in 1977 to 20.4 per cent in 1980. Unions were faced with the difficult choice of offering concessions or accepting a plant shutdown, often to see their plants close anyway as they watched their effectiveness erode. Branch plant locations were most severely hit. For example, in Los Angeles, the second largest producer of cars in the world after Detroit during the 1950s, all of the assembly facilities were permanently shuttered, as were most of the parts providers.

Imports began to make serious inroads in the US market. In contrast to 1978, when GM reached 47.8 per cent, Ford 23.5 per cent, Chrysler 11.1 per cent, American Motors 1.5 per cent and imports 16.1 per cent of the US market, by 1988 GM's market share had dropped to 35.9 per cent, Ford 's to 21.5 per cent, and Chrysler's to 11.2 per cent; American Motors had dropped out of the market altogether (1986), while imports had captured 31.4 per cent.[26] The growth of trade translated into a balance of payments problem. In the four years from 1982 to 1986, the US trade deficit attributed to vehicles and parts rose from $1.2 billion to $10 billion[27], while the ratio of imports to consumption increased from 13 per cent to 20 per cent.[28] Most of this deficit was the result of unreciprocated trade with Japan (see figure 3.1).

Figure 3.1 *US exports and imports of auto parts by selected trade partners, 1982 and 1986*

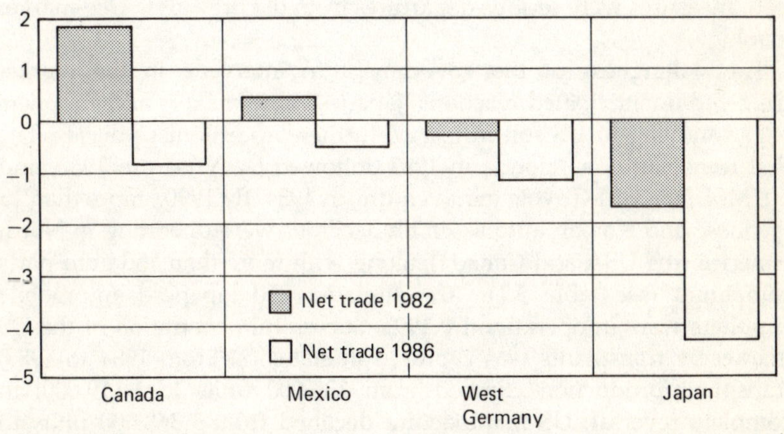

Source: US Global Competitiveness: The US Automotive Parts Industry, USITC Publication 2037 (December 1987).

Rapid import penetration contributed to a market that was becoming progressively more saturated and fragmented. In contrast to 1950, when only one-fourth of US residents owned a car, by 1977 the figure was one-half. Because of the crowded market, product differentiation became ever more significant. Specialty vehicles, recreation vehicles, sports cars like the Corvette, and luxury cars such as Cadillac were showing greater profits than the common passenger car.

The poor performance of US car makers in their most basic markets spawned a number of studies comparing inefficiency in US plants relative to Japanese facilities. The studies invariably showed that higher wage rates, lower output to value added ratios, and other productivity measures consistently favored Japanese producers.[29] In addition, these new entrants carefully targeted their market so that, as their products gained consumer confidence, the demand for US-made cars began to dissipate.

The pressures to change were relentless. Government responses were inconsistent and defined by crisis management. The first major intervention was to save the Chryler Corporation from near bankruptcy. Only reluctantly did the Carter administration agree to provide a federally guaranteed bail-out after it was convinced that the social and economic consequences of bankruptcy were unacceptedly high. Next, and due to lobbying by American car makers for trade protection (ostensibly so that they could retool in response to mounting governmental regulations and new demands created by the energy crisis), the government adopted Voluntary Import Restraints in 1981. Both measures were serious departures from the prevailing free-market ideology.

The willingness of the government to intervene in the market triggered unanticipated reactions. Japanese auto makers and suppliers began moving to US soil in fear of further protectionist policies. The first transplant was Honda in 1982, followed by Nissan in 1983, and NUMMI, the GM–Toyota joint venture, in 1984. By 1990, more than 13 Japanese and Korean auto assembly facilities were operating in North America (the USA and Canada), along with more than 150 auto parts companies (see table 3.1). An estimated 250 Japanese automobile suppliers were in operation by 1991. Successful penetration of the US market by transplants was captured in statistics. From 1984 to 1989, transplant production climbed from 138,000 units to 1,119,000; in complete reversal, US manufacture declined from 7,368,000 units to 5,703,000.

The soft market inspired new terminology in the industry as trade journals warned that the nation would become plagued by "over-

Table 3.1 *US auto industry sales and income (dollar values in millions – rounded)*

	GM	*Ford*	*Chrysler*	*AMC*	*Total*
Net sales					
1990[1]	124,705	97,650	30,620	–	252,975
1989[1]	126,932	96,146	35,186	–	258,264
1988[1]	123,642	92,446	34,421	–	250,509
1987	101,782	71,643	28,873	–	202,298
1986	102,814	62,716	22,586	3,463	191,579
1985	96,372	52,774	21,256	4,040	174,442
1984	83,890	52,366	19,600	4,215	160,072
1983	74,582	44,500	13,240	3,300	135,622
1982	60,026	37,067	10,040	2,900	110,033
1981	62,698	38,247	9,971	2,600	113,516
Net income (loss)					
1990	(1,986)	86,068	–	1,058	–
1989	4,224	3,835	323	–	8,382
1988	4,856	5,300	1,009	–	11,165
1987	3,551	4,625	1,318	9,494	–
1986	2,945	3,285	1,404	(91)	7,543
1985	3,999	2,515	1,635	(125)	8,024
1984	4,517	2,907	2,400	15	9,839
1893	3,730	1,867	701	(147)	6,151
1982	963	(658)	170	(154)	322
1981	333	(1,060)	(476)	(137)	(1,339)
Net income (loss) as % of sales					
1990	–	–	–	–	–
1989	–	–	–	–	–
1988	–	–	–	–	–
1987	3.4	6.5	4.5	–	4.6
1986	2.7	5.2	6.2	(2.6)	3.9
1985	4.1	4.8	7.7	(3.1)	4.6
1984	5.4	5.6	12.2	0.4	6.1
1983	5.0	4.1	5.2	(4.4)	4.5
1982	1.6	(1.8)	1.7	(5.3)	0.3
1981	0.5	(2.8)	(4.7)	(5.2)	(1.1)

[1] Total sales revenues.

Source: Ward's Automotive Yearbook, various issues.

capacity." In 1987 it was projected that North America would have 61 assembly plants in 1990, nine more than in 1988, with the capacity of generating two million cars in excess of those demanded. Added to the more than four million imported cars, excess capacity in North America was projected to reach six million vehicles in 1990.[30] But this did not materialize because US plants continued to close.

In the drive to regain their competitive position, US manufacturers initiated a multi-pronged and sometimes confusing array of responses. They continued to close older plants, introduced technology aimed at compressing product development-cycle times from the customary five or six years to 2.5 or three years, attempted to increase the cost effectiveness of small-lot production, lowered costs of large-volume manufacture and assembly, and made existing plants more responsive to model changes and product variability. These adjustments occurred while simultaneously meeting CAFE, safety, and emissions regulations, improving quality, and reducing costs. Yet, because the recessions, competition, and loss of market share were felt unevenly by the auto makers, their strategies for recovery were quite distinctive.

After a brush with near bankruptcy in 1979, Chrysler realized significant profits in the mid-1980s which it began to channel into a policy of niche marketing by acquisition. In 1987 Chrysler bought out American Motors Corporation and Lamborghini, and in 1989 it bought an interest in Maserati. These acquisitions once again forced the company to near insolvency. Fiscal constraints required closure of older domestic and foreign plants, sale of its interest in the Spanish auto company SEAT, and a concentrated focus on the North American market. In 1989, faced with long-term debt, underfunded pension liabilities that approximated $7 billion, and creditors that were urging a massive sell-off of plant and equipment, Chrysler embarked on a drastic cost-saving plan.[31] It cut approximately $3 billion from its total budget of $27 billion, and personnel were reduced from 92,000 to 69,000. But expenditures for new product development were spared and Chrysler spent some $900 million annually on research. Staffs were reorganized to emulate Honda's system of product development, and they were housed in a new design, development, and production center – the Chrysler Technology Center – in Auburn Hills, Michigan, which opened in 1992. With the introduction of new models in 1993, it was hailed by some analysts as the best American car company.

By contrast, Ford adopted dual strategies of cost reduction and internationalization. This was first visible abroad. After a series of costly European strikes during the late 1960s, in 1976 Ford introduced the "world car" (Fiesta), which combined vertical disintegration with

Table 3.2 *US auto industry vehicle sales, payroll, and employment*

	GM	Ford	Chrysler	AMC	Total
World vehicle sales – units (thousands)					
1990	7,451	5,805	1,984	–	15,240
1989	7,905	6,337	2,381	–	17,073
1988	8,108	6,441	2,567	–	17,116
1987	7,766	6,115	2,451	–	16,332
1986	8,576	5,984	2,198	288	17,046
1985	9,305	5,634	2,157	392	17,488
1984	8,256	5,667	2,034	442	16,400
1983	7,800	5,002	1,494	383	14,679
1982	6,244	4,324	1,182	287	12,036
1981	6,762	4,400	1,283	311	12,756
Worldwide payrolls – hourly and salary (millions)					
1990	–	–	–	–	–
1989-	–	–	–	–	–
1988	–	–	–	–	–
1987	27,145	11,670	4,363	–	43,177
1986	28,146	11,290	4,137	610	44,119
1985	25,639	10,175	3,843	730	40,387
1984	22,505	9,800	3,386	963	36,654
1893	19,605	9,125	2,400	913	31,721
1982	17,043	8,863	1,796	845	28,547
1981	19,257	9,325	2,083	744	31,409
Total average world employment – hourly and salary (thousands)					
1990	–	–	–	–	–
1989	–	–	–	–	–
1988	–	–	–	–	–
1987	673	350	123	–	1,146
1986	734	382	115	20	1,251
1985	762	369	108	22	1,310
1984	748	384	100	24	1,256
1983	691	380	97	26	1,194
1982	657	379	74	22	1,132
1981	741	405	88	21	1,255

Source: Ward's Automotive Yearbook, various issues.

multiple sourcing, parallel production, and increased automation worldwide to capture economies of scale in global markets and reduce sourcing from existing suppliers. Though this was conceptually plausible, in fact the company could not overcome cross-national logistical barriers.[32] When this appeared to be a limited strategy, and after suffering from a net income loss in the USA during the early 1980s (table 3.1), the company sought recovery through reorganization. First it reduced employment (see table 3.2) – during which even engineering and technical staffs were affected, their numbers declining from approximately 17,000 in the late 1970s to about 6,000 or 7,000 in the early 1990s. Then it increased the extent of out-sourcing, which was combined with a strategy of internationalizing certain activities, including design and development. Engineering for some models was externalized to domestic suppliers, while for others it was transferred to Asian and European partners. In addition, the company consolidated operations, streamlined product offerings, improved design, engaged in low-cost sourcing and manufacture where possible, often from international sites, and entered into joint ventures. In order to integrate and coordinate these complex European and US operations, it introduced matrix management. This was combined with policies of international product specialization where product design and manufacturing capabilities were delineated by region. Coordination for the North American Escort was handled by Mazda. Ford of Europe oversaw compact-sized cars, including the European Sierra and the US Tempo-Topaz, as well as four-cylinder engines, while Ford US coordinated development of larger cars and engines. To augment these activities, Ford established regional research and design facilities abroad. Thus the less successful "world car" strategy evolved into a strategy of regional specialization.

Because it was larger and more powerful, General Motors did not feel the need to change until the 1990s. Up to that point, it had maintained employment levels relatively constant even when others were decreasing their employment base (table 3.2). As opposed to either Chrysler or Ford, GM tried to combine a full model policy with cost effectiveness from technology acquisition and application and changes in labor relations. It acquired Electronic Data Systems Corporation (EDS) for $2.5 billion (and paid an additional $700 million to H. Ross Perot for his interest) and Hughes Aircraft Co. for $5 billion, and began a capital spending program ranging from $6 to $12 billion per year. This launched a series of internal experiments in the use of technology and labor. At one extreme, it transformed an axle plant at Saginaw, called "Vanguard," into a completely automated factory using sophisticated production processes and computer-integrated manufacturing, and no direct labor at all. At the other extreme, it established the Buick Reatta Craft Centre, where cars were brought to teams of workers on automated guided vehicles who assembled only 53 cars per day – fewer than could be made on a conventional assembly-line in one hour. At NUMMI, the GM–Toyota joint venture, it tried new forms of labor relations. Experimentation permeated the company, with practically every plant illustrating a different concept or stage of implementation. The most progressive ideas were channelled into Saturn, the independent subsidary which former Chairman Roger B. Smith once claimed would be "the key to GM's long-term competitiveness, survival, and success."[33] Augmenting changes within the firm was an increase in out-sourcing, especially in engineering services, such that by 1986 GM was doing business with some 761 engineering firms. International production and joint-venture activities also increased, and were consolidated around regional markets. And after much criticism about the lack of coherent segments, GM streamlined its product offerings. In 1984 it adopted a platform system with the C-P-C (Chevrolet, Pontiac, Canada) group aimed at the small to mid-sized segments and the B-O-C (Buick, Oldsmobile, Cadillac) group aimed at the larger segments. The reorganization was insufficient to prevent further market erosion, however, and, when faced with chronic underutilized capacity and model proliferation, it attempted to reduce the number of models while increasing variability. This objective was explained accordingly:

> Since 1986, GM has reduced the number of passenger carmodels offered by its five car divisions from 175 to 158. This number will decrease to 132 by 1992. The move toward product deproliferation is the result of a passenger car strategy aimed at cutting back on the number of models, body styles, trims, powertrains, and options to reduce costs and manufacturing complexity and focus more closely on quality. While there will be fewer *models*, there will be greater *style* differentiation and product exclusivity, as evidenced by the new models recently introduced.[34]

Under-utilized plant capacity was a problem for all the car makers, but it was chronic in GM. From 1971 to 1986, the number of cars made in small lots increased significantly (see table 3.3), in part because of efforts to reduce the break-even point, combined with a niche production strategy that included the manufacture of cars in specialty markets and out-sourcing of small-lot production to independent

Table 3.3 *Percentage of total production by lot size*

Lot Size (× 1000)	1971 GM	1971 FD	1971 CR	1976 GM	1976 FD	1976 CR	1981 GM	1981 FD	1981 CR	1986 GM	1986 FD	1986 CR	1987 GM	1987 FD	1987 CR
0-50	5	6	7	7	6	8	5	8	13	7	7	21	9	5	21
50-100	3	9	0	6	19	26	9	28	0	10	13	32	18	8	30
100-150	6	20	26	8	31	19	12	17	16	21	14	34	13	22	17
150+	86	65	67	79	44	47	73	48	71	62	65	13	60	65	32

GM = General Motors.
FD = Ford.
CR = Chrysler.

Source: Ward's Automotive Yearbook (1987, 1986, 1980).

Table 3.4 *GM plant cutbacks*

Plant	*No. of employees*	*Closing date*
Willow Run Assembly Plant, MI	4,014	summer 1993
Tarrytown Assembly Plant, NY	3,456	summer 1995
V-8 Engine Plant, MI	4,036	1995
Moraine Engine Plant, OH	549	summer 1995
Grey Iron Foundry, MI	600	summer 1994
St Catharines Engine Plant, Ont.	165	fall 1992
Detroit Plant 55, MI	270	end of 1993
Detroit Plant 57, MI	150	end of 1992
Deico Chassis Plant 20, OH	249	end of 1992
Deico Remy Plant 10, IN	375	1st qtr. 1992
St Catharines Casting Plant, Ont.	2,150	spring 1995
Lordstown Die Construction Plant, OH	279	1992
Total plants affected: 12	Total: 16,293	

Source: Automotive News (March 2, 1992), p. 34.

manufacturers. But, more importantly, it signalled that GM was operating very inefficiently. In 1992, after disclosing that it had been losing $1,600 on every vehicle made in the last year, GM announced the closure of 12 facilities, affecting more than 16,000 workers, and the prospect of closing another nine plants (see table 3.4). In addition, it reorganized the C-P-C, B-O-C structure to eliminate excessive layers of management and make the decision-making process leaner and more flexible.

When in 1992 GM was still losing market share and was reportedly 40 per cent less productive than Ford, the corporation took even more drastic measures.[35] The outside directors of GM's board voted to reorganize the corporate structure and rearrange the company's executive slate, with the result that the Chief Executive Officer was replaced, along with the President. Seen as a major intervention, the action made a poignant statement throughout corporate America. As noted by one analyst, "This is truly momentous – it's the culmination of the corporate-governance movement to make outside directors perform."[36]

The NUMMI Experiment

Of all the ideas introduced, one project that was perhaps most influential at the outset of the transition was NUMMI (New United Motor Manufacturing, Inc.), the joint venture between General Motors and Toyota, located in Fremont, California.[37] NUMMI became symbolic of change in the interpretation of antitrust legislation and the nature of industrial relations, and it presented significant alternatives to manufacture that opened the way to transformation of the industry.

When NUMMI started production in 1984, the decision to undertake a joint venture was new and controversial. The tie-up between GM (then the world's largest auto maker) and Toyota (then the world's third largest), the first of its kind in the USA, was challenged by Chrysler as a violation of antitrust laws. But the Federal Trade Commission approved the proposal on the following grounds:

> first that the joint venture would serve as a learning laboratory for GM, giving the company a chance to get first hand experience in the Toyota production and human relations system; and second, that since no clear harm from the joint venture could be demonstrated, laissez-faire economic philosophy would dictate that the two partners to the

> agreement should be allowed to proceed without government hindrance.[38]

The government then established strict ground rules for micro-level management, which in essence delineated the rules by which the venture would commence. The government, rather than GM and Toyota, decided the number of cars the joint venture would produce; how the price for the product would be determined; how long the joint venture could last; and how the two firms could communicate.[39] The message conveyed was that temporary tie-ups for purposes of improving market efficiency promoted rather than diminished competition, or, from another perspective: "substantial efficiencies were given more weight than speculative competitive effects."[40] The timing of this decision coincided with the passage of the National Cooperative Research Act (NCRA) of 1984, which permitted cooperative basic research and development among private firms; this also signalled a new leniency in the interpretation of antitrust.

When the plant opened, the entire facility represented a departure from prevailing practice. More than $400 million was committed to upgrading the plant. A new stamping plant using quick-die change and dedicated to producing sheet-metal parts was added, resulting in the first assembly/stamping joint operation in the USA Just-in-time inventory sourcing was introduced to coordinate the 1,450 parts initially shipped from Japan, as well as the 400 sourced from the USA. The Japanese concepts of *jidoka*, or stopping the line to correct defects, and *andon*, which refers to an electrical sign board, or the visual display of operations, were instituted. These changes in work organization far surpassed technological advancements, since the plant had a modest 170 robots used for spot and arc welding.

However, the most significant innovation was the method of labor relations. As a result of greater sub-contracting, reorganized work, and a simplified product, the workforce dropped from 6,000 when the plant operated solely under GM to 2,200 under the GM–Toyota joint venture, and consisted of employees of the former GM facility at Fremont screened for their ability to cooperate. Approximately 2,000 employees received on-site training in addition to 200 hours of on-the-job training. More than 400 hourly workers also travelled to Japan for training at Toyota Motor Corporation to learn how to perform multiple tasks within a team. Teams, which rotated tasks, consisted of five to eight persons from among hourly and salaried workers. They would meet approximately every two weeks to discuss tasks and issues of quality and make limited shop-floor decisions, such as those concerning job rotation. Team leaders were selected by management with concurrence of the union, and, for their added responsibilities, which consisted of administrative duties, filling in for absentee workers, and assisting slower workers, they were paid approximately $.50 more per hour. The teams were further clustered by threes and fours into groups which were governed by a first line manager.

With implementation of the team concept, job categories changed considerably. From a previous 80-plus job classifications under General Motors, the number was reduced to one for production workers and three for skilled categories – tool and die; tool and die try-out; and general maintenance (e.g., pipefitters, electricians, etc.) At other plants, the number of job categories could easily reach more than 160. Because team members were responsible for quality control and job content, industrial engineers were eliminated.[41] In addition to being the primary work unit, teams provided an informal mechanism for resolving grievances prior to the formal grievance procedure and presented a forum for creative problem-solving. Yet because of the cooperative rather than confrontational relations between labor and management, the team concept represented a direct assault on conventional labor relations. After considerable resistance, the idea was eventually accepted by the union leadership. NUMMI permanently altered work conditions in the industry by becoming a standard for efficient production, despite continued and arguably justifiable concerns of sophisticated speed-up among workers.

After the plant was established, producers of seats, plastic moldings and other parts located nearby. The agglomeration of parts producers around the plant anchored the activities in the community and created positive multiplier effects in ways not possible under prior branch plant policies. Absenteeism declined. Quality and productivity nearly doubled that of other General Motors plants and was nearly as high as in Japanese plants. Output expanded from 47 cars per hour at the former GM plant to 60 cars per hour. Based on the apparent success, GM introduced these concepts in some form at other plants over the next decade, as did Ford and Chrysler.

Change or Continuity?

Reconfiguration of production work fueled debates about the skill-enhancing or deskilling tendencies of the new automation and labor relations. Central to this was the operating team, or team concept, with its implied expansion of tasks, reduction of job titles, and relaxation of work rules. Proponents argued that it increased workers' control over work, and hence productivity,[42] while opponents countered that higher productivity was actually the result of faster-paced work and neo-Taylorism.[43] Automation and team systems were introduced jointly as well as independently, since there is no implicit link between the two, although some have argued that skill-enhancing technology and cooperative teams are attributes of small-scale, specialty production organized into networks.[44] That is, while advanced technology and team work applied to mass production perpetuated the degradation of work, their combined use in specialized production or network configurations had the opposite effect.

Evidence to support the effectiveness of either new technology or labor relations suggests that changes in labor were far more significant. Among the most consistent observations about technology were that companies rarely use automation to its fullest potential for achieving flexibility and, further, that, when applied, technological developments tended to exceed by far the ability of organizations to adjust.[45] MIT analysts John Krafcik and Daniel Roos found that not only was there little correlation between the use of robotics and high productivity, but many firms neglected to use them for enhancing productivity.[46] Others have observed that the purpose of technology was often not to increase flexibility, but to reduce worker control.[47]

Krafcik and Roos further found through correlations and regressions that management style (i.e., team concept) was positively correlated with productivity.[48] On the basis of such statistical analysis and the experience of plants such as NUMMI, innovative labor relations appeared to have had a much greater effect on productivity than extensive automation, but the case is nowhere near closed.[49] When automation was introduced into the assembly process, skilled trades and production workers were affected differentially, with skilling among trades and deskilling among production workers.[50] On the other hand, despite the multiple skilling in plants using the team concept, increased productivity in part was the result of longer hours or faster-paced work as opposed to the enhanced problem-solving attributes of teams.[51]

Although argued to be a form of "neo-Fordism," the team concept, along with a workforce disciplined by high unemployment, contributed to higher productivity. As the transition progressed, the US automobile industry became leaner and more productive, and supported by government policies, though still chaotic in application, that were more oriented toward encouraging efficiency than to a strict adherence of *laissez-faire* principles.

Towards Redefinition

For all three auto makers, the crisis was met with increased joint ventures and alliances (see figure 3.2). Initially equity holdings

Figure 3.2 *Major auto-making joint ventures, 1990*

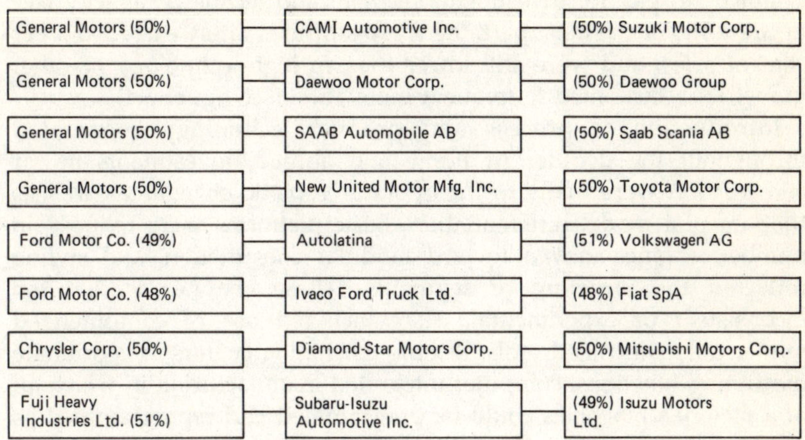

Source: Ward's Automotive Yearbook (1991).

Figure 3.3 *Research and development expenses, 1977–87*

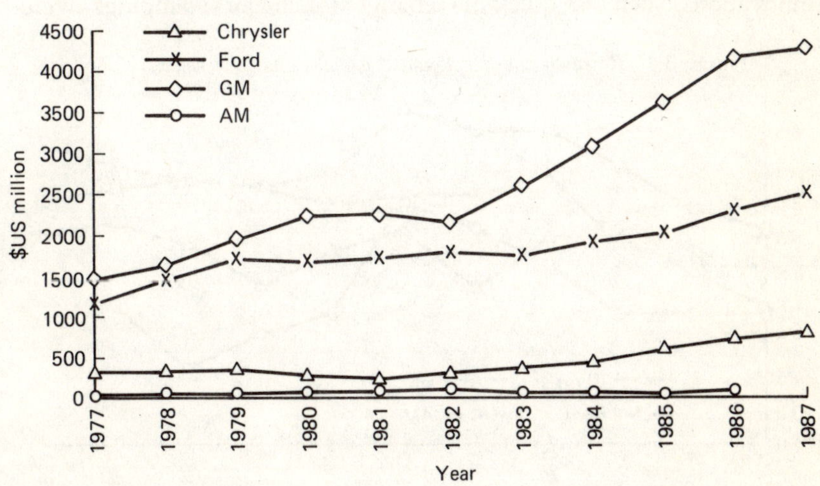

Source: Various annual reports.

intended to expand segment offerings and markets abroad predominated. Later, joint-venture activity in the USA increased with the purpose of consolidating parts production, share in the knowledge of markets or production techniques. The most well known of these was the NUMMI joint venture between General Motors and Toyota.

As the three US auto makers embarked on major changes, from 1978 to 1987 the extent of funding for research and development more than doubled to pay for investments in plant and technical capacity (see figure 3.3). For the most part, these expenditures rarely exceeded 5 per cent of sales, and were still lower than in high-technology or other industries accustomed to frequent innovation (see figure 3.4).

Introduction of process and product technology accelerated throughout the decade. At home and abroad, investments in car construction were made to incorporate cosmetic changes as well as fundamental model differentiation. Basic platforms were reduced in number, engines moved toward modular construction, and styling reflected the targeting of segments. These changes were often inconsistent or experimental. They included use of computerized numerically controlled tools, flexible machining centers to coordinate machining functions, computer-integrated manufacturing in which all of a factory's machines could be programmed and reprogrammed as needed, and manufacturing automation protocols which could link dissimilar machines and different plants. Investment in process technology frequently aimed at reducing the costs and break-even point of parts requiring long production runs to be cost effective. Innovations such as quick-die change for major stampings were

Figure 3.4 *Research and development expenses as % of sales, 1977-87*

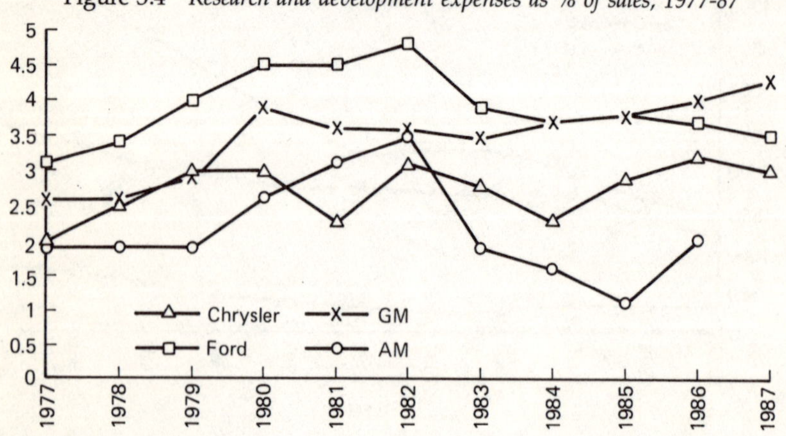

Source: Various annual reports.

borrowed from Japanese manufacturers, allowing the time required to change major dies to be reduced from hours to minutes.

Throughout this period, rationalization, redefinition of production-line work, and the introduction of advanced technology provided critical cost savings that were augmented by out-sourcing and greater coordination among suppliers. Both manual and research-intensive work were contracted out until the UAW successfully limited the extent of out-sourcing of production work in their 1988 contracts. Manufacturers combined vertical disintegration with out-sourcing of both manufacture and service functions. The primary functions that were out-sourced consisted of engineering services, prototype development, and sub-assembly. Since passage of the National Cooperative Research Act of 1984, joint research projects were initiated by General Motors, Ford, and Chrysler in such areas as battery and composites development. Only in instances where anticompetitive effects could be found, as in collusion, were joint research and development activities ruled illegal.[52] Thus more research and development activity was shared among car makers and with their suppliers.

Contract engineering grew to approximately 50 per cent of all engineering services for auto makers in contrast to prior years, when it performed a largely overflow function. Contract engineering companies provided low-cost services and fast turn-around due to use of temporary workers (often resulting in turnover rates of 400 to 500 per cent), flexible work rules, and ease of decision-making. Many of these were start-ups created by former "Big Three" employees who could enter into business because of low capitalization requirements and low barriers to entry. Of the more than 1,000 engineering and design (E&D) service firms in 1990, most consisted of only 1 to 20 people, although the largest 24 accounted for over one-half of the employment. These companies began to experience a shake-out as more full service boardwork, modelling, manufacturing engineering, and line production was required of them. Engineering service providers began to change in orientation from E&D engineering solutions suppliers to "systems suppliers." With consolidation of E&D firms, along with single sourcing policies by major auto makers, these activities began to concentrate within Michigan.

Another change occurred in the acquisition of parts with adoption of just-in-time inventory sourcing and use of parts sub-assemblies single sourced from first-tier subcontractors. Credited to the influence of Ford's "Q101" quality evaluation program and Japanese transplants,[53] supplier reorganization took the following configuration:

> in describing the changes, the terms black box, gray box and white box often are used along with the somewhat disliked terms first, second and third tier.
>
> A black-box company can supply a self-contained pre-tested system, which an OEM [original equipment manufacturer] customer may know little or nothing about but can simply "plug in" to a vehicle being assembled. A fuel-injection system or antilock braking system of the type supplied by West Germany's Robert Bosch GmbH is a typical example. An airbag system is another.
>
> A gray-box supplier is most often described as a company that could build sophisticated black box-type components, but instead works closely with OEM engineers to custom- produce a product.
>
> White-box suppliers have little or no in-house engineering capabilities. They do nothing more than build to OEM specifications.
>
> A typical first-tier supplier provides major built-up components to an assembly plant, such as transmissions.
>
> In the second tier are suppliers of partially assembled components such as wire harnesses.
>
> A third-tier company is most often described as a maker of "commodity" products, such as nuts and bolts.
>
> Many suppliers cross the lines, however. A company might be a first-tier supplier to one OEM, and a second-tier supplier to another. Likewise it might make black-box products for one OEM, and gray-box products for another.
>
> In the old structure, components would flow into the OEMs from a huge number (more than 2,500) of independent and captive suppliers, and the OEMs would manage all assembly, design and marketing processes . . .
>
> However, under the new scenario, each automaker relies on about 150 first-tier suppliers that are deeply involved in the design process.[54]

Subcontractors began to share in research and development and take responsibility for sub-assembly and quality control. The multiple-tiering system minimized the number of parts brought to final assembly, and reduced the time parts were held in inventory. Nonetheless, the sharing of research and creation of explicit tiers proved difficult to implement because of the extensive cooperation required. To share in the cost of research, as well as to gain access to larger markets, suppliers followed the example of the assemblers and also began to enter into joint ventures. According to one supplier survey conducted in 1990, 57 per cent of the respondents were involved in at least one joint venture or partnership.[55]

A significant amount of prototype and small lot production was also transferred to foreign affilitates, engineering and design houses, and body conversion shops. Consequently, small producers expanded into body and chassis engineering, manufacturing engineering, computer-aided design, electronics applications, model and prototype construction, stamping, and die manufacture, thereby displaying total production capability.

Through vertical disintegration, the assembly function became leaner, more dependent upon subcontractors and affiliate producers, and increasingly defined by an agglomerated spatial distribution of production. First-tier suppliers began to coordinate some sub-assembly operations. In terms of international distribution, most high value-added goods production remained in the USA, while low value-added products were to a large extent sourced from low-wage foreign sites.

The New Industrial Geography

With these changes, the industrial geography has begun to look vastly different from the period of branch plant proliferation. In contrast to the 1950s, when branch plants were widely dispersed, the assembly function has become more consolidated around a loose North–South corridor running through the Midwest and into the South. The pattern of new transplants and new domestic plants, combined with the closing of older domestic plants, revealed a preference for greenfield sites, presumably to lower-wage, less-unionized areas located within this broad manufacturing belt.[56]

Assembly and component manufacture concentrated in the Midwest or mid-South-Central region of the country to take advantage of proximity to suppliers using just-in-time inventory sourcing, with the majority of facilities located within a three-hour radius of Detroit. Agglomeration was particularly evident among transplants,[57] as opposed to the sourcing from generalized Midwest locations preferred by US firms.[58] Research and development of major parts manufacturers also displayed clustering around the area of the most intense productive activity.

Concentration in Michigan facilitated interaction among firms and spawned a critical mass of employers seeking a skilled engineering workforce. This same skill base was drawn on by auto assemblers looking for outside engineering capacity. Across the nation, Southern California also emerged as a center for advanced concept design because of its reputation as a bellweather for marketing trends. Thus research was divided nationally by market versus manufacturing orientation.

Within North America, the manufacturing belt spread into Canada, but particularly into Mexico, to take advantage of cost savings. As these preferences materialized, employment in US assembly firms declined by approximately 23 per cent from 1978 to 1988, and by 19 per cent in major components.[59] At the same time, employment in the Mexican transportation parts sector rose to approximately that in Canada (see table 3.5). With an increase in the USA of non-unionized Japanese transplant parts plants and a downturn in the number of unionized parts firms, plus the shift of capacity to Mexico, unionization among auto-parts workers declined. The result was a growing dualism in the wages of auto assembly and parts workers in the USA. In contrast to 1950, when parts sector wages were 96 per cent of assembly wages, by 1983 they had slipped to 69 per cent.[60] Thus one of the consequences of economic integration was increased labor segmentation within the North American region.

Table 3.5 *Employment in the North American auto parts industry (thousands)*

	1965	*1973*	*1978*	*1984*	*1988/89*
US auto parts employment	570	725	783	618	635
Major auto makers			428	300	289
Unionized independents			155	98	79
Non-union independents			200	220	267
Canadian parts employment	56	91	94	82	103
Mexican parts employment			5	33	99
Transportation Maquilas			5	29	94
Export engine plants				4	5
North American total	625	816	876	700	738

Notes:

1 Compiled from Herzenberg, dissertation in progress, and Shaiken, 1990, based on BLS and Stats Canada employment data, UAW figures on membership in "Big Three" components plants and independent parts firms, and Mexican government data on Maquila employment.

2 Employment in engine plants estimated using figures for one plant and then projecting over the total engine export total assuming a constant employee/engine ratio.

3 The figures in the final column are all for 1988 except for employment in Mexican transportation Maquilas, which is for 1989.

The Emerging Industry

By the early 1990s, the US auto industry was beginning to show signs of recovery, despite continued losses, particularly by GM. The global recession was forcing retrenchment in Japan and Europe. US auto makers had begun to distinguish themselves by strategy and structure and were responding to the increased competitiveness, market fragmentation, and constant technological change in recognition that these were now permanent features in the market. Government policies were supportive of cooperation as a means of achieving competitiveness, which aided in the industry's transition.

As a consequence, the integrated firm structure of the USA began to take redefinition. The out-sourcing of parts production, engineering services, prototype development and small-run vehicles created production capacity among smaller firms. As the internal functions of the integrated firm were externalized, many activities needed to support industrialization were becoming externalized as well, such as training, research and development, and marketing. Critical phases of production – development, parts fabrication, small-scale assembly, and distribution – were increasingly handled by independent producers rather than by one integrated firm. As this has occurred, support activities, such as sales and marketing, which had been controlled by large producers and acted as barriers to smaller firms, were becoming freed up and available to newly emerging small competitors. State supported agencies, such as the Michigan Industrial Technology Institute, were created to share in the generation and transmission of research and development, training, technology transfer, and marketing.

Despite these changes, neither the industry nor government policies displayed a coherent commitment to either a low-cost approach toward industrialization or to one based on increased variability, quality, and a shorter time for bringing products to market. They seemed to straddle both strategies. As one of many examples, during its 1992 reorganization GM continued to stress strong supplier relations, as it simultaneously forced cost reductions on its suppliers. Similarly, the government seemed eager to support such policies as the passage of the North American Free Trade Agreement to lower the cost of manufacture and widen the market base, as it simultaneously encouraged activities for sharing the costs of research and development. These actions suggested changes in the direction of a quasi-integrated or quasi-market structure of industrialization. However, they were not sufficient to support the full extent of flexibility possible. Scenarios for further development were instead apparent abroad, and in the movement of the industry along the technological frontier.

4

European and Japanese Models of Industrialization: A Study of Contrasts

Alternative Paths of Industrial Development

Alexander Gershenkron observed some thirty years ago that the timing of a nation's industrialization shapes its institutions, and these institutions, in turn, become determinants to development at later points in time.[1] To rephrase this, the institutional setting that propels a nation forward in one instance can cripple development in another. What is paradoxical is that, while institutional stability is necessary to ensure growth, during periods of change institutions must be resilient and adaptable to new situations. Yet history has shown repeatedly that adaptability is extremely difficult to maintain, since interest groups are created and political-economic concepts become codified into law or accepted as convention. This paradox is currently evident, since the conditions shaping industrialization are now sufficiently different from those of the postwar era to require new institutional arrangements. Yet the possibilities for change are limited by the lack of appropriate mechanisms for adjustment.

What are these mechanisms? It was previously argued that the opportunity a country has to influence its industry's development lies in the way capital, labor, and product markets are constructed, and will reflect its philosophy toward economic intervention. So, for example, early industrializers with a *laissez-faire* orientation would confront a different set of possibilities for affecting economic change than, say, late industrializers inclined toward governing the market. In their developmental capacity, nations face the additional choice of whether to ease the negative effects created by declining industries, to champion growing industries, or to assist industries in transition.[2] To return to the previous examples, an early industrializer embracing *laissez-faire* principles would have far fewer options for intervening on behalf of growing industries, for instance, than would a late industrializer having development as its prime objective.

The stage of industrialization and the economic philosophy of a nation are imbedded in the structure of an industry. This is perhaps most visible in the experiences of the auto industry of the UK, the first industrializer, in contrast with that of Japan, the most recent industrializer. For nearly three centuries, British institutions remained relatively constant, yet they set the context for development under new situations. Ultimately, change came only by dismantling the existing industrial structure. Japan, on the other hand, was not only a stunning newcomer among industrialized nations which successfully combined a neo-mercantilist approach toward industrial development with novel institutional arrangements, but it revealed an ability to redefine itself as the circumstances surrounding industrialization changed. As opposed to the USA, which supported the emergence of the vertically integrated firm, in Japan the model was that of the quasi-integrated firm. The UK represents a nation that was stymied from developing in either direction. Yet a third model is found in the European countries with a corporatist tradition. Here, Germany will provide an illustration of a quasi-market form of industrialization. As these cases show, quasi-integrated and quasi-market forms of industrialization have withstood the pressures to change and are becoming transformed into quasi-disintegrated and other horizontal configurations. However, a lack of institutional resilience takes national industries out of the competitive arena.

European Manufacturers and Economic Adjustment

Although the automobile industry originated in Europe, Europeans could not achieve dominance in the world market. Car makers confronted extremely fragmented markets and historically lower income levels. Driving customs varied across countries, making designs for multiple markets costly. Until creation of the EEC in 1957, trade barriers limited market accessibility. In addition, high sales, license, and gasoline taxes put a premium on fuel efficiency. These diverse conditions encouraged product innovation, but they inhibited standardization. In most instances, manufacturers produced for limited segments, at low volumes, and with little interchangeability of components by "family" groups. Long product runs were necessary to secure economic returns at low volumes. Small-scale manufacturers and design houses often co-existed with large-volume producers.

Across Europe, the necessity to improve productivity and increase flexibility came after the oil shocks of the 1970s, followed by a period of labor unrest. The effect on large firms was to stimulate out-sourcing, build up reliance on international production strategies, and increase automation. Small manufacturers, engineering consultants, and design houses profited by a surge of alliances with large auto makers aimed at addressing limited markets and at producing sub-assemblies. Although vertical disintegration favored small firms, that were also vulnerable to take overs by large manufacturers. These two tendencies created a competitive tension between large and small companies. Large, mobile multinational firms, on the other hand, could capture scale economies locating in sites offering cost advantages. The tension could be resolved in either direction, but it could only favor small firms with support of state policies. Perhaps the most striking examples of the extreme are found in the UK, with its lack of state support, and Japan, with its proactive state. In the UK, the situation was resolved at the expense of domestic small firms. Once small-scale assemblers were decimated, the domestic British auto industry faced total collapse. This was not the case, however, in other European countries displaying strong state support for making small firms competitive. Although in the UK this was manifested as an issue of large, foreign versus small, domestic firms, the underlying problem was actually a function of the industry's structure and of government policies.

Restarting the Engine of the British Auto Industry

From 1914 to 1960, the British automobile industry was secure in its domestic market. It even emerged periodically as a formidable world competitor. But then in the 1970s it nearly disappeared altogether, only to reappear again in the late 1980s as foreign firms linked with the remnants of British manufacturers who used the UK primarily as a platform for entering the European market. In contrast to the industry in the USA, that in the UK did not establish large-scale manufacture. Instead it was fragmented, and weak in the face of stronger competitors. Because the UK had few options for intervention on behalf of its industry, the methods employed during periods of intense competition were usually as crisis intervention applied too late. And because the UK did not provide appropriate support for its small-scale manufacturers, its local talent was overtaken by more poweful multinationals. How did the nation fail its industries?

Capital as a Lever in Development The root of the problem can be traced to the formative years when key relationships were originally defined. One distinctive factor shaping the industry was the structure of the capital market. The capital markets were initially linked with development of the textile industry in the late eighteenth century. Because of low barriers to entry, it was relatively easy for small family ventures to become entrepreneurial by building on the existing "putting-out" system which consisted of many small firms. Firms could finance investment through retained earnings or the private funds of family and friends, practices that over time led to joint-stock forms of corporate organization and development of the stock market.[3] Banks were largely regional in orientation, but because small firms did not need to rely on them for industrial finance they developed the practice of short-term lending to industries, and in relatively small amounts.[4] These regional banks eventually disappeared, since they were never large enough to provide sufficient capital for firms operating in the national market, much less for international conglomerates, and they had become essentially superfluous to small firms. It therefore became tradition early on for firms to rely on internally generated funds or issues of equity to generate capital. As a consequence, in contrast to France, Germany, or Japan, for instance, the UK was left with no national industrial banks that could take an equity position in firms or play a role in their management, and hence participate in industrialization.

The role of capital was particularly striking in the automobile industry, where internally generated funds were restricted by the high cost of capital investment, therefore forcing the majority of financing to come from public issues. As early as 1905, 72 per cent of the capital of major firms was generated by new share and debt issues and only 4 per cent by retained earnings. By contrast, in the USA prior to 1926, the eight leading firms raised nearly 80 per cent of their capital from internal sources.[5] The result was that the UK afforded greater ease of entry than the USA. Between 1897 and 1913, there were 81 entrants into the industry, none of which gained market dominance.[6] By some observations, the legacy of too many firms with too much capacity played a role well into the 1970s and contributed to the collapse of the industry.[7]

Labor Markets as a Complement to Development Yet another significant factor influencing the industry was the structure of labor markets. As Britain industrialized, nascent firms were influenced by the existing craft tradition and skilled workforce coming largely out of metal-working. This skilled workforce controlled the pace of work, its content, and even pay, despite the fact that the relative abundance of skilled workers depressed wages and became a deterrent to the use of unskilled labor. The central position occupied by skilled workers encouraged the organization of trade unions focussed on protecting wages and shop-floor control.[8] Because unions were organized around crafts, the labor movement evolved into a highly vocal but fragmented presence, often engaged in fractious fighting within plants. One consequence was resistance to any new technology or work organization that would result in a decrease in labor, a decline in wages, deskilling, or a deterioration of shop-floor control. Another was a tendency to engage in overstaffing. Thus, as the British industry confronted the need to restructure, it faced fewer options than its competitors.

This pattern of labor utilization was repeated in the auto industry. The first workers were drawn primarily from the Amalgamated Society of Engineers or the United Kingdom Society of Coachmakers and were highly skilled, although by 1914 large segments of production work were already undertaken by unskilled labor.[9] The prominence of skilled workers forced management to coordinate production with them. The high degree of "labor independence" meant that management was never quite as successful in introducing the controls Alfred Chandler associated with managerial capitalism of the USA or that were apparent in large, complex firms elsewhere.

The relative ease of access to capital and the highly skilled labor force were important determinants in this industry. Because of the greater experience, compared with their US counterparts, of British workers in metal-working, they were more versatile in a wide range of manufacturing tasks, and because British firms could amass substantial funds at the outset, they could manufacture virtually the entire vehicle.[10] By contrast, US firms began largely as assemblers dependent on an extensive supplier base and on an unskilled labor force. As a result, British firms operated far below the level needed to capture scale economies. They also faced far more complex management problems because they were more integrated.

Consequently, profit maximization was driven by a logic based on harnessing a skilled but fragmented workforce:

> between 1905 and 1920, British producers adopted a strategy markedly different from the Fordist one. The Fordist strategy ensured high levels of productivity by combining rigid managerial control, flow production technology, and relatively high wages paid on fixed day rates. In contrast, the British strategy can be characterized as one with weak managerial control over labour, low wages, low capital–labour ratios, low levels of machine integration along flow principles, and piecework payment systems. This strategy allowed a relatively unproductive technology to generate relatively high levels of profits on invested capital.[11]

Context for Trade To protect this vulnerable industry, England erected tariffs of approximately 33.3 per cent between 1915 and 1956. The tariffs stayed at this level until the Dillon Round of the GATT negotiations (1962-8), when they dropped to 22 per cent, and then again with the Kennedy Round (1968-72), when they were set at 11 per cent. In keeping with its *laissez-faire* orientation, Britain opened its market, but the gesture was unreciprocated and it remained excluded from the EEC until 1973. As the tariff walls began to drop, the industry was completely reconfigured.

The Industry Takes Off Initially, the high tariff prompted foreign firms to locate facilities in the UK. The British car industry, which began in 1895, was no match for the more efficient Ford Motor Company when it started assembling cars in Manchester in 1911. By 1913, 6,000 of the 25,000 cars made in England were Fords.[12] In 1929, GM acquired Vauxhall, and in 1931 Ford opened another plant in Dagenham. These large powerhouses began not only to dominate the industry, but to change its structure as well. Rather than manufacture the majority of their inputs, as was practice for the domestic firms, they sourced locally and stimulated a major supplier industry. Such companies as Lucas (engines), AE (pistons, rings, and bearings), GKN (bearings), T&N (brake and clutch linings), and BBA (brake and clutch linings) developed as prominent suppliers. Up to World War II, the industry began to take definition around four segments: prestige domestic car makers producing 150 to 2,600 units per year (e.g., Rolls Royce, Aston Martin, Lotus); mid-sized domestic specialist manufacturers (such as Rover, Morris, or Jaguar); large foreign manufacturers (Ford, GM-Vauxhall); and a strong components industry (see table 4.1).

After the war, the British industry was stimulated by pent-up demand. In 1950 Britain became the world's largest exporter of cars,

Table 4.1 *Share of UK car production by firm (%)*

Austin	*BMC*	*Nuffield*	*Standard*	*Ford*	*Vauxhall*	*Rootes*	*Others*
23		20	11	14	9	11	12
19		21	13	15	11	11	10
17		22	11	19	9	14	8
	39		10	27	9	11	4
	37		9	28	13	12	3
	British Leyland					Chrysler	
		48		27	11	13	1
		48		26	8	17	1
						Talbot	
			Jaguar	34	13	6	1
		42	3.5	30	13	10.5	1
	Rover Group					Peugeot	
		41	4.0	34	16	4.0	1

Source: Reprinted from *Long Range Planning*, 22, G. Rhys, "Smaller car firms – will they survive?", pp. 22–9. Copyright (1989), with kind permission from Pergamon Press Ltd, Headington Hill Hall, Oxford OX3 0BW, UK.

overcoming the USA, and by 1958 it was making more than one million cars annually. But it was the large car makers who benefited the most from the expanding market. Smaller companies began to merge, such as Austin and Morris, which formed the British Motor Corporation (1952), or were bought out – Jaguar bought out Daimler (1961) and Leyland took over Standard-Triumph (1961). The body-making tradition was absorbed by the larger firms, as Ford bought out Briggs (1953) and BMC took over Fisher and Ludlow (1953).

Seeing an apparently strong industry, the British government determined that firms could only expand in areas of high unemployment, for which they were issued Industrial Development Certificates. Consequently, Ford opened a plant in Halewood near Liverpool (1963), Vauxhall expanded into Ellesmere Port (1963) on the other side of the Mersey, and Rootes went to Linwood, Scotland (1963), to be close to the Ravenscraig steelworks. While, in the short term, unemployment in these areas was alleviated, the dispersal removed plants from their supplier base, added transportation costs, and required that plants bring in a new labor force unaccustomed to industrial work. The increase in unit costs put Rootes at the brink of insolvency, which opened the door for Chrysler to purchase an interest in the company

(1964) and later buy it out (1967). Further, the government established the Industrial Reorganisation Corporation (1966-71) to encourage mergers in the parts industry, where poor performance appeared to be the result of organizational inadequacies. The IRC provided financing to individual companies on only seven occasions, but in two of these instances vehicle makers were involved – during the 1968 merger of BMC and Leyland to form BMLC, and when Chrysler took control of Rootes.

Crisis and Intervention But, by the late 1960s, the market for cars had begun to change substantially. With formation of the EEC in 1957, continental companies began to widen their markets and reorganize accordingly. Britain had opened its market, but was not part of the EEC until 1973. The time gap made it easy for foreign firms to penetrate the British market, but hard for British firms to reciprocate. During this period, foreign car makers used the UK as a base for servicing non-EEC markets through the export of cars in kit form (CKD) for overseas assembly. They had little incentive to upgrade British capacity or invest in new model lines.[13] The share of imports in the UK car market grew markedly from 3 per cent in 1961 to 10 per cent in 1969, 14 per cent in 1970, and 27.4 per cent in 1973. With the emergence of a more unified European market, Ford created Ford of Europe (1967) and began to consolidate its operations. During this time, Japanese car makers were becoming prominent, and Japanese production surpassed that of both Britain and France (1968). Then came the OPEC oil crisis of the 1970s, and imports grew even faster. By 1975 the share of imports was 33 per cent, and by 1980 it was 56.5 per cent.

The 1970s was a difficult decade for all car makers, but in particular for British Leyland and Chrysler. British Leyland faced almost continual reorganizations and labor difficulties, none of which resulted in sufficient restructuring to increase productivity or the scale of operations. A series of unprofitable decisions led to the company's collapse in 1975. The government responded by nationalizing it through the National Enterprise Board. Later, in 1977, it began a serious rationalization of the company. Chrysler, on the other hand, was provided with funds to apply to its own recovery. This was still not sufficient, and in 1978 Peugeot took over Chrysler Europe and formed Peugeot-Talbot.

As Ford, General Motors, and Peugeot-Talbot began to integrate their production and components purchasing on a European basis, they put a cost-squeeze on British suppliers through policies of multiple sourcing.[14] This was undertaken in conjunction with the import of cars built in European plants but sold as "British" cars. In contrast to 1975, when only 2.5 per cent of imports into the UK new car market were "tied imports," by 1980 this figure was 24 per cent. These tied imports had a very low British-made parts content. Thus, the UK parts industry began to decline. In 1979 it employed some 157,000 workers and contributed 59 per cent of total domestic demand, but by 1987 this number had dropped to 91,100 and the level of contribution was approximately 28 per cent of the market. Even research and development were affected. In 1983, Peugeot-Talbot shifted its design out of Britain.

The car makers also initiated policies of single sourcing from larger parts producers, to the detriment of small, and especially British, manufacturers. The purpose was better to control price, quality, innovation, and delivery, and to increase the subcontracting of major sub-assemblies. These actions favored certain kinds of firms:

> large components manufacturers who have the resources to develop scale economies, devote large budgets to research and development and quality control, and utilize their organizational strength to improve on delivery ... This new development, however, is not just a preference for large firms, but for multinationals with a global presence, that is, companies with the capacity to supply to assemblers anywhere in the world.[15]

The lack of British competitiveness surfaced as low productivity. In contrast to 1955, when the UK displayed the highest productivity in Europe, by 1973 it was the lowest, at 5.3 cars per person, and this dropped again to 4.7 in 1978.[16] Low productivity was attributed to overmanning, as well as to chaotic production methods. The effect on employment was devastating. From 1979 to 1987, employment fell by

Table 4.2 *Employment in major vehicle firms (thousands)*

	1979	*1987*	*% change*
Vauxhall	23	10	56
Rover (BL)	147	73	50
Ford	80	45	44
Talbot	24	7	68

Source: G. Rhys, *Motor Industry in the European Community* (Hertford: Institute of the Motor Industry (1989)), p. 67.

nearly 40 per cent (see table 4.2) due to plant closures and rationalization, and the multiplier effect was felt throughout the supplier industry.

To shelter the industry from continued import threats, the government had begun talks with Japan in 1975 over voluntary import restrictions on cars brought into Britain. Then, in 1981, the European Commission requested that Japanese car makers restrict their exports to Europe. Because Europe remained relatively closed to direct foreign investment, and in an effort to overcome these restrictions, Britain became a preferred location for Japanese manufacturers. The first to initiate a move was Honda, which started manufacturing passenger cars at BL's Cowley plant in 1981. Through this arrangement, BL adopted Honda's most recent technologies with the intent of revitalizing its manufacturing systems. In 1982, the cars were recognized as UK cars by the Italian government, but the EC issued a policy the following year requiring indirect control of imported Japanese vehicles. As a result, Honda entered into a joint venture with BL (1984), followed by other manufacturers.[17] When Nissan began manufacture in Washington (Tyne and Wear) in 1986, the venture proved so successful that the next year it doubled its 1992 production goal to 200,000, and in 1988 created the European Design Centre. By 1989, Nissan Motor Europe was established as an integrated management company.[18] 1989 was also the year Toyota began construction at Burnaston, near Derby, for manufacture in 1992 and when Honda invested in the Rover group (formerly BL). For Honda, this meant access not only to Rover's sales system, but also to the high technology of British Aerospace, which had been taken over by Rover in 1988.

The British Industry Reconfigured The introduction of Japanese manufacture in the UK had a significant effect on the structure of the industry and on industrial relations. The Japanese car makers had all agreed to an 80 per cent local content, but this included research, marketing, and other inputs besides components. In this instance, "local" referred to the EEC, not Britain, *per se*. Thus, and in continuation of the trend, the Japanese car makers began to source primarily from large national or international suppliers, and not from the many small domestic suppliers. There was also a significant amount of relocation by Japanese suppliers. In some instances, these were subsidiaries of the car makers (e.g., Calsonic, Hashimoto, and Yamato are subsidiaries of Nissan); in other cases, they were independent suppliers (e.g., Ikeda – car seats; Calsonic – radiators and exhausts; Yuasa – batteries; Nippon-Seike – dashboard instruments).[19] The purchasing patterns for both Japanese and non-Japanese car makers signified a major loss of indigenous capacity:

> A return to the old system in Britain based upon a multitude of indigenous companies supplying assemblers sourcing the entire car locally is inconceivable. Instead, the absence of a national giant (Rover) and the delivery of the car industry into the hands of the multinationals, for the variety of reasons ..., has led to the decline and concentration of the car components industry in fewer and foreign hands.[20]

During the 1970s, Ford and Vauxhall (GM) rationalized their labor force by releasing both production workers and engineering staffs. The engineering workforce established engineering and design houses to which the car makers subcontracted sub-assemblies, prototypes, and specialty cars. Some of the prominent firms included International Automotive Design (IAD) and Hawtal-Whiting, companies which were emerging as second-generation design houses. In contrast to first generation design houses, such as those in Italy for example, these newer firms were not so much stylists as systems integrators which incorporated styling into their product. They were as equally concerned with aspects of manufacture as with the product itself.

Industrial relations in Britain prior to the collapse of its auto industry was at best a test of wills. Throughout the 1970s, all firms, except perhaps Ford, faced severe problems of managerial authority. British Leyland had the most difficulties, with low productivity due to the introduction of measured day work and "mutuality," in which even minor issues had to be negotiated, compounded by strikes.[21] Vauxhall had a "right to manage" strike in 1979, and Talbot faced "contested mutuality" over flexibility and overmanning and a three-month strike in 1979 over wages. After the plant closures and lay-offs, and with introduction of Japanese styles of labor-management, labor relations changed to include team concepts – even in US subsidiaries – and job assignments changed to reflect new production methods, such as occurred in the USA. By the end of the 1980s, productivity in the British car industry had improved dramatically. One indicator of change came on May 1, 1989, when *The Times* reported that a British Rover plant had a higher level of productivity (cars made per person) than Nissan's Washington (Tyne and Wear) plant.[22]

To what can change in the British car industry be attributed, and what is the prognosis for the future? It is fair to say that the British industry is essentially non-existent, since the most important car makers are now foreign. The industry had trouble adjusting to change because of a fragmented labor movement, an inability to manage without resorting to drastic measures, and government policies directed at rescuing a declining industry, but not in guiding development in a growing industry. The only option appears to have been collapse of the national industry in order to reconstruct a new basis to industrialization.

Ascendence and Transformation of the Japanese Car Industry

The Japanese auto industry offers a poignant contrast to the British case because of Japan's late rise as an industrializer. Although the auto industry of Japan seemed to burst onto the international market with unexpected force during the 1970s, as with all overnight sensations, development was actually a long time in progress. The manufacture of automobiles began in 1904, only one year after Ford was established in the USA, and during the 1920s the industry expanded rapidly. Some of its growth was due to the 1918 Aid for Military Vehicles Act, which authorized the army to establish the Army Military Vehicle Force. The military build-up generated orders for trucks from the *zaibatsus* (industrial combines) of Kawasaki Shipbuilding and Mitsubishi Shipbuilding, as well as from Hatsudoko Seizo (later to become Daihatsu). But most of the growth resulted from the establishment of Ford in Yokohama (1925) and General Motors in Osaka (1927). Within a few years, the weak domestic industry was overtaken by the foreign assemblers. By 1929, only 437 vehicles were made by domestic companies, in contrast to 29,338 by foreign firms; there were also 5,018 imported vehicles.[23] Near demise of the domestic industry was averted in 1939 when all of the foreign firms closed their Japanese plants. The Japanese car makers so thrived in their protected environment that by 1957 Toyota had established United States Toyota in Los Angeles, and by 1980 Japanese companies were the leading producers of automobiles in the world. What happened to warrant this dramatic turn of events? The rise of the Japanese industry has become the object of intense study and equally intense debate in recent years. Though the circumstances are by now well known, it is nonetheless worth reviewing if only to put into perspective the significance of government guidance in accelerating industrial growth.

The Significance of Reciprocal Consent The operative word here is guidance, since Japan's ascendence as a late developer with few natural resources required conscious creation of a comparative advantage. In contrast to nations that attempted a similar feat through despotic governance, here it was accomplished through reciprocal consent between firms and the state in achieving desired market outcomes.[24] Reciprocal consent refers to a process by which market jurisdiction is constantly negotiated by the state and the private sector and results in an interdependence between public and private power. Through this relationship, the Japanese quasi-integrated form of industrialization crystalized. This was quite apparent after World War II, but it was already evident during the prewar period of growing militarism.

Genesis of the Auto Industry It is therefore appropriate to start at 1926, when the army expressed fear that the local industry would succumb to foreign firms. Their concern led the government to establish an advisory board to the Ministry of Trade and Industry called the Committee for the Promotion of Local Industry. The committee then formed a Special Commission on the Feasibility Study of the Automobile Industry, which released a report in 1931 recommending creation of a "domestically manufactured standard model" car to alleviate inefficiencies and redundancies in the domestic industry.[25] Through the actions of several branches of government, support was voiced for the creation of national industry leaders. In the wake of these discussions, Nissan was established (1933). Then, in 1936, the Automobile Industry Act was passed, which introduced ownership restrictions and local content requirements, as well as production limitations on foreign firms. A few years later, import tariffs were raised from 50 per cent to 70 per cent, the yen was devalued, and a foreign exchange licensing system was implemented – all actions intended to benefit the domestic industry. Finally, when the Military Motor Vehicle Act was passed in 1939 stipulating that only cars for military or government use could be manufactured in Japan, Ford and GM were forced to withdraw from the market.

It was during this period that Toyota was established in Koromo (later renamed Toyota City), near Nagoya (1937). Like Nissan, Toyota rose to the position of national leader, but unlike Nissan, which attempted to replicate US "best practice," Toyota began a lengthy process of development based on a:

> sequential learning process of technology absorption and incremental innovation: from technological improvements made through learning-by-doing, to learning-by-interaction between users and producers, and further to human resource development to cope with such learning.[26]

This practice has also been referred to as "reverse engineering," because it involves the manufacture of a product that is similar to one in existence by redesigning it without access to either direct foreign investment or the transfer of blueprints for product or process design.[27] To catch up with established car makers, and to take advantage of the pool of engineers, researchers, and professors in local universities and industries, the company opened a motor vehicle industry research and development institute at Shibaura, Tokyo, in 1937.[28] In addition, Toyota adopted existing technology by using or copying state-of-the-art designs or parts taken from the most advanced US products.[29] The designs were then modified by Japanese engineers, who through their revisions began to master the products as well as critical design skills. As in the case of Nissan, Toyota learned mass-production methods by sending its engineers to work with Ford, but because Toyota knew the early years of operations would lead to mistakes, the company often limited its production runs. As a result, it was common for them to use multipurpose machinery run by multiskilled workers instead of specialized, single-function machines that provided economies of scale to large-volume manufacturers. To strengthen its basic research ability and build on their acquired technology, in 1940 Toyota opened the Toyota Science and Chemical Institute in Tokyo. And, to establish a sales network, the company took over several GM sales agencies. This emphasis on research, and a flexible use of equipment and labor combined with government intervention in securing the market, marked the beginning of a powerful alliance forged in later years.

Postwar Industrial Consolidation World War II left the auto industry depressed, and restructured. During the US occupation, Japan passed the Anti-Monopoly Law of 1947 patterned after the Sherman, Clayton, and Federal Trade Commission Acts, and adopted the Law for the Termination of *Zaibatsu* Family Control and the Law for the Elimination of Excessive Concentrations of Economic Power, aimed at reorganizing holding companies.[30] These antitrust policies have remained largely inoperative over the years, but initially they forced redefinition of the family-based *zaibatsus* into *keiretsus*, or industrial enterprise groups, that were instrumental in managing industrial growth.

The *keiretsus* have been among the more contentious of Japanese institutions because of their seeming violation of antitrust. There are two kinds of *keiretsus* – horizontal and vertical – and they overlap. Horizontal, or inter-market, *keiretsus* consist of firms and industries that are affiliated through direct or indirect council membership. Of the six main *keiretsus*, three are descendants of *zaibatsus* – Mitsubishi, Mitsui, and Sumitomo – and have at their center companies that were formerly direct subsidiaries of the *zaibatsu* holding companies, while the other three have particularly strong ties to banks.[31] All are associated with the auto industry through membership or affiliation (Mitsui, Toyota; Mitsubishi, Mitsubishi; Sumitomo, Mazda; Fuji, Nissan; Sanwa, Daihatsu; Dai-Ichi Kangyo, Isuzu). The characteristic that makes them horizontal is that they link banks, financial institutions, life insurance companies, trading companies, and a wide range of industries – from trade and commerce to construction, real estate, shipping, warehousing, and manufacturing – through shareholding, lender-borrower, buyer-seller, and director relationships. At different times, banks in the group have provided initial capitalization, arranged mergers and tie-ups, and helped establish overseas assembly plants and sales outlets. In 1988, 98 of Japan's 200 largest industrial firms maintained some affiliation with one of these industrial groups.[32]

Vertical *keiretsus* have at their core manufacturing companies which organize the supplier and distribution network hierarchically in a quasi-integrated firm structure. Just as the enterprise groups provide a level of financial and technical support for its companies, so the companies provide a measure of support for their supplier base. In the case of Toyota, this was by: (1) making used production equipment available (machine tools and others) at nominal prices; (2) providing teams of experienced workers to start-up projects; (3) conducting programs for training production workers; and (4) providing financial assistance.[33] The notable features between primary and supplier firms vary from one case to another. Some suppliers are very independent, while others are not. The supplier firms are further organized by associations (*kyoryokukai*) that promote the exchange of ideas and other cooperative activities for the improvement of product quality and efficiency (see table 4.3).

The outbreak of the Korean War and postwar era strengthened the role of the *keiretsus*, and solidified the definition the industry would take for the next several decades. 1945 to 1960 marked the reconstruction period, when the system of regulating and allocating materials, financing, and prices was dismantled and replaced by fiscal austerity programs imposed by the Dodge Line polices of 1949 and antitrust legislation that laid the foundation for vigorous competition and the opening of the economy. But these were met by a combination of new controls, interventionist policies, and a reconcentration of power among industrial groups. The immediate effect of the postwar economic orientation was a deep economic depression that generated

Table 4.3 *Associations of ancillary firms, 1968 and 1979*

Primary firm	*Association*	*Number of member firms, 1968*	*Number of member firms, 1979*
Daihatsu Kōgyō	Daihatsu Kyōryoku Kai	73	
Daihatsu Motor Co.	Daihatsu Kyōyū Kai		143
Fuji Heavy Ind.	Shinwa Kai	98	
	Fuji Gunma Kyōryoku Kai		158
	Fuji Mitaka Kyōryoku Kai		54
Hino Motors	Hino Kyōryoku Kai	79	247
Isuzu Motors	Isuzu Kyōryoku Kai	228	
	Isuzu Kyōwa Kai		269
Mitsubishi Motors	Mitsubishi Kashiwa Kai	67	344
	Mitsubishi Kyōryoku Kai	289	
Nissan Motor Co.	Nissan Motor Takara Kai	107	112
	Nissan Motor Shōhō Kai	34	49
Toyota Motor Co.	Kyōhō Kai	182	25
	Kansai Kyōhō Kai		25
	Kantō Kyōhō Kai		64
	Tokai Kyōhō Kai		136
Toyo Kogyo	Tōyū Kai	54	
	Tōkō Kai	45	

Source: Konosuke Odaka, Keinosuke Ono, and Fumihiko Adachi, *The Automobile Industry in Japan* (Tokyo: Kinokuniya, 1988), pp. 67, 258.

numerous strikes by a newly unionized workforce expressing its strength after the passage of the Union Labor Law of 1945. The unrest, and a need for truck replacement parts created by the outbreak of the Korean War, generated a substantial demand for trucks, so the General Headquarters of the Supreme Commander for the Allied Powers authorized Nissan, Diesel Motors, and Toyota to meet the new demand. The accumulation of capital and industrial rebuilding that followed from US military policies of "Special Procurements" of Japanese products provided the basis for subsequent development.

To circumvent growing union antagonism, industries began implementing a system of permanent employment. The debates over the origin of lifetime employment tends to fall into arguments over the influence of traditional social relations versus postwar employment practices. However, a compelling case can be made for integrating the two. Labor economist Robert Cole contends that during the course of industrialization, corporate groups found it in their interest to adopt principles similar to those found in the ideology of the family-based commercial and manufacturing confederations of the Meiji period that provided permanent tenure for male members.[34] Though these institutions had changed their employment policy by the end of the Tokugawa period, the legacy nonetheless served as an ideological and structural model for the practice of permanent employment. This strong precedent provided a cultural rationale for emphasizing company loyalty rather than individual status which was convenient during periods of labor unrest and expansion of the economy when companies wanted to reduce labor turnover. Born out of tradition and necessity, the system of reward by age and length of service (*nenko*) created the requisite material inducements and negative sanctions for securing desired worker loyalty. It also led to reduced labor mobility and access of entry into employment within the core segment of the labor force.

Growth by Design As the government began to chart its course for economic recovery after the war, it met with divided opinions over the role of government involvement in stimulating the automobile industry. Discussions began in September 1949 over the Industrial Rationalization resolution and continued till 1951. It was led on one side by the Bank of Japan, which argued on behalf of unrestricted importation of automobiles and parts, and on the other by the Ministry of International Trade and Industry (MITI), which favored greater protection. The compromise resulted in the Amended Law for Introduction of Foreign Capital (1951), along with high protective tariffs (20 to 50 per cent), a commodity tax system that favored domestic autos, import restrictions based on the allocation of foreign-exchange, and foreign-exchange controls on foreign direct investment.[35] With the 1951 signing of the San Francisco Peace Treaty and the Japan–US Security Treaty, Japan re-joined the international economy from a position of protected growth.

The issue of fragmented and weak markets requiring technological competence was confronted by Japan through corporate policies designed to capture innovation and government policies designed to promote growth by means of market intervention. Several companies entered into agreements for technological cooperation. Nissan joined with Austin (1952), Isuzu with Rootes (1953), Hino with Renault (1953), and Shin-Mitsubishi Heavy Industries with Willy-Overland (1953). Toyota, on the other hand, continued with its policy of "reverse engineering."

MITI also became more actively involved in stimulating the industry. In 1952 it announced a policy for the development of the domestic automobile industry, and in 1955, when the government formulated a five-year plan for economic self sufficiency, it outlined a program for the development of domestic passenger cars. MITI appeared to operate from a position that combined growth and Schumpeterian concepts of efficiency. This was later confirmed by the Director-General of MITI's International Trade Administration Bureau, S. Fukukawa, when he stated:

> The basic philosophy underlying the industrial policy of Japan is the principle of free competition in the market place. So our greatest concern has been to devise measures for tapping the ingenuity and vitality of private individuals and firms by ensuring the maximum efficiency of the market mechanism. But there are problems which cannot be dealt with effectively by individual firms or the market mechanism... achieving optimal resource allocation from a long-term dynamic viewpoint which cannot be accomplished by the market mechanism alone. [This is an area] in which industrial policy can – and should – play a useful role.[36]

MITI's objectives were accomplished through policies targeted at groups of firms according to sector, technology, size, or region, which were coordinated with actions by financial institutions.

MITI could effectively shape markets through a range of instruments that included: (1) tariffs and quotas; (2) control of foreign exchange; (3) influence over credit allocation in public and private banks; (4) technology import licenses; (5) accelerated depreciation allowances; (6) land subsidization; (7) influence over cartel legalization; and (8) creation of joint public–private companies.[37] To prevent cut-throat competition and develop infant industries, MITI authorized the creation of a number of cartels among small firms. In order to build a high-growth economy, it channelled resources toward developing such high-volume capital-intensive industries as the automobile industry. Toward this end, it applied quotas on cars lasting from 1950 to 1965, and tariffs that lasted until 1978. It coordinated investment projects, such as a seven-year tie-up from 1952 to 1965 between Austin and Nissan, and in 1966 arranged a merger between Nissan and Prince Motor Industry. And, in a crucial move, it removed import quotas in 1965. This forced rationalization, and moved the auto industry towards export competitiveness. It was not necessary for MITI to have continuing control in the industry for it to have a lasting effect. Nor did it have final authority. As one illustration, in 1955 it attempted to introduce small, inexpensive passenger cars known as the "People's Car" by subsidizing manufacturers, and in 1961 it introduced the "producers' group concept," where producers would be divided into groups of two or three firms to manufacture in mid-range cars, specialty vehicles, and mini-cars. However, the car makers instead chose to retain control over their segment structure.[38] Firms could and did behave in ways counter to MITI's policies, sometimes with preferred outcomes – as in Honda's choice to enter the car market without MITI's concurrence. But what it did provide was sectoral guidelines for business enterprises and officials in charge of credit allocation, research funding, and educational planning. When the influence of MITI over developments in the gasoline-powered automobile industry later waned as the latter became stronger, it shifted focus to new strategic sectors, such as semiconductors, computers, telecommunications, and electric vehicles.

The Japanese Development Bank was another major actor in that it provided loans to the automobile industry. In 1951, 4 per cent of investment came from this source.[39] With the 1965 passage of the Law on Temporary Measures for Promoting the Machinery Industries (Machine Industry Law), the automobile parts industry – selected as one of the seventeen industries for promotion – specifically benefited. Through this law, the Japan Development Bank lent funds to first-tier parts firms, and the Small Business Finance Corporation assisted secondary suppliers. The purpose of the legislation was to establish a "rational production system, to modernize facilities, promote exports, develop new technologies, and set overall raw material policies."[40] The initial legislation had a five-year time limitation that was extended twice, and the list of eligible firms was expanded to include not only automobile parts providers, but also automotive industry equipment and tooling, internal combustion engines, and industrial vehicles. Over a fifteen-year period, 34.8 billion yen were loaned to 529 firms. Of the loans made by the Japan Development Bank, 32.1 per cent went to manufacturers of automobile parts between 1961 and 1965, and 54.2 per cent between 1966 and 1974.[41] Such extensive financial and technical support assured the development of a strong parts and equipment industry in a short period of time.

There were other benefits as well. The auto industry (1951) and parts industry (1956) received special depreciation allowances (50 per cent for the first year, and, for "important" equipment, 50 per cent for three years) for "rationalization" (i.e., labor saving) equipment under the Enterprise Rationalization Promotion Law.[42] In addition, between 1951 and 1959 the Society of Automotive Engineers of Japan and the Midget

Motor Manufacturers Association of Japan were provided with subsidies for projects totalling 369 million yen.[43] Further, when companies could prove that imported machinery was essential for manufacturing, they could obtain import tariff exemptions under special provisions of the Tariff Law and the Provisional Tariff Measures Law. Through all of these provisions, the industry moved rapidly toward applying efficient methods of manufacture.

A Refocus Toward Internationalization These policies of industry promotion and protection developed the industry beyond the stage of an "infant industry." During the 1960s, the Japanese economy began to grow rapidly, and the auto industry became increasingly competitive. The government had previously announced "Basic Guidelines for Trade and Foreign Exchange Liberalization" (1958), which encouraged firms to construct or expand facilities devoted to passenger car production. By the time trade liberalization was adopted (1965), the mass-production system was in full operation. Japan became a member of OECD in 1964, which further secured its international status. Honda (1959) and Nissan (1960) had previously established sales companies in the USA, followed by movement abroad by Japanese car makers. By 1964, Japan had surpassed France in the number of cars manufactured.

When Japan joined OECD, the Japanese cabinet adopted a policy of liberalizing capital transactions in the auto industry, to take effect in 1971. This policy permitted foreign companies to expand in Japan by investing in joint ventures. It resulted in ties not only with foreign firms, but also among Japanese firms. Nissan and Prince merged (1966); Toyota established ties with Hino (1966) and with Daihatsu (1967); Chrysler and Mitsubishi entered into a joint venture (1971); GM forged a relationship with Isuzu (1971); and Ford linked up with Toyo Kogyo (Mazda) (1979) (see figure 4.1). To illustrate how Japanese firms dealt with structural adjustment, when Toyo Kogyo faced excess manufacturing labor, it shifted factory workers into the sales division over the period from 1975 to 1980. The joint ventures strengthened the smaller Japanese companies *vis-à-vis* Toyota and Nissan, while solidifying the position of these two front runners. The 1971 legislation also marked the end of the Machine Industries Law and other programs, and brought to a close the period of overt industry protection and promotion.

As the Japanese companies began to penetrate world markets, attention focussed on the Japanese system of production. In reality, this referred to the Toyota system of production. Toyota maintained its own unique structure, although descriptions about the Japanese

Figure 4.1 *Inter-firm linkages in the automobile industry between America and Japan, 1988.*

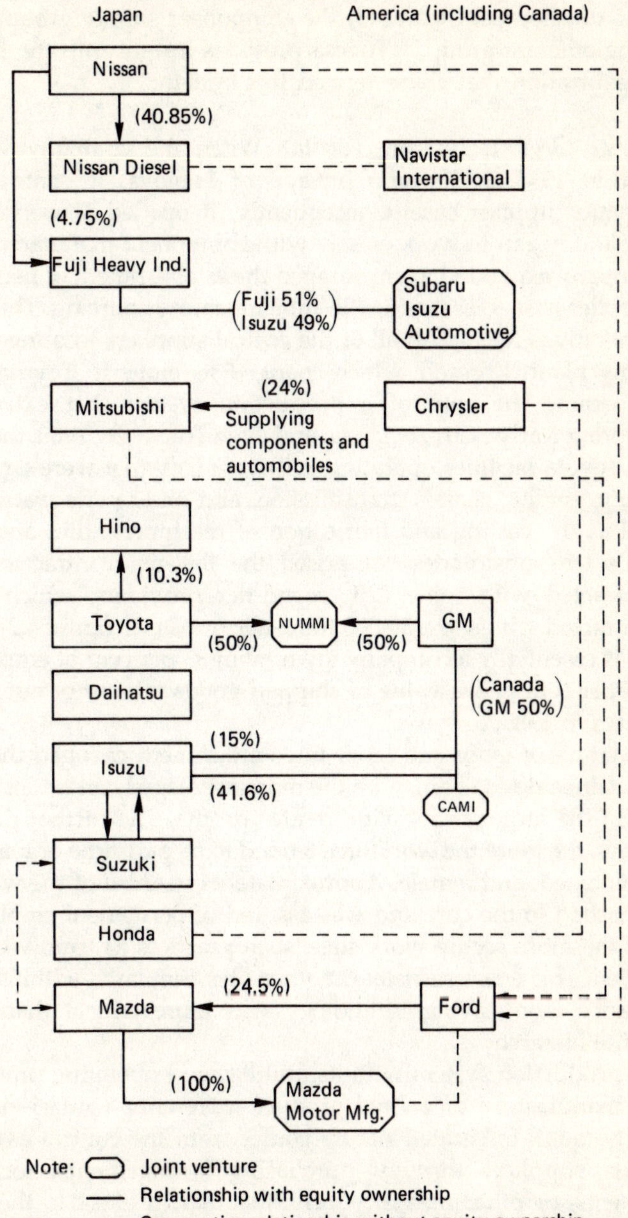

Source: Ken-Ichi Imai, "Japanese business groups and the structural impediments initiative," in *Japan's Economic Structure: Should it Change?* ed. Kozo Yamamura (Seattle: Society for Japanese Studies, 1990), p. 188.

firms appear to be fairly consistent.[44] In general, Japanese production consists of spatially interconnected industrial systems based on four types of group interaction: (1) the work team in the plant, (2) the product development team, (3) the component supply group, and (4) the conglomerate group.[45] Toyota provides insight into the hierarchical organization that characterized this system.

Industrial Organization in Toyota When the company was first formed in 1937 in Koromo outside of Nagoya, it confronted an inadequate supplier base. Consequently, it opened a specialty steel factory and began to work closely with component manufacturers. As the company expanded, it encouraged the establishment of tiers among the supplier base to assure just-in-time inventory sourcing. This had an agglomerative effect, with all of the critical suppliers locating near the assembly plant. Koromo, which changed its name to Toyota City in 1959, became the core of a production system that extended to neighboring Kariya City, Nagoya, and even Tokyo. By 1980, there were eleven Toyota facilities operating in Toyota City that were engaged in assembly, engine, chassis, transmission, and other parts manufacture, as well as the casting and fabrication of machinery, dies and molds. Toyota's ten subsidiaries comprised the first-tier contractors which subcontracted with some 220 second-tier providers, which in turn subcontracted with some 30,000 third-tier firms (see figure 4.2). Toyota City was essentially a company town, with 83 per cent of employment and 95 per cent of the value of shipped goods in auto or auto-related industries in 1985.[46]

The nature of labor and labor force attachment changed the higher up the value-added chain, with the more privileged conditions of work found in the larger firms with greater profits. The further down the hierarchy, the more the workforce tended to be part-time or temporary, non-unionized, and female. Approximately one-third of the workforce was attached to the core and was assured of permanent employment. Within the more secure work sites, such practices as team work were employed. This was less visible at other sites. Similarly, within the first-tier plants, labor-saving technology was more critical than further down the hierarchy.

This production system with its multilayered operating units linked in the manufacture of a final product represents a quasi-integrated firm. The quasi-integrated nature comes from the control assemblers exert on suppliers through purchasing arrangements, technology agreements, or other means, which is similar in effect to the control an integrated firm maintains over its subsidiaries. However, the

Figure 4.2 *A schematic view of the Japanese automobile industry in the 1970s*

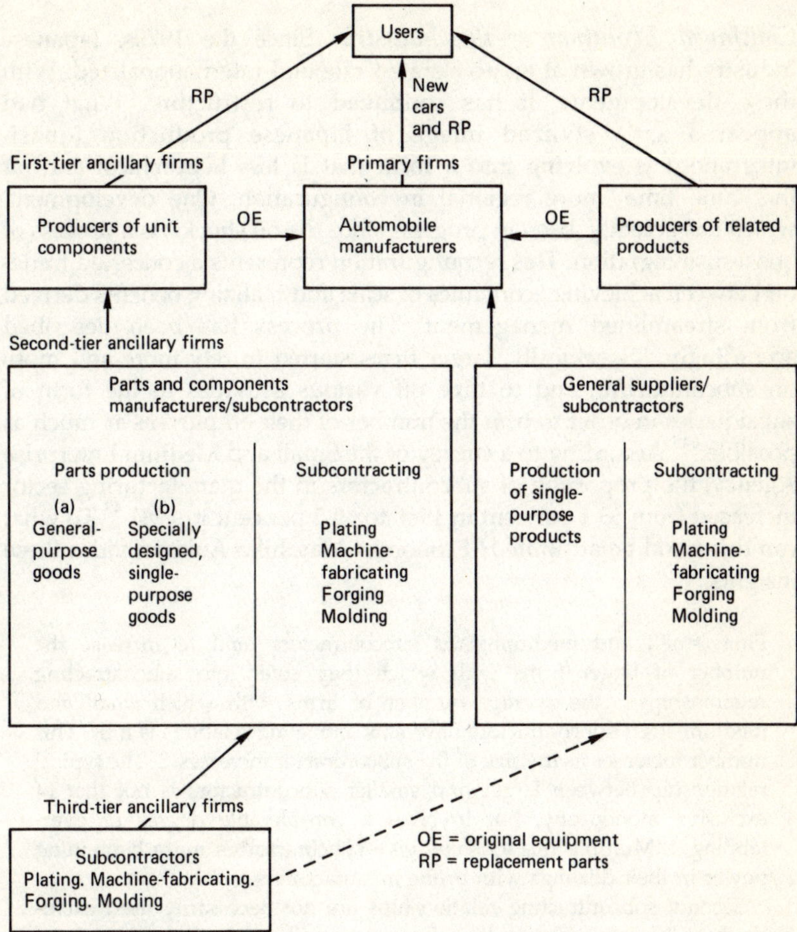

Source: Konosuke Odaka, Keinosuke Ono, and Fumihiko Adachi, *The Automobile Industry in Japan: A study of Ancillary Firm Development* (Tokyo: Kinokuniya, 1988), p. 2.

disintegrated nature of the relationship allows for greater flexibility in the arrangements. The need for proximity in the interaction among firms results in the agglomeration of activities with metropolitan areas

– a pattern that continues to evolve as companies join forces and change the location of manufacture.

Continued Evolution of the Industry Since the 1970s, Japanese industry has grown at an accelerated rate and internationalized. With these developments, it has continued to restructure. What had appeared as a stylized image of Japanese production (quasi-integration) is evolving into a form that is less heirarchical and, at the same time, more regional in configuration. One development, which has actually been in progress since the oil shocks, is a process of quasi-disintegration. This reconfiguration represents a concerted trade-off between achieving economies of scale and realizing benefits derived from streamlined management. The process has been described accordingly: "Specifically, larger firms started to rely more and more on subcontracting and to hive off various activities in the form of subsidiaries in order to trim the number of their employees as much as possible."[47] According to a survey of the Small and Medium Enterprise Agency, the proportion of subcontractors in the manufacturing sector increased from 53.1 per cent in 1966 to 65.5 per cent in 1981.[48] To what can this trend be attributed? Economist Masahiko Aoki provides these insights:

> First, small and medium-sized subcontractors tend to increase the number of larger firms with which they enter into subcontracting relationships ... the average number of firms with which small and medium-sized subcontractors have subcontracting relations is four. This number increases as the size of the subcontractor increases ... The typical relationship between larger and smaller subcontractors is not that of exclusive monopsony, but involves a considerable degree of overlapping ... Multiple relationships give subcontractors more bargaining power in their dealings with prime manufacturers.
>
> Second, subcontracting relationships are not necessarily used exclusively to lower labor costs. In many cases, small and medium-sized firms that have had long-term relations with larger prime manufacturers have accumulated their own technological and managerial expertise as well as the ability to develop new part products. Such situations involve a certain degree of "knowledge sharing" ...
>
> Third, the exclusive absorption of shocks by subcontractors in terms of fluctuating earnings and employment does not seem to be as widespread as it used to be: various types of risk sharing between prime manufacturers and subcontractors seem to have become more prevalent ... the buffer function is regarded as the primary factor ... by fewer than 10 percent ... one-third of manufacturers thought that subcontract-

> ing reduced the cost of production, and about three-quarters of the subcontractors regarded "reliable long-term relations" as the primary factor. This indicates that, contrary to the stereotyped dual-structure hypothesis, larger prime manufacturers with diversified finished products and financial viability act as partial insurers of business opportunities, earnings, and employment for smaller subcontractors in exchange for insurance premiums in the form of semimonopolistic gains.[49]

The extensive sharing among firms is leading to a change in Japanese industries. Rather than the prior hierarchical system of companies, a number of small and medium-sized enterprises have freed themselves from the restrictions set by larger firms, and in turn are redefining the traditional balance of power.[50] The new configuration is more horizontal in nature, with more overlapping, multiple relations, and more balance especially between first-tier suppliers and the primary manufacturers. In contrast to the quasi-integrated firm, this represents a form of "quasi-disintegration."[51] As opposed to the USA, where venture firms are spun off at the initiative of large firms which retain control over the final output, here subcontractors maintain considerably more independence.

With quasi-disintegration, research and development has been pushed downward into the supplier base. First-tier suppliers are increasingly entering into product development decisions with the major companies. This trend has been critical for adoption of simultaneous engineering – or the concurrent undertaking of design, development, and manufacture – steps that had traditionally been undertaken sequentially. Simultaneous engineering will be re-examined in the final chapter. With quasi-disintegration, not only are subcontractors more independent, but so are final assemblers. Since substantial portions of sub-assembly are undertaken outside of the final assembly plant, assemblers can locate away from the center of intense firm interaction. Indeed, Toyota's newest facility in Japan is not near its other facilities, but at Tahara. Furthermore, final assemblers are now in the position to increase their use of automated technology, since the tasks requiring human applications are reduced. Again, Nissan's newest plant in Kyushu is also its most automated. Another complement to the horizontal configuration is a tendency to shift less value-added manufacture to nearby low-wage nations. Countries such as Thailand, Malaysia, Indonesia, and the Philippines are becoming integrated into a *de facto* Southeast Asian economic region. This level of integration is occurring concurrently with the integration of North

America and Europe, where major parts providers have followed major assemblers for manufacture.

While Japan's techno-economic paradigm is unique, the lessons are, in fact, widely applicable. The government's policy of targeting industries on the basis of their growth and its organizational strengths for promoting such industries have been key to Japan's competitive success and critical in creating a stable economic environment for industrial development. For the most part, Japanese industrial policies have been directed at promoting adjustment rather than preventing its occurrence. Although MITI was extremely influential as a coordinator of a broad range of instruments, it was not a final authority in determining the industry's outcome. Despite the strong state presence, this is not an instance of state-led growth, it is an instance of proactive and sometimes uneven guidance. According to one assessment, MITI acts as a "broad policy architect, ad hoc working problem solver, formal regulator, regional policy arbiter, and informal administrative guide. In some industries it has a strong statutory authority, in others only a broad and sometimes weak influence."[52] The government provided a coherent purpose and long-range goal for encouraging development, but industries maintained considerable latitude over how this was accomplished. The process of reciprocal consent facilitated continual change in the industry. As the industry reconfigured, the nature of government support also shifted toward encouraging the production of vehicles using new fuels, for example, and toward solving the diseconomies of excessive congestion created by the just-in-time inventory system. The multiple levels of industrial organization and support for small firms were additional factors that both assured a strong supplier base and helped to create the conditions that led to their independence from the final assemblers. This is in direct contrast to the UK where appropriate support was not only lacking for major firms, but even more so for the small, domestic supplier base. Finally, the structure of the capital and labor markets assured growth when needed and rationalization when necessary. Only recently have banks been supplanted by the stock market as a source of industrial funds, and has permanent employment been threatened by lay-offs. While these developments appear to represent a shift toward Anglo-American market structures – as if to suggest a linear progression towards maturity – instead they are stages in the evolution of the *Japanese* system.

Germany: An Illustration of Quasi-Market Industrialization

After the high cost of reunification, and with the distractions caused by European economic integration, the German economy and industry appear to be in a state of disarray. One might wonder if anything can be learned from this example. Germany's costs of production are notoriously high. German workers enjoy the highest hourly wages. Total labor costs, including social costs, come to approximately $40 per hour. Although Chrysler's labor costs are also a reported $40 per hour, workers in Germany average only 37 hours of work per week, compared with the US rate of 40 hours per week, and this figure should drop to 35 hours per week during 1993.[53] The wage bill doesn't even take into account the liberal holidays, medical leave, and high absentee rate. All of these factors lead to an industry that is trailing behind world leaders with respect to productivity (see table 4.4).

When given the choice of purchasing a car of comparable quality, Americans – who constitute the largest export market for German cars – are looking elsewhere since German cars have become over-priced relative to value. In 1992, the sales of VWs in the USA had fallen to their lowest level since 1960, while the sales of Mercedes Benz had dropped 35 per cent since the mid-1980s, a figure that was somewhat better than BMW at 50 per cent, and Audi at 75 per cent, but Porsche fared the worst, with sales of only 4,400 cars in 1991.[54]

Table 4.4 *The six major West German automobile manufacturers in 1985 (passenger cars and domestic operations only)*

Manufacturer	*Employees output units*	*Output units*	*Sales (million DM)*
VW	159,991	1,734,991	48,531.40
VW	123,598	1,376,241	38,920.60
Audi	36,393	358,612	9,610.80
Opel	57,273	903,150	14,794.70
Daimler Benz	109,000	537,909	23,862.00
Ford	45,991	505,231	14,443.50
BMW	46,814	431,085	14,246.40
Porsche	7,915	54,458	3,567.90

Source: Peter J. Katzenstein (ed.), *Industry and Politics in West Germany: Toward the Third Republic* (Ithaca: Cornell Iniversity Press, 1989), p. 117.

The precipitous drop in sales forced German auto makers to take serious ameliorative measures. One was to establish overseas sites for auto manufacture. BMW announced plans to build a $250–300 million assembly plant near Spartenburg, South Carolina – where they can pay non-union wages – for manufacture of 60,000 roadsters in 1995. Their expected labor-cost savings is on the order of $3,000 per car. Mercedes Benz is currently making trucks in Mexico, but is reportedly gearing up to make luxury cars, possibly as early as 1993. Mercedes Benz also opened a new $1.6 billion assembly plant in Rastatt, Germany, in which work is undertaken by groups of workers in eight- to twelve person teams.

Is this enough? When industry analysts ask why Germany can't compete, they come up with the answer that German manufacturers are making the same mistakes US firms made one decade ago:

> But are Germans on the right track? These "solutions" have a haunting ring to them. They are exactly the same approaches the Big Three undertook in the early 1980s, namely, moving manufacturing operations to lower-cost locations overseas, and making huge investments in new, high-tech facilities. In retrospect, most American executives recognize this was a strategic mistake. They didn't attack their problems head-on. Instead they tried to manange their problems, or buy their way out of them.[55]

In fact, the German solutions represent a far more radical departure from prior policies than just following in the footsteps of American firms. For companies who sold their products on the basis of "German engineering," and which were relatively immobile until recently, something has changed significantly for them to feel they could – or even should – begin to internationalize production now. Rather than this being an instance of German firms simply trying to capture low costs, it is instead indicative of more complex production strategies. A brief examination of the German situation demonstrates how these actions parallel trends evident in both the US and Japanese industry.

Retracing Steps to the Present As a counterpoint to the prior cases, the German situation will be reviewed from the perspective of the West German experience. Obviously, the full picture is far richer, but well beyond the scope of this discussion. The intent here is only to lay out a profile of the West German context – as background to contemporary Germany – in order to understand the logic driving the industry's actions.

The distinctive nature of West German institutions have by now been well documented.[56] Historically, German policies reflected a "social market" approach toward facilitating market trends, although this has arguably been weakened by unemployment, recession, and other economic problems that have justified stronger actions. One thrust has been toward economic intervention in anticipation of sectoral adjustment as provided for in the Promotion of Economic Growth and Stability Act of 1967. In a decidedly corporatist approach, industry-led adjustments have involved the government, banks, businesses and labor. Adjustment mechanisms have favored creation of crisis cartels, subsidies, loans, and labor relocation and training, and not company bail-outs or labor compensation and income maintenance. One of many examples involves the 1970s crisis of VW. Here, the method of adjustment was jointly determined by the federal and state (*Land*) governments, the shareholders, and the trade union and focussed on rationalization and modernization, including a social program for the workers and a subsidy to the region for reinvestment.[57]

Yet other policies have focussed on shaping industrial growth, as opposed to decline, and are embedded in a process of "concertation." This refers to the concerted efforts of a number of independent actors in reaching a desired outcome. As an example, the manufacture and export of a product could involve the input of banks specifically oriented toward assisting small and medium-sized firms, research institutes engaged in basic R&D, technology transfer centers, vocational education programs, and export promotion programs. The collective process has resulted in a decentralized, region-based form of industrialization.[58] Such is the basis to the German *Mittlestand* – which translates to medium-sized companies but refers to a middle-class ethic and business tradition – that constitute the bulk of specialized and craft-based manufacture.

The decidedly embedded form of industrialization supported a widely diverse auto industry in Germany, evident by the extent of industry concentration, which is lower in Germany than in all other leading producing countries except Japan. Domestic producers include Volkswagen, which operates with Audi, Daimler-Benz, BMW, and Porsche. Ford and GM (through their subsidiary, Opel) also manufacture here (see table 4.4). GM and Ford are credited with introducing mass-production methods to Germany (they were established in 1925 and 1929, respectively), later adopted by Volkswagen and Mercedes Benz.[59]

The strategy of German manufacturers has traditionally been to engage in the low-volume manufacture of high-margin products. When faced with competition, they have tended to move upmarket by improving on product design and quality, but not by undertaking price competition. Each of the domestic manufacturers operates in a limited segment range. Because of the limited ability of the domestic market to support the large number of manufacturers, all are export oriented, with the USA being a particularly important market. In 1986, VW and Audi sold 11.4 per cent of their production in the USA, Daimler-Benz 16.8 per cent, BMW 22.4 per cent, and Porsche 57.6 per cent.[60] For Daimler-Benz, BMW, and Porsche, this has meant competing in world market high-performance, specialty niches.

The structure of the mass producers and smaller producers tends to be quite distinct. Although the German industry is reportedly highly integrated, in fact this is more true for VW and Mercedes-Benz than for smaller firms.[61] Perhaps the most vertically disintegrated firm in the industry worldwide is Porsche. For years, Porsche's only production facilities consisted of an assembly plant, a research and development center, a sheet-metal pressing shop, and an administrative building.[62] It contracted out the manufacture of literally all parts except for those few critical to the integrity of the name. More recently, it also expanded into general engineering services. At the opposite end, the VW plant in Wolfsburg is one of the largest integrated facilities, with employment at the level of some 65,000 people.

Despite these differences, they operate with a common set of social inputs. One is the high skill level of the workforce upon which product development marked by technological solutions depends. One industry analyst describes it accordingly:

> At the center of the "German model" is the skilled worker and a specific understanding of skilled work as a "profession." This understanding includes the ... willingness to accept comprehensive responsibility ... and ... a large degree of self-regulation ... The strong anchoring of the German way in the structures of co-determination and the corporatist system of vocational education means ... a greater degree of institutional and legal limitation of the company headquarter's scope for action and decisionmaking.[63]

On the one hand, the high skill tradition is at the core of union–management relations known as co-determination, or what has been called "a firmly established productivity coalition between management and labor at the point of production."[64] On the other hand, it is responsible for a certain amount of innovation diffusion:

> underlying greater technical sophistication among German users and their ability to take responsibility for configuring and installing their own systems is an infrastructure of apprenticeship, polytechnical schools, universities, and technical institutes that produce multi-level manufacturing expertise among German adults ... Dense communications networks, overlapping memberships, and flows of people among these institutions generate wide diffusion of ideas ...[65]

Another critical input is the support of banks. Under the universal banking system, banks can engage in commerce, investment, and merchant banking, asset management, and insurance. They can take equity positions and sit on management boards. For example, Deutsche Bank holds a 28 per cent stake in Daimler-Benz.[66] Bank representatives sit on the supervisory boards of all of the auto makers.[67] For auto makers and suppliers, long-standing relationships with "house" banks (*Hausbanken*) as lenders is common practice. Because access to capital is relatively secure, there has been less incentive for firms to go public. It also supports a long-term investment perspective. As one analyst has noted, "German firms in sectors exposed to the world market tend to have long-term profit expectations and performance standards and high intangible investment in marketing and research, which pays only over a long period."[68]

A third critical input comes from support for research and development and technology transfer mechanisms. For example, the state of Baden-Württemberg, which houses Daimler-Benz and Porsche, is also the site of the Steinbeis Foundation (*Steinbeis Stiftung für Wirtschaftsforderung*), a non-profit organization created in 1971 for the purpose of transforming basic into applied research. It contracts with research scientists and development engineers in universities, research institutes, and private industry and transfers technology to small and medium-sized firms. Another non-profit research organization nationwide is the Fraunhofer Gesellschaft. Combined with the many universities and technical schools, the network for innovation is extremely dense. In a comparision between the UK and Germany, one observer noted:

> one of the more insightful distinctions to be made between the UK and [Germany] is the notion that they represent radically different institutional models of innovation: the UK being a 'mission-oriented' country, [Germany] being a 'diffusion-oriented' country ... In the former, the primary goal of public policy has been to encourage the development of technological capabilities in fields considered to be nationally significant. Examples from the UK would include military projects ... In contrast,

> 'diffusion-oriented' countries have put less emphasis on developing new prestige technologies, than on promoting the widespread diffusion of advanced technological capabilities throughout the economy via strong institutional mechanisms for technology transfer (e.g. education and training, especially its vocational component, and co-operative research networks etc.).[69]

All of these inputs result in a strong base for supporting a technically competent supplier network in the auto industry. For the most part, suppliers work closely with assemblers in quality control and research and development. One often-cited example is the case of Daimler-Benz and Bosch jointly developing the antiblock system (ABS). Bosch also maintains a 20 per cent sourcing limit from subcontractors in order to learn from a range of providers, but compensates them by engaging in long-term partnerships.

The joint outcome of access to skilled labor, patient capital, and technically competent suppliers is a level of innovative capacity that is critical to the German strategy of increasing productivity through higher value added. These underlie the creation of "German engineered" products and define the basis to regionally defined production systems. The extensive external provision of goods and services treated as public goods makes this a "quasi-market" system, in contrast to the quasi-integrated system of Japan or the vertically integrated system of the USA. Historically, this foundation has made mobility difficult. German firms could not move to low-wage sites without abandoning the entire structure. But, as in the case of Japanese manufacturers, this system has responded to exogenous changes through adaptation.

Toward a More Horizontal and International Structure An example of adaptation can be found in BMW. Clearly, not all firms are following this strategy, but the ability for BMW to do so is illustrative of the possibility for change. As in the case of US and Japanese firms, BMW is adopting a even more horizontal configuration, and combining this with a concerted international regional strategy. Its strategy is one of "collaborative manufacturing" with suppliers, in which BMW acts as the system integrator.[70] A reported 55 to 75 per cent of total production costs are out-sourced, with approximately 80 per cent of these involving collaborative work with specialist subcontractors.[71] At the same time, BMW is planning on opening a new plant in Spartanburg, South Carolina (1995), in recognition that a purely export strategy is neither cost effective nor responsive to regional markets. Now that US suppliers have begun to change, and given a strong network of

Japanese suppliers, BMW will have a choice of subcontracting with established European suppliers and shipping the products to its Southeast coast site, or establishing a new set of collaborative arrangements in the USA. This action by BMW merely confirms the trends evident in the USA and Japan.

Charting a New Course

The three cases illustrate several key points. One is that countries which are successful in regenerating their industries are distinguished by dense institutional structures through which multiple levels of interaction between the public and private sector can occur. In Japan, this was expressed as reciprocal consent among actors engaged in achieving desired market outcomes. In Germany, where the market was less governed, it was expressed as concertation. Both allowed a certain diffusion of costs and risks as well as innovation to permeate society.

Secondly, these cases illustrate the repeated tendency toward the externalization of activities by firms – resulting in models of collaborative manufacturing – that were combined with strategies of international regionalization. Rather than being contradictory strategies, these are actually complementary and can be fostered by appropriate public policies. However, the new demands for innovative capability can present an added burden for early industrializers, and, as illustrated in the next chapter, for developing countries attempting to use the automobile industry as a means for technological advancement.

5

Emerging Nations: Profiles of Interdependent Development

The Paradox of Flexible Production and Development in Industrializing Nations

The current trends in international industrialization pose difficult issues for industrializing countries. They must come to terms with the fact that the current period of international competitiveness based on flexibility and technological competence may preclude the introduction of innovative products by industrializing countries. It is hard to know whether continued *de facto* regionalization will place developing countries at a permanent technological disadvantage *vis-à-vis* advanced industrialized nations. Yet unresolved is the question of whether the gobal scale of competition necessarily favors multinational corporations over small or domestic producers involved in automobile or parts manufacture. Some argue that it is no longer possible for developing countries to become export competitive in complex manufactured products.[1] The effect of automation is thought to create a "comparative advantage reversal" in developed countries.[2] According to some auto industry analysts, "visions of massive finished unit exports, even from developing countries who rapidly learn best practice from the world's multinationals, are not realistic."[3]

History is filled with examples of industrializing countries becoming economically and technologically dependent upon advanced industrialized nations once key sectors, such as the automobile industry, are dominated by multinational corporations.[4] The problem has been stated accordingly:

> ... international capital, centered in the metropolitan "core" of the world economy, imposes hierarchical, externally rooted structures of control upon the less developed "periphery" so that it may be more readily exploited... The less developed countries thus are compelled by economic necessity to import capital, machinery, and technology, thereby becoming dependent upon foreign suppliers, financial institutions, and transnational corporate managements... inasmuch as these economies do not produce either their own capital goods or technologies, they are "structurally incomplete" and must maintain a "dependent articulation" with a world economy dominated by transnational corporations in order to function at all.[5]

A labor corollary is expressed as the new international division of labor. In concept, the distribution of production across core and peripheral nations consists of disarticulated ties binding developed and developing nations.[6] A frequently cited example is the maquiladora or in-bond industry in Mexico that, in actuality, reveals both an international and a gender division of labor.[7]

However, the situation is even more complex. It is now increasingly common to see advanced industrializing countries engaged in sophisticated production activities requiring skilled labor and capital intensity.[8] Current pressures toward the decentralization and regionalization of design and production are pushing the extent of research and development. Unstable markets recast the necessarily imperialist nature of transnational firms, while simultaneously placing new emphasis on the ability of industrializing nations to influence their developmental paths. The crux of the issue lies in recognition that the technological basis of competition creates multiple risks and prohibitive costs that must be externalized by firms. In the process of externalization, firms solidify industrial linkages, integrate multiple stages of production, and depend on the local provision of infrastructure and service functions supporting research and development related activities. This mutuality of interests between firms and states provides an avenue for developing countries to determine their technological trajectory, along with a basis for "creating" the advantage associated with high technology sectors. Yet several conditions must exist for this to occur: "A virtually universal condition for the existence of viable relationships is the localization, or indigenization, of both labor and management... A second, widely affirmed condition is local participation in equity ownership."[9]

Industrializing countries have an opportunity to develop their research and development capability, especially as it complements the interests of auto manufacturers wanting to expand their regional functions. The question is whether they will.

The following cases provide examples of how developing countries have entered the international economy given the current strategies of auto makers. The differences among these countries could not be more dramatic. Some are more successful than others – indeed, one country no longer exists – but each illustrates a key point about the changing nature of industrialization and the possibilities for insertion into the international economy. The countries examined here are Mexico, Brazil, South Korea, and the former Yugoslavia.

Postwar Industrialization: Dependent Development

The period after World War II was one of economic growth stimulated by consumer demand. In many developing countries, the economic expansion presented an opportunity to industrialize. To compete successfully in manufacturing, they commonly adopted national policies favoring development through import-substitution. Critical inputs to such sectors as chemicals, steel, automobiles, capital goods manufacture, or those industries which fueled local consumption were primary targets of intervention. Prevailing theories of regional development based on international trade suggested that industrialization would occur in those sectors in which the country maintained a comparative advantage, predictably in the manufacture of low-value added inputs. To move beyond this stage toward capital intensive manufacture, and ultimately to research and development, required extraordinary efforts. Latin American, Asian, and European experiences illustrate the way this was attempted during early phases and how this has changed in more recent years.

The Brazilian and Mexican Auto Industries: From Expansion to Retrenchment Latin America has an extensive history of automobile production. Motor-vehicle manufacture in Brazil dates from 1919, that in Mexico from 1924. Industrialization evolved through four distinct phases: the importation of finished vehicles; growth based on local assembly; domestic components manufacture; and the export of vehicles and parts. Initial production consisted of the assembly of complete knock-down kits, but after World War II, when demand was strong, policies were directed at stimulating domestic parts production.

Decrees in 1947 and 1954 set quotas on the importation of finished automobiles and materials into Mexico. In Brazil, imports of automotive parts were banned when local sources were available. President Kubitschek furthered the industry's promotion in 1956 by creating the Automotive Industry Executive Group (GEIA) to oversee development of the manufacture of a full range of automobiles and a parts industry capable of supplying the entire industry. GEIA stipulated that between 90 to 100 per cent of parts be locally sourced, and established import, exchange, and fiscal benefits for meeting these requirements.

These policies complemented development in the USA and other advanced industrialized nations. In the USA the era of "Fordism" was characterized by high productivity derived from mass production, combined with mass consumption sustained by rising real wages secured through collective bargaining pacts and governmental policies of demand management, which jointly functioned as pillars to a self-sustaining virtuous growth cycle. Complementary strategies of import-substitution industrialization in Mexico and Brazil attempted to reproduce the Fordist model of industrial development. Growth was stimulated by tariffs on consumer goods, imported capital goods, and incentives to domestic consumer goods providers. Over-valued exchange rates favoring imported capital goods assured capital-intensive manufacturing. Subsidies on food and services for the expanding numbers of industrial workers fueled the consumer base. Though these policies of generating production behind protected markets were creating sectoral and distributional imbalances, growth was sustained through traditional exports, net foreign investment, and debt-financed imported capital and intermediate goods. As long as both industrialized countries and these industrializing countries enjoyed continued economic expansion, their objectives were mutually reinforcing.

Throughout the 1960s and early 1970s, stable patterns of international investment, trade, production, and employment were linked with high rates of economic growth. In Mexico, motor-vehicle production (including trucks and buses) doubled from 1960 (49,807) to 1965 (114,521), and then tripled between 1965 and 1975 (to 356,624). In Brazil, motor-vehicle production grew seven times from 1960 (133,041) to 1975 (930,234).[10] During the so-called Brazilian miracle years of 1968 to 1974, auto industry output grew at a compound annual rate of 22 per cent, nearly twice as fast as real gross domestic product at 11.2 per cent, and was essentially the driving force behind the country's growth.[11] For both countries, expansion of the industry seemed to lie in successful policies of import-substitution industrialization.

The policies proved both effective and problematic. Markets became fragmented due to a large number of producers, producers operated well below capacity, and domestic parts production was costly yet of low quality. As of 1960, foreign inputs still represented 80 per cent of the total value of Mexican vehicles in a market consisting of nine manufacturers.[12] Consequently, in 1962 Mexico issued another Auto Decree with the stated objectives of, first, stimulating backward linkages, especially in such high-value added products as engines and drive trains, through a 60 per cent local content requirement on the value of automobiles, and, second, expanding the extent of domestic participation through local parts manufacture involving 60 per cent Mexican participation – goals that could not be met. Instead, the excessively high number of producers for the size of market and relatively underdeveloped supplier base exacerbated a looming balance of payments problem.

To counter chronic trade and market structure imbalances, Mexican decrees were issued in 1969 and 1970 which reiterated the 60 per cent local content requirement, and introduced a condition that manufacturers balance imports with the export of auto parts. Auto parts exports increased dramatically, but not local content. By 1970, only 36 per cent local content was attained. On the other hand, the ratio of auto parts exports relative to assembled vehicles grew from 3:2 in 1965 to 4:1 in 1970, and 50:1 in 1980. At the same time, the industry was becoming more concentrated in foreign hands. In contrast to 1963, when 62 per cent was foreign owned, by 1971 this had risen to 84 per cent.[13] Auto production continued to grow, such that Mexico surpassed Argentina in 1974 to become the second largest Latin-American producer of automobiles after Brazil.

Brazil suffered from similar problems. The limited domestic market and a proliferation of vehicle models and plants combined with high domestic content requirements created capacity under-utilization, inefficiency, and high costs. In 1962 there were six firms manufacturing vehicles – a number that rose to eleven in 1965.[14] By 1962 Brazilian capacity was 40 to 50 per cent under-utilized. A vehicle that cost $1,600 in 1965 to manufacture in Detroit cost $3,000 in Brazil.[15] Economic pressures led to high inflation, negative real GNP growth, and labor unrest, all of which helped to provoke the military takeover of 1964 and a subsequent austerity program aimed at depressing and controlling wages. During the austerity years of 1964-8, most auto makers sustained losses. By the end of the period, four of the original auto makers were no longer in the market and all of the firms with Brazilian ownership had passed into foreign control.[16]

To jump-start the industry, the government instituted policies that stimulated effective demand by increasing the purchasing capability of the highest-income segments of the population. Between 1970 and 1974, an estimated 50 to 60 per cent of consumer credit was used to finance automobile purchases.[17] But, as in the case of Mexico, the growth was creating a balance of payments outflow, only here it was due to remittances of profits, royalties, and interests, since nearly all of the terminal sector and many of the major parts firms were foreign owned.

Industrial development based on the imported technology and production processes of transnational corporations proved difficult to sustain over time. The period of accelerated expansion in Brazil came to an abrupt end with the oil shock of 1973. Oil prices quadrupled, trade deficits rose, and auto production plummeted. In an attempt to halt the slide, Brazil instituted the Fiscal Benefits for Special Exports Program (BEFIEX) in 1976 which offered special fiscal benefits for exports, and in 1977 exempted the auto industry from price controls. In Mexico the crisis peaked in 1982, when the automobile trade deficit rose to 57.7 per cent of the total trade deficit. With issuance of a 1983 Auto Decree, local content requirements were waived and exports were encouraged.

The initial outcomes of these attempts at import-substitution industrialization were the collapse of domestic auto markets, the denationalization of the Brazilian industry, and the absorption of the Mexican industry by US interests. It appeared to pave the way for a pattern of dependent development based on a "new international division of labor," although the actual form of economic integration proved more complex as the industry continued to internationalize. From the surface, failure of the industry represented a failure of import substitution industrialization and an indictment of protectionist policies, but that too appeared less convincing when the process endured further scrutiny.

Assessing the Reasons for Failure The quality of development in both these countries was problematic from the outset. Not only did the industry operate well below levels needed to achieve economies of scale, but the transnational companies were transferring older technology to these less developed markets on which they could continue to extract rents.[18] Further, domestic ownership was never a condition of manufacture in the final assembly industry, so, with denationalization, these countries could never remain in command of their technological trajectory.

Nor was technological development supported in the parts industry. In Mexico, the parts industry did not exist before the shift from assembly to manufacture. The key was the 1962 decree requiring 60 per cent local content in the assembly of autos and 60 per cent local content for the manufacture of engines, as well as the stipulation that assemblers produce only engines. However ambitious it may have been, Mexico in 1962 did not have the required technology, machinery, or tooling needed to produce most auto parts, nor did most Mexican entrepreneurs have the necessary capital resources to enter into production.[19] Auto companies had to establish engine facilities and link up with local parts manufacturers to meet the local content requirements. Rather than resulting in the development of an indigenous industry, it instead led to domination of the Mexican auto parts industry by foreign (and particularly US) joint-venture firms that possessed both expertise and capital. Mexican firms that benefited from the 1962 decree were either producers of such low-technology items as interiors, suspension springs, glass, and batteries, or members of the Mexican Grupo Monterrey or Chihuahua-Comermex Group, which were "legally, financially, and adminstratively linked conglomerates of financial and industrial enterprises ... [or] industrial concerns linked to banks through interlocking directorates"[20] that had sufficient capital and market power to enter into the industry. These firms were the minority of parts manufacturers and remain "the only thoroughly Mexican parts firms in terms of technology, ownership, and management."[21]

In Brazil, the domestic auto parts industry was undermined by national policy. Prior to Kubitschek's creation of GEIA (1956), domestic auto parts manufacturers had created a syndicate, Sindipecas (1951), to represent their interests. The syndicate was sufficiently influential to convince a Subcommission on Jeeps, Trucks and Automobiles created by President Vargas (1952) to establish guidelines that would favor domestic parts suppliers in the industry stimulation plan it was drafting. By one account:

> The auto parts suppliers and the state agreed that the industry, when set up, would be "horizontally" organized – the assemblers would produce only the principal components and subcontract the rest to a thriving national auto parts sector. The assembly sector would be predominantly multinational while the auto parts sector would generally be reserved for domestic capital.[22]

The problem was that this was never adopted, and when GEIA was established, in 1956, it focussed instead on efforts to create a mass-production industry in Brazil rather than on securing the parts market for domestic manufacturers. The encouragement of eleven car makers to manufacture in Brazil – with the idea that a shake-out would eventually narrow the number of producers – meant that parts producers were operating in a very fragmented and unstable market. These conditions, combined with conflictual supplier relations, instead led assemblers to integrate vertically. As of the 1970s, assemblers were as much as 70 per cent integrated, while suppliers were as much as 80 per cent integrated.[23]

Thus, while both countries in fact suffered from operating in inefficient protected markets, the problem was not rooted in import-substitution industrialization, *per se*, as much as the way in which it was implemented. By contrast, Japan, which also protected its infant industry, had instead forced the industry to adhere first to domestic and then to export market discipline. Further, it provided national guidance needed to develop the industry. As noted by one scholar:

> The point is... that the Mexican state had potential power and alternative courses of action that it did not employ... [due to] organizational constraints... With a complex entity like the state, ... internal constraints may stem from a lack of the organizational coordination necessary to wield its potential power to full effectiveness.[24]

Both Mexico and Brazil engaged in policies directed at disciplining the labor market and stimulating consumption among high-income segments of the population. This was compatible with competition based solely on price which forced downward pressures on wages and inputs. They attempted to duplicate the US Fordist model of development without either supporting the adaptive learning mechanisms needed to develop indigenous technological capability, or strengthening the domestic institutions that could have guided industrialization through reciprocal consent, concertation, or some other variation. In fact, had they provided stronger support for the supplier base and been more responsive to the needs of small manufacturers operating in specialty markets, they might have attracted European manufacturers dependent on quasi-market relationships.[25] Instead, their own policies limited them to trying to replicate an inappropriate model for development.

Insertion into the International Economy The oil shocks of the 1970s plunged the world economy into recession, depressed the market for cars, and forced these two countries into economic crisis. Both abandoned their import-substitution industrialization strategies and took an outward orientation. Since then, they have begun to see their industries recover – for Brazil this has been tentative, while for Mexico it has been meteoric. The most tangible evidence of a turn around is seen in the extent to which automobile exports have contributed to the growth of their economies. In 1980 exports constituted approximately 10 per cent of vehicle production in Brazil and 4 per cent in Mexico. By 1987 these had risen to nearly 30 per cent and 27 per cent respectively. Like the UK, these countries had lost their national industries and much of their domestic supplier base. Most of the growth has been foreign dominated – reflecting an extension of the global sourcing and export platform policies of foreign car makers. As summarized by one industry analyst:

> while the form of export expansion which characterizes the Mexican motor industry is likely to be increasing integration with the US motor industry along the pattern which has occurred in Canada since the mid-sixties, the Brazilian pattern has been described more generally as one of "sub-imperialism" whereby the country becomes an export base for foreign capital with markets in less developed Third World countries. The most clear example of this type of strategy in Brazil is that of VW which exports not only to other Latin American countries, but also to North Africa and the Middle East and to sub-Saharan Africa.[26]

This characterization is factually correct but the interpretation is predicated on an unyielding relationship between developed countries or transnational corporations (TNCs) and the industrializing world. In both Brazil and Mexico, policies of externalization and the regionalization of production by car makers are creating conditions for greater state assertion.

To retrace the steps, in Brazil, the crisis of the 1970s was realized as balance of payments problems created by increasing imports. Between 1970 and 1974 imports grew five-fold. The price of regular gasoline increased by 242 per cent from 1973 to 1977, consumer credit was tightened, and effective demand for cars plummeted.[27] In the face of major industry losses the government instituted two major programs: the BEFIEX program (1976), which provided tax reductions of 70 to 80 per cent on machinery and capital goods imports and 50 per cent reductions on the import of components, raw materials, and intermediate goods to companies agreeing to export a certain value of production; and the National Alcohol Program (PROACOOL), designed to promote the use of alcohol-powered vehicles. Although these actions turned the nation toward export promotion, they inadvertently increased the cost of manufacture, since the cars produced for the domestic market used one kind of fuel while those for export used another.

Oddly enough, these incongruent policies reinforced the role of Brazil as a South American center for the manufacture of vehicles. Because Brazil had discrete design requirements, car makers had to redesign cars for this market. Some began to establish design labs for adapting basic designs for the Brazilian, and even Latin-American, market. One such example was GM's $20 million technology center in Sao Caetano do Sul (it recently closed due to the company's financial retrenchment). According to a trade journal:

> The installation of a high-technology research and development facility in Brazil puts General Motors do Brasil in the mainstream of GM product development. The operation, with 200 employees, is on a par with similar centers in Europe and the Far East. The center takes GM do Brasil a step up the ladder in the corporation's hierarchy – a trend being followed by many of GM's competitors in Brazil.[28]

VW adopted a similar policy. VW do Brasil not only produces for South America, it also develops models for the regional market. Policies aimed at the regionalization of production and markets are supplemented by a system of integrated parts production. For example, some parts are made in Brazil for shipment to Mexico and the USA. Thus, while Brazil does indeed function as an export platform for Europe and the USA for some manufacturers (see table 5.1), it is also poised to develop the lead capacity for autos designed in and for the region. The emergence of Latin America as a distinct region is highly possible though still in transition.

Yet another development unique to the region is Autolatina – a joint venture between Ford and Volkswagen of Brazil and Argentina created in 1988 and based on a complete removal of trade barriers, which took effect in 1993. The purpose of the joint venture is to update technology, improve operating efficiencies and make better use of manufacturing facilities. It also reinforces tendencies toward regionalization by both the car makers and the countries of Brazil, Argentina, Uruguay, and Paraguay, which make up the regional trade area known as Mercosur. Other car companies are looking to follow suit by integrating facilities, and even parts, in the manufacture of autos within the region.

Although these trends offer opportunities for Brazil to expand its technology base, currency and economic reforms currently preoccupy

Table 5.1 *Brazil: exports, 1984 (by firms and countries of destination)*

	Fiat	*Ford*	*GM*	*VW*	*Mercedes*	*Others*[1]	*Total*
Germany	2,424	2,424					
Belgium	1,448	1,448					
Denmark	2,849	2,995	5,844				
France	5,558	5,558					
Netherlands	3,434	3,434					
Italy	43,001	1	43,002				
Finland	4,940	4,940					
Norway	5,387	2	5,389				
Sweden	8,001	8,001					
Portugal	602	45	647				
Switzerland	757	757					
USA	2	1	18	5,415	22	5,458	
Others	358	3	7	114	36	518	
Subtotal 1	58,714	22440	5	627	5,529	105	87,420
Venezuela	6,242	8,161	19,301	33,704			
Uruguay	1,079	1,600	906	1,108	12	7	4,712
Peru	23	23	4	1,256	436	127	1,869
Bolivia	80	95	61	301	9	100	646
Chile	126	78	284	179	172	21	860
Ecuador	1,920	1	52	3	1,976		
Colombia	1	4,630	3	2	4,636		
Argentina	9,216	11,305	80	20,601			
Others	64	119	84	700	631	64	1662
Subtotal 2	16,830	10,077	27,190	14,853	1,392	324	70,666
Algeria	2,302	3	2,305				
Iraq	21		20,003	20,006			
Nigeria	13,576	13,576					
Egypt	125	596	7	728			
Indonesia	837	837					
Others	188	134	156	302	44	163	987
Subtotal 3	2,492	259	157	34,480	881	170	38,438
Total	78,036	32,776	27,352	49,960	7,802	589	196,515

[1] includes Volvo, Scania, Puma, Gurgel, Toyota, Sta Matilde.
Subtotal 1 refers to total exports to Europe, North America, Japan, and Australia.
Subtotal 2 refers to total exports to Latin America.
Subtotal 3 refers to total exports to Africa and Asia (and Middle East).

Source: Motor Vehicles Manufacturers Association of the United States, *World Motor Vehicle Data* (1986).

the country. The institutional network necessary to develop internal capability is still not in place. Recent government calls for the development of an inexpensive "people's car" has led to the courting of Fiat and VW, although Brazil also has a fledgling specialty car maker, Gurgel, which is attempting to do the same. In a repeat of history, the government has the option of favoring the development of foreign firms, or of incubating domestic capability – as it has done in aeronautics, for example, with widely acknowledged success. Thus, the Brazilian path of development still has considerable room for maneuver.

Mexico is charting yet another course. The lack of success of the previous auto decrees stimulated yet another decree in 1977 that lowered the local content requirement to 50 per cent for the assembly of cars, and extended the requirement to the manufacture of parts. However, this was simply too little too late. From 1977 to 1981, the deficit surged from 20 per cent to 57.7 per cent of GNP. Then, in 1982, Mexico suffered a collapse of the peso and economic crisis. The market for cars suffered a 41 per cent drop, followed by a 40 per cent decline in auto production. The response was a 1983 decree that waived local content requirements on cars for export, thereby shifting the emphasis of national industrial policy from import-substitution to export promotion.

Multiple industrial strategies are now evident among auto makers. One is the manufacture of high-value added products, such as engines, which were previously assumed to be the domain of advanced countries. As of 1982, six Mexican plants were making engines for export (see table 5.2). An example of the high level of technical capability is the state of the art Ford plant at Chihuahua, which opened in 1982 with the capacity of making 500,000 units. When it opened, this plant utilized the most advanced technology in engine manufacture and a skilled labor force, and paid workers a fraction of US or Japanese wages. However, as many have argued, the issue was not simply wages, but productivity, or inputs relative to outputs, as well as quality. To the surprise of many, these engines were found to be of comparable quality and to require similar labor input as those made in US plants.[29] Ninety per cent of the engines made at the Chihuahua plant are for export. In 1982, Mexico exported 320,301 engines. By 1988 this had increased to 1,428,937.[30]

Another strategy of car makers is to assemble completed vehicles using advanced production techniques. The Ford plant at Hermosillo is a prime illustration of this approach. Opened in September 1987, this is the only Ford facility in North America to combine stamping,

Table 5.2 *Plants making engines for export, Mexico, 1982 and 1988*

Firm	*Location*	*1982*	*1988*
Ford	Chihuahua	1,000	277,224
Chrysler	Ramos Arizpe	135,620	210,109
GM	Ramos Arizpe	137,947	543,535
VW	Puebla	45,301	211,248
Nissan	Aguascalientes	–	53,539
American motors/ Renault	Torreon	–	133,282

Source: Asociacion Mexicana de la Industria Automotriz (AMIA).

manufacturing, and assembly. In the original model, 65 per cent of the parts by value were sourced from Japan, 32 per cent from Mexico, and the remainder from the USA. Mazda, which is 25 per cent owned by Ford, provided the basic design and major components. In the new model which went into production April 1990, 75 per cent of the parts by value came from the USA, approximately 15 per cent from Japan, and 5 per cent from Mexico.[31] The plant is linked with Detroit and Japan through computers and telecommunications, making it fully integrated with centers of decision-making. As a result of expanded productive capacity throughout Mexico, from 1985 through 1989 there was an annual increase of 142 per cent of autos imported into the USA.[32] In 1989, Mexico ranked fifth behind Japan, Canada, West Germany, and South Korea in the number of assembled vehicles imported into the USA.[33] There are now five major producers exporting cars from the country (see table 5.3).

Continued and expanded sourcing of low-value added parts is yet a third strategy, of which growth of the maquila program is the clearest testimony. In 1979 there were 38 maquiladoras engaged in transport equipment production. By 1985 this had grown to 65, and by 1990 it was 152. Employment during the same years grew from 5,035 persons to 40,145, and then to 85,556. Compared with other maquila sectors, value added per employee, an indicator of relative capital intensity, was highest in transport equipment.[34] This is a reflection of what some call "second-wave" maquila activities, in which increasingly sophisticated technology and work organization are utilized.[35] Nonetheless, wages remain low compared with those of other industrializing nations. The average hourly wage in the maquiladoras in 1990 was $1.63, in contrast with $2.25 in Singapore, $2.94 in South Korea, and

Table 5.3 *Mexican car production, 1989*

Firm	*Domestic*	*Export*	*Total*
Chrysler	57,058	45,643	102,701
Ford	47,580	39,580	87,160
GM	22,839	40,292	63,131
VW	76,256	23,057	99,313
Nissan	70,005	17,228	87,233
Total	237,738	165,800	403,538

Source: Ward's Automotive Yearbook (1990), p. 304.

$3.91 in Taiwan.[36] Maquila products made for autos ranged from electrical wire harnesses to electronic controls, interior trim, and seat covers, and, for the most part, entered the USA under duty-free provisions (see table 5.4).

To encourage further investment, Mexico relaxed restrictions on foreign investment in May 1989, thereby allowing 100 per cent foreign ownership. Added incentives came with a December 1989 decree that permitted foreign car makers located in Mexico to import models not made in the country, beginning November 1, 1990.[37] The overwhelming positive investment climate has stimulated new capacity. Nissan announced planned expenditures of $1.2 billion for a new car assembly facility in Aguascalientes, 300 miles north of Mexico City, expansion of its engine, stamping, and transaxles plants and aluminum foundry in Aguascalientes, doubling of its grey iron foundry capacity in Lerma, and enlargement of its domestic market assembly plant in Cuernavaca.[38] When completely operational in 1995, the new assembly plant is expected to make 16,000 vehicles a month for export to Japan, the USA and Latin America.

As in the case of the Ford Hermosillo plant, this is a fully integrated manufacturing facility. It falls short of total design capability, however, despite an increase in the number of staff working on research and development in Mexico from 260 to 400 persons. The lack of design capability of Mexican facilities is a major concern, since the possibility of a free trade agreement between Mexico and the USA puts pressure on Mexican plants to compete on equal footing with their northern neighbors. As noted by Nissan Mexicana President Shoichi Amemiya: "Industries keep innovating, and what we sell today could be obsolete tomorrow… Mexico has no innovative capacity to renew its products

Table 5.4 *Auto-related maquiladoras, 1990*

Industry	*Number*	*Product*
Total	149	
Parts producers	103	
Assemblers/ Subsidiaries	46	
GM	29	
		16 Wire harnesses
		8 Engine controls, solenoids, electrical components
		3 Interior trim, dashboard
		1 Stereos, electronics
		1 Ceramic magnets
Ford	9	
		4 Interior trim, seat covers
		3 Climate controls, steering columns, catalytic converters
		1 Radios, electronics
		1 Glass
Chrysler	6	
		4 Wire harnesses
		1 Electronics
		1 Interior trim, seat covers
Honda	2	
		2 Seat covers

Source: UAW Research Division.

as quickly as Japanese, European and US auto makers do."[39] It is this drive toward greater innovation that may push Mexico into a new stage of development. This issue will be re-examined in the final chapter.

Industrialization under export promotion is turning out to be quite different than under import-substitution. The number of car makers and model lines have been drastically reduced. Production has been modernized and the geographic distribution of production has shifted as the assembly and manufacture of autos and parts are concentrated in the north. An increasing number of parts requiring advanced technology, such as engine production, are made here, along with traditional low-value added parts. Cars for export are progressively representing new models, while new plants are characterized by the adoption of Japanese and US concepts of labor relations. Due to just-in-time inventory sourcing, agglomeration economies are developing around new facilities.

The new initiatives have had stunning results. One is that, with the manufacture of high-value added products such as engines – the legacy of local content policies – the export of engines to the USA quadrupled from 1982 to 1988.[40] The second is that, with increased sourcing of low-value added parts, particularly from maquiladoras (in-bond plants), the output of car parts from maquiladoras destined for the USA more than doubled between 1985 and 1990.[41] The third is that, with the increased assembly of complete vehicles shipped to the US market, Mexico ranked fifth worldwide in the number of vehicles imported into that country in 1989.

The picture that is emerging in North America is one of Canada, the USA and Mexico blending into one region for the assembly of autos and manufacture of complex parts. The assumption that capital-intensive production would remain in the USA was dispelled with Mexico's engine and assembly plants.[42]

However, Mexico, like Brazil, may have reached the limit of its created comparative advantage unless it intervenes on behalf of its industry to make its local capacity not just export competitive, but innovative as well.

Late Industrialization and the Auto Industries of South Korea and the Former Yugoslavia

In recent years, South Korea in particular and the former Yugoslavia to a lesser extent (since the civil war it has ceased to be a major contender) have impressed the world with their unexpectedly strong showings in auto export markets. At first this was somewhat confounding because of their relatively short history in auto manufacture. But now the ingredients for successful late industrialization are becoming apparent. In contrast to Latin America, where early penetration of direct foreign investment curtailed the power of the state to effect development, South Korea's bureaucratic authoritarian rule, following from Japanese colonization, essentially orchestrated industrial growth. In socialist Yugoslavia, governmental intervention was also a critical factor in industrialization. In both cases, "well-organized bureaucratic authoritarian states with an explicit project of fostering capital accumulation *preceded* the involvement of the transnationals and shaped the character of that involvement".[43] In South Korea and Yugoslavia, as in Latin America, import-substitution industrialization strategies, such as protective tariffs, and overvalued exchange rates shielded the initial stages of industrialization, but the role of the developmental state was far more important. In South Korea, politically insulated state development agencies could set terms for firm participation in industries designated for development, provide tariff exemptions, offer preferential loans, allocate foreign exchange, and distribute import licenses. The influence of the state was enhanced by state-linked private-sector conglomerates that included banks and trade associations. In both countries, the presence of a strong state laid the groundwork for creation of a domestic industry. However, the fact that the cars they produced were of exportable quality and were successfully distributed abroad was largely a function of broader trends in the industry – the inability of car makers in developed countries to make low-cost cars, growing fragmentation of the market, tendencies toward industry alliances, and, perhaps most importantly, the availability of independent design, marketing, and other critical services that supported new entrants into the industry. In this respect, South Korea and the former Yugoslavia are illustrative of the newly rising competition from developing countries.

South Korea: The State as Protagonist The South Korean auto industry has realized an unusually rapid growth. From its inception in 1962 at 3,000 units per year, it expanded to 600,000 cars and commercial vehicles by 1986, at least half of which were for export. Much of this meteoric rise can be attributed to participation by a strong state. To a large extent, the state structure was the outcome of Japanese and US influences. Japanese colonization left an imprint on the South Korean economy in the form of an interventionist state bureaucracy, and in *chaebol* business enterprise groups which structured local capital formation. The US occupation helped strengthen the maufacturing base and the state's role as arbiter of growth through procurement policies and financial aid. Jointly, these two countries contributed to the creation of a bureaucratic authoritarian regime that aggressively promoted industrial development. The extent of government participation in industrialization is particularly evident in the auto industry.

Development of the industry went through four phases: knock-down kit assembly (1962-7); localization and take-off (1968-74); local model production (1975-81); and product development (1982 to present).[44] The automobile industry was launched in 1962 with government adoption of the First Five Year Development Plan and enactment of the Automobile Industry Protection Law. Through this legislation, the importation of parts for assembly production was exempted from tariffs, but the import of completed vehicles and parts not for final assembly was prohibited. South Korea already had an extensive supplier base that was a residue of the Korean War, since the replacement market for Korean and US military vehicles was supplied largely by domestic production. The first assembly plant was established in 1963 by the Saenara Motor Company with a $3.5 million loan and technical assistance from Nissan. It was taken over by Shinjin Motor in 1965 after a foreign exchange crisis. In 1967 this became the Daewoo Motor Corporation.

Then, according to one account: "in order to promote competition in the automobile industry, the government allowed Hyundai and Asia to enter into passenger car assembly production."[45] Hyundai Motor was established in 1967 and began assembly operations in 1968 with technical cooperation from Ford. In order to accelerate complete domestic manufacture of small cars by 1972 and of standard automobiles by 1974, and to expand domestic content, the government announced the Automobile Industry Basic Promotion Plan (1969). Through a number of incentives, emphasis was given to local sourcing:

> Production volume was allocated according to the actual performance of the domestic content schedule. Tariff exemptions were provided for the raw materials used in the local production of parts and components. The assemblers received preferential allocation of foreign exchange for importing medium-sized passenger cars. Investment was encouraged in such functional items as engines, transmissions, and axles. Preferential loans were provided to firms which had investment in parts and components manufacturing. As a result of these intensive efforts, the domestic content ratio increased rapidly, reaching over 70 percent in 1974...[46]

As the industry picked up, Asia Motor started in 1970 with the assembly of Fiat, while Kia Industrial Company began producing passenger vehicles in 1974. In all cases they operated under 100 per cent local ownership, although Kia was the only one to begin without foreign capital imports.

After the oil crisis of the 1970s, the government adopted the Long-Term Automobile Promotion Plan (1974) directed at developing indigenous models with 100 per cent domestic content for export. To augment this strategy, the government also began to promote development of the supplier industry. This requirement put an unreasonable demand on the industry, however, because most suppliers operated on a small scale, using poor equipment and unskilled workers, and had very limited innovative capacity. Further, despite the fact that the assemblers were linked with *chaebols*, such was not the case for suppliers. The Japanese *keiretsu* industrial system of vertical organization was not replicated in South Korea, although the horizontal, or inter-firm, *keiretsu* structure was. Consequently, supplier firms received insufficient technical assistance, financing, or even supply of raw materials. According to one survey:

> 70 percent of 81 ancillary firms surveyed did not receive any kind of assistance from the primary firms and only about one-fourth of them had technical assistance. Any assistance, in the form of credit lending and loan guarantee or supply of raw materials, was either very small or negligible. This very weak assistance from the primary to the ancillary firms is, in fact, the most important characteristic of the subcontracting system in Korea, being very different from the Japanese subcontracting system in which various forms of support and assistance are provided by assemblers.[47]

The consequence of this weak linkage structure was that assemblers maintained a competitive cost pricing relationship with suppliers, who, in turn, with little incentive to upgrade the quality of the product, would cut corners to make the most inexpensive product. Not surprisingly, a 1976 survey by the Korean Automobile Association found that only 10 per cent of 1,200 products met international standards, 30 per cent were slightly below, and the remaining 60 per cent were significantly below standard.[48] Improvements in the supplier industry therefore required foreign licensing.

Insufficient support for the supplier base was a serious oversight. Foreign firms and banks were largely uninterested in local investment since they were initially focussed on other developing countries. It was therefore incumbent upon the state to gain control of domestic financial resources. To compensate for this omission and to up-grade the quality of parts production to make them export competitive, the state encouraged mergers and joint ventures; in 1978 it designated certain firms to be recipients of low interest loans and technology transfer assistance and offered preferential taxes and credits if they located in the Industrial Complex in Changwon. Through these policies the government created an autonomous supplier base which had access to financial and research assistance normally available only by association with an auto maker. It also began to explore the possibility of promoting a horizontal type of subcontracting system so that supplier firms could both specialize and broaden the base of purchasers, thereby benefiting from scale economies.

As the industry took a more outward orientation, the economy expanded rapidly. Although the nation appeared responsive to making structural adjustments as warranted, one area remained a major weakness. By the early 1970s unemployment was at 5 per cent, but few real benefits were passed on to workers. As the government did not rule by consensus, its legitimacy required suppression of voices that could challenge its authority. In 1961 unions were banned; this ban was later lifted, but was partially reinstated in 1971. Industrial-relations policy consisted of authoritarian rule-making powers and decision-making over industrial disputes vested in the government. Wages were kept low, and regulations regarding the conditions of work were minimized. As a consequence, labor protest came in the form of either high turnover rates or protest movements.[49] Even minor disputes erupted into major conflicts, often with political overtones. The outcome of these policies was a lean and well-focussed approach toward industrialization, but one that remained seriously flawed as the country progressed toward democratization.

Against this background, the auto industry developed along two distinct lines. One was in accordance with a policy in independent development exemplified by Hyundai, and the other was a policy of partnership adopted by Daewoo. A comparison of the two shows that Hyundai's greater command over resources and product lines was crucial to its success.[50]

The Hyundai *chaebol* started as a construction firm that diversified into shipbuilding and automobile manufacture. Hyundai Motor Company entered into car operations as an assembler for Ford, but after seven years in this role, and using technical licenses acquired from Ford, it began to address the export market as a domestic company. During its first phase of manufacture (1974-9) Hyundai acquired technology (mainly through licensing rather than joint ventures) for body styling and body design from Italy, and for engine, transmission, and axle design and manufacture from Mitsubishi. These were applied towards the development of a new product, the Pony. Prior to entering into developed market economies, it began exporting to Latin America (starting in 1976), the Middle East, and Southeast Asia. In 1978 it established the first automobile research and development laboratory in South Korea, focussed on attaining emissions and noise control and the safety standards required for entering into Europe and North America. During the second phase (1979-81), it began development of a product that could be exported to industrialized nations. In the third phase (1981 onwards), Hyundai initiated development of the Excel. With each phase it acquired more design and development expertise on which to build future products. By 1983 it had entered the Canadian market, and by 1987 had penetrated the US market, each through exclusive relations with independent dealers in Canada and the USA. In 1986 the Excel was selected as a "Product of the Year" by *Fortune* magazine.

In contrast to Daewoo, which shared 50 per cent ownership with GM (1972) and sold its products under the GM nameplate, Hyundai had a corporate policy which retained local ownership, managerial control, and product identity. Its policy was modified with the purchase of a 10 per cent interest by Mitsubishi in 1982 followed by an additional 5 per cent in 1985, but Mitsubishi's role was limited to providing technical assistance and supplying parts. As a consequence of this relationship, the company adopted Japanese production methods in the mid-1970s with the assistance of Mitsubishi and Hino Motor.

Since the outset, the company has maintained a high level of investment in research and development. By 1986 it had committed 79 billion won (approximately $91 million) toward R&D, 10 per cent of which was for basic research, 40 per cent for applied research, and 50 per cent for development.[51] Hyundai established central research and development facilities at Mabuk-ri, outside of Seoul, to develop engines, transmissions, and advanced technologies, followed by the Hyundai Technical Center located in Detroit (1986), for the purpose of acquiring advanced automobile technology. The commitment to R&D is further reflected in the high percentage of technical staff on its payroll compared with Daewoo (see table 5.5).

By contrast, Daewoo's development was dominated by its foreign partner. Until 1982 Daewoo was dependent on GM for parts, technology, product, and management. After that managerial control was transferred, and the relationship changed to one of joint partnership. GM's policy was to introduce older products, but these were often inappropriate to the local conditions. Daewoo licensed far fewer technologies than Hyundai, and, until it changed its relationship with GM, these were limited to GM or its affiliates. Because more of its parts were sourced from GM or its affiliates, it had a lower local content ratio (70 per cent for the Gemini, 1975) than Hyundai (85 per cent for the Pony).

As a result of these policies, Hyundai was much more successful in both the domestic and the international market. As of 1986, Hyundai produced 43 per cent of the cars for the domestic market in contrast to Daewoo's 19 per cent (Kia provided 35 per cent, Asia 1 per cent, and

Table 5.5 *R&D Efforts in Hyundai vs Daewoo Motor Corporation*

	Hyundai					*Daewoo*				
	1977	*1980*	*1983*	*1985*	*1986*	*1977*	*1980*	*1983*	*1985*	*1986*
R&D person	253	312	1,122	1,676	2,254	67	265	254	406	495
R&D invest. (mil. won)	1		20	39.1	79	0.5	3	3.7	28.2	17.4
R&D intensity[1]	4.2	3.5	10.5	9.7	8.7	1.3	3.3	3.8	4.7	4.3
R&D intensity[2]	1.1		3.5	3.7	4.1	0.6	1.8	1.3	7.7	4

[1] R&D person/total employment.
[2] R&D investment/sales.

Source: Jinjoo Lee, *Two Different Development Paths*, working paper of the the Korea Advanced Institute of Science and Technology, Seoul (October 1987), p. 15.

Keohwa/Dong-a 2 per cent). Similarly, Hyundai dominated the export market, with 70.4 per cent of cars exported compared with Daewoo's 1.5 per cent (Kia had 1.4 per cent, Asia 24.2 per cent, and Keohwa/Dong-a 5.3 per cent). Clearly, some of Hyundai's success lies in its so-called "self-reliant" strategy, which allowed it to incorporate knowledge into its process of development. This was combined with significant support from the government. By contrast, Daewoo was severely hampered by external constraints.

There remain some caveats, however. Despite similarities with its Japanese mentors, Hyundai continues to display significant departures. It does not provide high wages, employment security, or control over suppliers. Links of equity shares, technical assistance, financing, and supply of materials between the assembler and suppliers tend to be weak, so in this respect the system bears greater resemblence to the vertically (dis)integrated system than to the quasi-integrated structure. In spite of these weaknesses, the timing of this eclectic model has proven particularly fortuitous due to changes evident in the international automobile industry. This last point is particularly striking in the Yugoslavian auto industry.

Benettonization of the Yugo The former prominence of Yugoslavia in the international auto industry was remarkable on several counts: it was a commentary on the role of market socialism and of non-aligned and Eastern Bloc countries in the world economy; it showed the diversity that was beginning to appear among products in the entry level market; but, most of all, it illustrated how independent providers of research and development and product distribution complement auto manufacturers and re-create functions of the integrated firm in a disaggregated form.

Since it was a small country, foreign trade had always been an important determinant of economic growth in Yugoslavia. From 1952, when the Soviet model was abandoned, to the early 1990s, Yugoslavia had undergone several stages of import-substitution and export-led industrialization. The country developed a model of decentralized enterprise-level planning within a socialist context. Following adoption of the Constitution of 1974 and subsequent laws enacted to implement the concept of self-management, a system of local control over production was established in units smaller than the firm, called the Basic Organ of Associated Labor (BOAL).[52] The difficulties of this path were evident as persistent trade deficits forced reforms of fiscal institutions and monetary policies, but also created a critical attitude toward dependence on foreign technology and foreign investment.[53] Despite performance problems and setbacks, Yugoslavia emerged as a country with strong social and political infrastructure combined with enterprise autonomy.

Auto making at Zavodi Crvena Zastava, the manufacturer of Yugo America, began in 1953. Since then it has grown into a complex comprised of 87 manufacturing plants including stamping mills and foundries. This nearly self-contained enterprise employed more than 50,000 workers and produced most of the material used in cars made for domestic consumption.[54] In some ways the company was quite progressive, as seen in the organization of the BOALS, yet in other ways, as in the use of traditional assembly-line technology, it was not at all advanced.

A major change in Zastava's evolution occurred in 1984, when it was approached by Global Motors, a holding company for distributing cars in the USA, about the prospect of exporting the Yugo to the USA. This coincided with an economic crisis in Yugoslavia precipitated by a mounting foreign debt. Zastava agreed to the offer and the Yugo was introduced to the USA in August 1985. After that, Zastava upgraded its auto design by working with independent designers, improved product quality by instituting Western-style manufacturing processes and labor relations on the line producing export Yugos, and began using more US parts in the export cars. The higher efficiency and greater worker satisfaction of the Yugo America side of the plant was spreading throughout the facility and creating critical self-appraisal of the entire system.[55]

In terms of relative productivity, the Yugo was not very competitive. However, it was not on these grounds that the company was a pioneer.

It was in the relationship with Global Motors that Yugo America gained a competitive edge against larger producers. The concept behind Global Motors was reminiscent of the Italian retailer Benetton. Benetton contracts backward to clothes-makers and forward to distributors, and is responsible for keeping a pulse on the market. Global Motors ideally wanted to do the same. It looked for products from developing countries with "competitive labor and a national mandate for industrialization."[56] In return, it was going to provide product certification management, marketing and distribution, technology transfer, financial assistance, quality assurance programs, specific plans for dealer facilities, and dealer development. Global Motors had planned to introduce cars from Malaysia and elsewhere and, in the process, expand the segments it was to offer. In its industry brochure, it wrote:

> Global Motors intends to revolutionize the way cars are imported and sold in this country [USA].
>
> Global Motors Automotive Centers will combine a range of different brands and multiple services in one facility. These new centers will offer dealers greater efficiencies, higher profitability, and a full range of customer satisfaction programs.
>
> The new Global concept borrows from marketing ideas already practiced by non-automotive retailers. National outlets, with a uniform design and function, provide marketing continuity and assurance beyond standard automotive signage programs.[57]

In fact, this did not happen. Global Motors filed for bankruptcy in 1989, in large part because the product was poorly received in the USA.[58] Yugo sales had dropped from 48,000 in 1987 to 31,000 in 1988, and the model was experiencing serious competition from the Hyundai Excel. Although the Yugo and Global Motors did not take off, a poignant lesson remains. Just as Hyundai entered into the USA and Canada through independent dealer networks, so could Yugo America, only in this case the grand scheme was to be marketing driven. The point is that the externalization of functions that occurred in the auto industry included ties with sales and marketing. This relative autonomy of sales opens new possibilities for the sourcing and distribution of autos worldwide.

Development in Retrospect With hindsight, Brazil and Mexico suffered from excessive reliance on an inappropriate model for economic development and neglected to develop the internal institutions that would have nurtured technological ability, primarily in the supplier industry. Based on the Anglo-American concept of market structure and economic logic, they suffered from insufficient mechanisms for state guidance of market-competitive firms or of industry structures that spread capitalization, from lack of market access, and, most importantly, an absence of innovation. South Korea has attempted to replicate older Japanese models of firm interdependence, but this has not penetrated deep within the industrial structure. Further, though state guidance is strong, it is repressive, and could fail based on issues of legitimacy rather than on ability to intervene in the market. Finally, for Yugoslavia, an overwhelming problem of quality control damaged its name beyond repair in the markets it most wanted to influence. In contrast to Brazil, Mexico, or Daewoo in South Korea, which were dominated by foreign firms with an explicit export agenda but also export capability, Yugoslavia suffered from inadequate entree into the international market.

Despite these setbacks, recent trends in internationalization, regionalization, and agglomeration evident in the industry pose new opportunities for industrialization by developing countries. These are apparent in the changes in product development and manufacture that are occurring worldwide.

6

Assessing the Prospects for Development under Flexible Production

Re-examining Concepts of Flexible Production

Flexible production was originally a response to increased trade and investment flows; monetary, supply, and financial volatility; changing technology; and shifting patterns of consumption. Now it is being propelled by yet other considerations. In the automobile industry these consist of efforts to reduce the time required to bring a product to market and attempts to introduce new types of vehicles using non-gasoline fuels. Because of these two dimensions, the industry resembles high-technology sectors instead of one that is old, mature, and on the decline, since massive investments are required in research and development that may not be appropriated from marketing. These trends essentially accelerate the product life cycle. They also reinforce tendencies toward multi-state and sub-state regionalization because of the need, on the one hand, to target regional markets correctly, and, on the other, to externalize design and manufacture. A brief glimpse into these emerging trends illustrates why they are both cause and consequence of flexible production.

Product Development and Production Networks

The necessity to compress the time required to bring a product to market has become a major driving force in the industry. The impetus behind this emphasis on speed is an ability correctly to identify rapidly changing market preferences, given market competitiveness and fragmentation. A local orientation coincides with tendencies toward regionalization created by the need to lower costs by locating in low-wage sites, minimize the negative effects of monetary fluctuations, obtain market feedback, or circumvent trade barriers. The most signficant innovation by which firms shorten the time required to bring products to market is through what is sometimes referred to as simultaneous engineering, concurrent engineering or integrated manufacturing, and it involves a reconceptualization of the way products are developed and manufactured.

The concept of simultaneous engineering can be distinguished from traditional, and particularly US manufacturing by the sequence of events. The US tradition is to design first and then, through discrete steps, undertake manufacturing engineering, manufacturing, assembly, and quality control. Simultaneous engineering turns the process around and brings manufacturing engineering, quality engineering, and test engineering into the design process from the outset.[1]

This process has several desirable outcomes. One is the shorter time needed to bring products to market. A 1989 study of auto makers by Kim Clark revealed that the development lead time in the USA averaged 62 months when product and process engineering occurred sequentially, while in Japan, where product and process engineering overlapped, the average was 43 months.[2] Another advantage is increased receptivity to changes in the product market or in addressing particular market segments. Yet a third benefit is derived from higher quality resulting from the incremental and constant nature of improvements and innovation, coupled with cost savings derived from lower inventory, production delays, and scrappage. Lastly, simultaneous engineering introduces flexibility in product output and mix that is lacking in "production-heavy" manufacturing processes.

In principle, a type of matrix structure is adopted by a firm in which product planning and development become strategically linked with manufacturing. When implemented, staffs are reconfigured such that product designers work in teams with manufacturing process designers. Suppliers of major components or production tools also enter into the process at the outset. The level of integration often extends well into manufacturing functions, and may involve rotation of engineering tasks between design and manufacturing, or use of production workers in process design. The deployment of workers into strategic project teams requires replacement of the rigid structures associated with functionally segregated, vertically defined organizations. The concept is based on a series of feedback loops linking sales, design, development, and production among a group of manufacturers (see figure 6.1). For this reason, research and development are usually located near sales and production. As noted by Masahiko Aoki, "This model implies that research and development are best carried out in geographic proximity – or at least with intimate communications links – to the site of production and sales so that close contacts can be maintained."[3]

The integrity of the process depends on creation of management practices and tasks that generate iterative problem-solving. Because of employee resistance to redefined job assignments and firm resistance to supplier involvement in product or process design, this concept has been particularly difficult for Americans and Europeans to implement. Consequently, Japanese producers have provided most leading-edge examples, although there have been successful exceptions, with Chrysler being the most notable. Japanese manufacturers transported their ideas to international sites as they relocated. The MIT Commission reported that "Japanese producers introduced product development teams including product planners, product engineers, process engineers, and representatives of the manufacturing plants. The product

Figure 6.1 *Looped model of industrial activity*

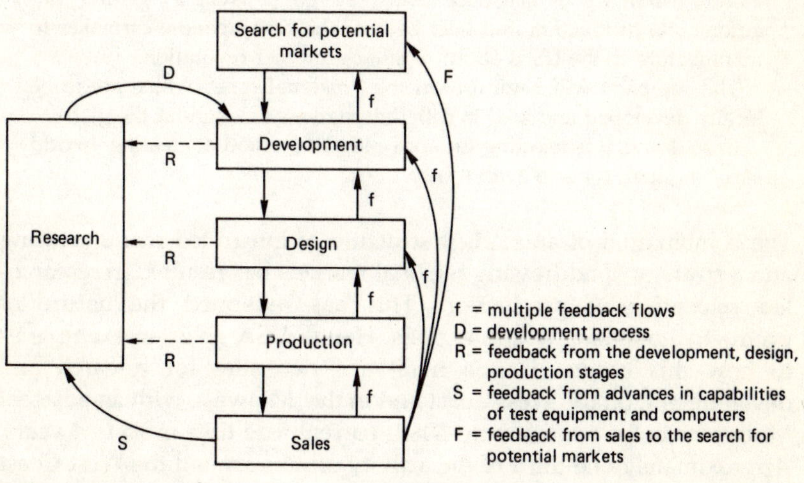

Source: Masahiko Aoki, "Frontiers in corporate globalization," *Japan Echo*, xvii, Special Issue (1990), pp. 26–32.

and process engineers were from the supplier as well as the assembler firm."[4]

The movement abroad has been evolutionary, rather than concerted from the outset. Honda, one of the most internationally organized companies, provides a clear illustration of the transformation. The former chief of Honda's R&D, Nobuhiko Kawamoto, explains how the placement of international R&D changed to include integrated manufacturing accordingly:

> At the beginning . . . the role of these [R&D] centers outside of Japan was to act as a sort of sensor, to gather information and to feed that information back to Japan. With the shortening of the development cycle, their responsibilities have expanded. In essence . . . we are dividing the work load by major market and region, the result of which is that we expect the research activities of these (offshore) centers to become even more independent in the future. Honda R&D North America and Honda R&D Europe are cases in point; both subsidiaries are expected to expand their activities to include total product development.[5]

A recent newspaper article makes this transformation even more explicit, with the title "Honda junks world-car tactic for regional-model strategy"(Nobuyuki Oishi, *Nikkei Weekly*, October 5, 1991). In this article, the Honda position is presented in the following manner:

> Honda Motor Co. which once defied the government by getting into automobile production and later became the first Japanese carmaker to manufacture in the US is about to launch another revolution.
>
> The company will begin producing "regional cars," which are to be locally developed and sold in different markets throughout the globe.
>
> In so doing, it is rejecting the conventional method of creating "world cars" in Japan for sale everywhere.

The combination of an explicit structure of integrated manufacturing and a strategy of addressing regional markets has resulted in research-led relocation of production. This has redefined the nature of productive relations within regions. Honda USA gives an example as to how this occurs. Honda maintains two sites for research and development, on the West Coast and in the Midwest, with an adjacent Midwest site for manufacture. Their current lead time is 3.5 to 4 years. Approximately one-third of the activity centers around the West Coast R&D function, and the other two-thirds is under the direction of Midwest research, development, and manufacturing. Throughout the entire process, one team leader (usually from R&D) heads a core team that remains intact at both sites. The core team is augmented by people from various capabilities as required. As the process moves from initial design to advanced prototype development, workers from the assembly plant check the prototype(s) and offer feedback as to manufacturability. Seen as a whole, the process resembles a relay, with a core team in place the entire time.

Honda, along with other companies that use this method, involves its most critical suppliers in the core team. Since the concept is still new to many suppliers, the latter generally require a certain amount of training. Suppliers who have undergone a changeover have found it necessary to redefine the entire company, since requirements placed on their staff were vastly different. External suppliers and process equipment manufacturers are particularly important in the following areas: (1) fabrication of production tools; (2) prototype construction; and (3) major parts manufacture. These functions combine with assembly to create a network of production activities. This is explained in the following discussion:

> Product development involves a significant amount of what one might call cognitive activity…
>
> Much of the development process… involves what we might call a design, build, test cycle...In the middle of this design, build, test cycle is a set of production activities – building prototypes, executing simulations, and so forth …
>
> Another example of manufacturing activities embedded in the development process is fabrication of production tools and equipment. Take, for example, the problem of actually building and testing major body dies and tools to be used in the production process. [When integrated with design and development, this can vastly cut down on the lead time]… the lead time for a major body die in the Japanese industry is on average about 13 to 14 months. The same kind of die requires, again on average, almost 28 months in Europe …
>
> Where did these differences come from?… One is that the Japanese firms are much more overlapped… The second major difference is that the cutting and finishing operations – the actual production of the part – occur in about 2 to 3 months, as opposed to nearly 10 months in the case of the US.[6]

There are very broad implications behind the trend toward adoption of simultaneous engineering. One is that the distribution of global economic activities is changing, since research and development functions previously tied to headquarter locations are becoming mobile. A second is that tasks both internal to and across firms are becoming completely restructured as speed becomes a critical variable. Third is that the nature of industrial integration across countries, and between developing and developed countries in particular, appears to take on entirely new dimensions, since research and development must operate closely with manufacture.

Industrializing countries confronting the redistribution of productive activities face several choices. One is that they could be left out of the product development process and manufacture only models that do not require shortened development times. Another is that auto makers could attempt to bring them into the loop by requiring that assembly functions be tied to R&D functions in their home site (i.e. USA, Germany, or Japan). Alternatively, these countries could develop their own R&D capability for servicing the regional market. This last alternative requires that they support not only primary firm functions, but supplier, process manufacturer, and prototype activities as well.

Evidence of growing innovative capability in industrializing countries is already beginning to surface. For example, in Mexico, Japanese and US firms are involving Mexican firms in the process of simultaneous engineering, and this is increasing the innovative content of domestic manufacturing. Indications are that some non-US foreign manufacturers are choosing Mexico rather than the USA within the North American market to circumvent established US engineering conventions. These manufacturers import their own engineers for key tasks until they can be replaced by a new generation of engineers. US firms are also becoming more responsive to a Mexican presence in design and development. For example, Chrysler involved six Mexican firms in the design of an engine. The process began in 1990, and lasted 1.5 years. The expectation is that Mexican firms will take the lead in this product in the future. In Brazil, US and European firms are establishing design centers, making the country the center of a South American region for manufacture of products for the South American market.

Both Mexico and Brazil are beginning to adopt policies that support these trends. In the past, Mexico had been a follower rather than a leader in encouraging creative links between the private sector and the country's scientific community. But by mid-1992 it had become increasingly apparent to policy makers with the Mexican trade ministry (SECOFI) and the National Council for Science and Technology (CONACYT) that the achievement of a sustainable competitive edge in such leading sectors as autos, chemicals, and telecommunications would require greater government support.[7] Recent decisions to develop a National Center for Industrial Innovation attest to this fact. In Brazil, stronger relations with

Argentina over Autolatina provide another indication of support for a regional industry.

These trends suggest several points. First, as firms are restructuring to become more innovative, they are including developing countries as an integral part of the process. Second, the regional dimensions of the restructuring are differentiated by developed nation centered regions, and those with industrializing countries at the core. Third, within both types of region, advanced industrializing countries are confronting new opportunites for developing innovative capacity. That is, rather than being held hostage to the demands of transnational corporations, they have genuine possibilities for participating in the direction of their growth.

The New Technological Frontier

A second factor that will accelerate flexible production is the introduction of alternative-fuel vehicles. During the oil embargoes of the 1970s, countries searched for means to reduce their dependence on gasoline-powered vehicles. Brazil went so far as to mandate use of alcohol-powered vehicles, although this proved to be a costly choice. Electric cars were marketed in several countries, but they had a limited range and were largely ignored by consumers. Public policies also neglected to make the use of electric vehicles worthwile. The issue of alternative-fuel vehicles has re-emerged recently, but it has not been due to continued oil dependence. Instead, the motivating force has been the need for clean air.

The most aggressive move in this direction has come from Southern California. The problem centers on the Los Angeles air shed, which is one of the most polluted in the world. In recognition of the situation, California adopted a Clean Air Act in 1988 which included the introduction of low-emission vehicles in their strategy for meeting air-quality standards. The federal Clean Air Act of 1990 later set similar standards. In 1990 California shortened the timetable for introducing low-emission vehicles, and the California Air Resources Board established rules for meeting the timetable. These actions essentially mandated use of electric and other low- or zero-emission vehicles, but they left open many other concerns. Public confidence had to be restored after the failed efforts of the 1970s. Infrastructure had to be built to accommodate the new vehicles. Existing technology had to be vastly improved for cars to have commercial appeal. And manufacturers had to feel this constituted a genuine shift in demand before they could justify major expenditures in a new technology – especially one intended to replace that in which it had a vested interest.

The response was disjointed, but nonetheless clearly in favor of the new technology. The US Department of Energy began support of long-term, high-risk research and development of new technology through its Office of Transportation Systems. Other programs supported measures for testing and evaluating private industry use of electric vehicles. Various Acts authorized manufacturers to apply credits toward the Corporate Average Fuel Economy (CAFE) standards for production of vehicles operating on methanol, natural gas, or electricity. At the state level, the California Air Resources Board, California Energy Commission, Electric Power Research Institute, Electric Vehicle Development Corporation, South Coast Management District, and Southern California Edison joined forces to create the Electric Vehicle Task Force in 1988 for the purpose of facilitating commercialization of electric vehicle technology in the state. The California Department of Commerce created the California Competitive Technology Program in the same year with the stated objective of aiding in the transfer and commercialization of new products or production processes. At the local level, the South Coast Air Quality Management District authorized funds in 1988 for a five-year Clean Fuels Program and later adopted a three-tier plan for improving air quality and achieving National Ambient Air Quality Standards, while the city's Department of Water and Power and Southern California Edison jointly hosted an international competition for the development and sale of electric vans and passenger cars by 1995, which they called the "Los Angeles Initiative."[8] Since then, New York and Massachusetts have joined California in mandating zero-emission vehicles, beginning in 1998, and thirteen other states are expected to follow.

The strong signal issued worldwide was that demand for alternative-fuel vehicles had been assured through public policy and supported by infrastructure development, and was to be promoted by commercialization programs. This provided sufficient incentive for firms to respond. Interestingly, they have done so largely as consortia, or through some joint effort in which the costs of developing the vehicles are shared. In the USA, under the auspices of the National Cooperative Research Act of 1984, approximately one-tenth of the 305 research and development consortia registered as of December 1992 were automobile related.[9] Among the most important for alternative-fuel vehicles are: (1) the United States Advanced Battery Consortium, registered February 7, 1991, by Chrysler, Ford, and General Motors "to conduct or direct joint research and development on advanced battery technology for future electric vehicles ... [with the objective of minimizing] inefficient duplication of effort and expense when researching various high risk/ high cost technology ... "; (2) the Low Emissions Technologies Cooperative Research and Development Partnership, registered July 14, 1992, by Chrysler, Ford, and General Motors "to identify opportunities for joining aspects of their independent research and development efforts pertaining to technologies for future low emission motor vehicles"; and (3) the Advanced Lead-Acid Battery Consortium, registered July 29, 1992, by 37 members not associated with the Big Three, including companies from the USA, the UK, Canada, Mexico, France, Germany, Italy, South Korea, Australia, and Japan, "to provide technology to accelerate the design and development of a lead-acid battery for immediate use in electric vehicles, together with the technology, related systems and equipment needed to support widespread usage of lead-acid batteries to power electric vehicles."[10] All of these consortia were created to undertake basic research and development.

Other efforts aimed at supporting basic research and development are surfacing in Japan and Italy. In Japan, electric automobiles were initially targeted by the Large-Scale Industrial Technology Research and Development Program of the Agency of Industrial Science and Technology of MITI. From 1971 to 1977, 57 million yen were allocated for the building of prototypes.[11] Then in 1977 the Electric Vehicle Council drafted an Electric Vehicle Market Expansion Basic Plan, which was directed at commercializing electric vehicles over the next ten years. The plan was subsequently revised in 1983, and in 1991 the following objectives were projected into the year 2000:

1 The First Phase (1991-3)
 ... introduction of EVs into the government agencies ...
 ... promotion measures will mainly be taken in the forms of financial support ...
2 The Second Phase (1994-7)
 ... to create broad public demands for EV introduction as well as to prospect lowering EV price.
3 The Third Phase (1998-2000)
 ... to bring down the price to such a level as the ordinary customers can afford EVs, as well as to arrange the mass production system and accessible service facilities ...
 ... providing incentives and arranging the infrastructure ...
4 The Fourth Phase (2000-)
 In this phase the public demand for EVs will be created to such a level that the demand and supply matches with each other in terms of price and performance.[12]

Figure 6.2 *Organization for research, development and demonstration of electric vehicles*

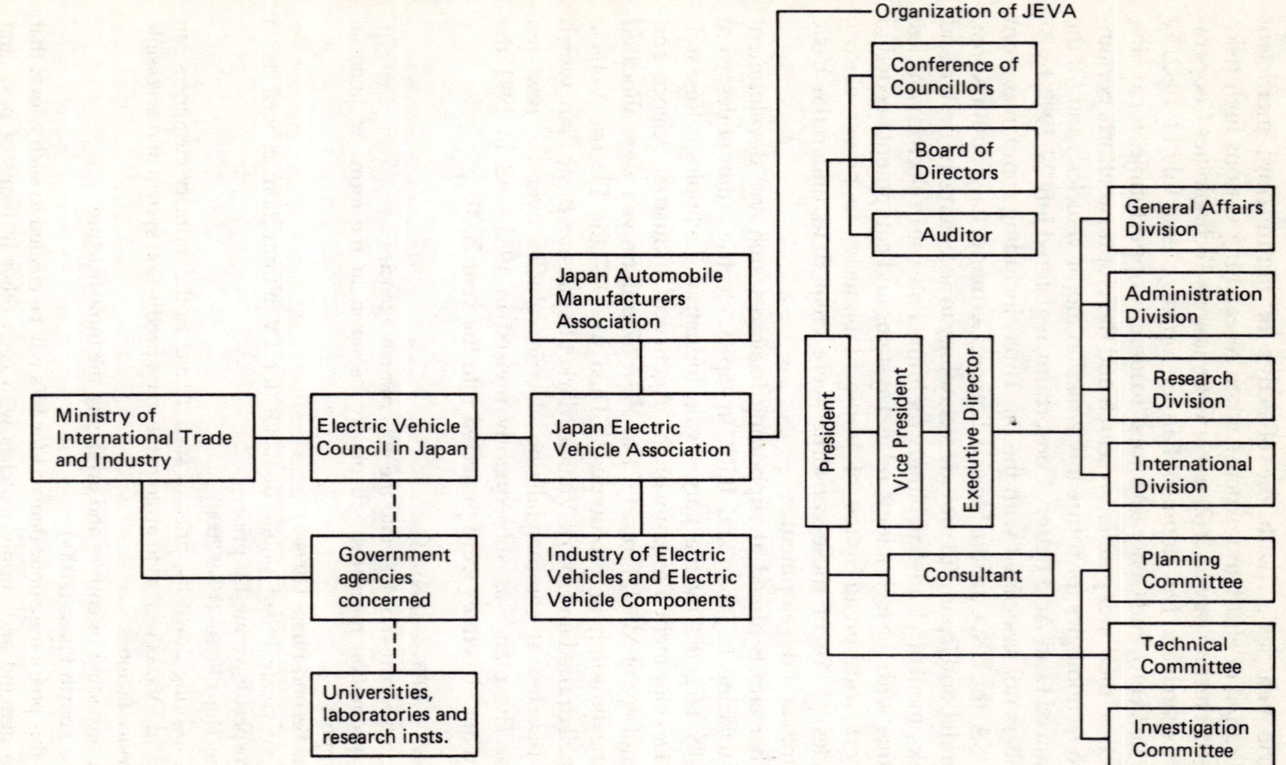

Source: Japan Electric Vehicle Association (May 8, 1992).

Implementation of the plan depends on a series of incentives and consensus in decision-making among the private-sector and public-sector agencies linked through the Japan Electric Vehicle Association (see figure 6.2). The concept is that these linked institutions will pave the way for introduction of the new industry within a short period and for a limited time. After that, the industry will have to be market competitive.

Another example comes from Italy. Through the Consorzio Bologna Innovazione, a project focussed on the testing of electric vehicles in the City of Bologna has been created that brings together the following participants:

CESI – Milano (Electric Technologies Research Center owned by ENEL, the National Electric Energy Company)
ENI Sud – a part of ENI (the largest Italian public chemical group) which produces electric vehicles
FIAT – electric minibus
Piaggio – low emission scooters
Lamborghini – electric vans.[13]

In addition, the West Genoa Science Park supported creation of two companies, Genesys s.r.l. and Altra S.p.a., which are engaged in aspects of electric vehicle research, prototype development, and manufacture. The Italian structure, as with Germany, involves more "concertation" – that is, more diffused decision-making in the manufacture of a new product.

In each case, it is recognized that joint activities and market guidance are needed for the new technology to succeed, but it is approached differently within each of the regions. The USA operates within a "free-market" context, in contrast to the governed market orientation of Japan and the corporatist policies of Italy. In the USA the focus has been on basic R&D, while in the other two cases it has been on sheltering the infant industry and on efforts to commercialize the product.

In a departure from the past, a new concept is being attempted in California that comes closer to the quasi-firm models of Japan or Europe than any other example in the US auto industry, albeit with considerable limitations. The project, called CALSTART, is a consortium of some 47 members representing Californian electric utilities; US businesses; federal, state, and local government agencies; US public and private educational and research institutes; and federal laboratories created as a demonstration through national legislation. The purpose of the consortium is to showcase Californian companies that make advanced electric vehicle components to worldwide automotive customers, to establish the infrastructure needed for the public to adopt electric vehicles , and to commercialize an electric bus and mass transit system (see figure 6.3). In contrast to the National Cooperative Research Act (NCRA) of 1984, which allowed firms to undertake joint basic R&D, this pushes the concept of antitrust further toward applied R&D than any other instance in the USA. It represents a third-generation interpretation of antitrust (with the NCRA being a second generation). In recognition that alternative-fuel vehicles are a difficult market for even established firms to enter, General Motors announced in 1992 that it would suspend plans to develop its Impact electric vehicle and begin a joint project with Ford. Increasingly, the costs, as well as the benefits, of any new technology are being shared by core firms, supplier firms, public entities, and other interested parties.

This high level of diffusion is not limited to industrialized nations. Mexico City and São Paulo, with their extensive air pollution, broad supplier base, and nascent advanced technology industry, also hold

Figure 6.3 *Organization chart, CALSTART*

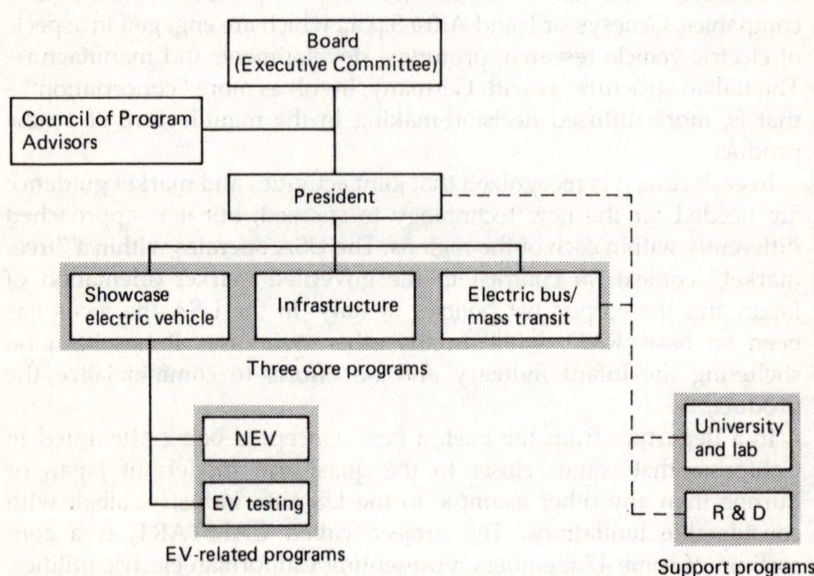

Source: CALSTART (December 1, 1992)

potential for entering into the development of new vehicles designed for their markets. However, this would depend on their willingness and ability to enter into a coordinative capacity with manufacturers as they simultaneously encourage market discipline.

The New Regions

How do the new trends in product development and in automotive technology reinforce tendencies toward flexible production, and what does this mean for regionalization? The conventional notions are, first, that regionalization is an aberration, and, second, if it is occurring, it is industrialized-nation-centric. For example, drawing on neo-classical trade theory, one would expect lower tariffs to lead to greater internationalization. This was the logic behind the "Enterprise for the Americas Initiative" unveiled by President Bush on June 27, 1990, which had as its objective support of democratic change, liberalization, and increased free trade within Latin America on the assumption that Western Hemispheric free trade would lead to a free multilateral global trading system.[14] But the historic decline in tariffs and increase in trade has instead been accompanied by a rise of quantitative restrictions on imports. Worldwide, approximately 40 per cent of trade is thought to be managed. By some estimates, only 5 to 7 per cent of global economic activities adhere to the rules of GATT. Robert Gilpin explains the situation accordingly:

> The two developments [i.e., economic globalization and economic regionalization] are in fact complementary and are responsive to each other. They reflect a world in which states want the *absolute* benefits of a global economy at the same time that they are seeking to increase their own *relative* gains through economic protectionism, the formation of regional arrangements, and managed trade.[15]

Among analysts who argue that regionalization is *de facto* if not *de jure*, most see the formation of blocs occurring in East Asia, North America, and Europe, with Japan, the USA, and Germany (among others) at their respective cores.[16] Within these continental delinations, the logic of the regions is remarkedly distinct. The unification of Western Europe is essentially politically motivated. By contrast, the East Asian region is driven not by state motives, but by the actions of firms themselves. Creation of a North American region, on the other hand, is motivated by lowering the costs of production associated with trade and foreign investment. Each of these regions shows measured increase in intra-regional trade.

However, it is not trade, nor even the initiating factor behind their creation that makes them so distinctive, but rather the techno-industrial foundation that is at the core of each region. John Zysman notes:

> Despite global interconnections among firms and world markets in many products, there are national technological trajectories ... We were very slow to recognize that there was more than one form of capitalist market economy. Those differences created certain types of firm strategies.[17]

Consequently, and as this study illustrates, there is a consistent tendency to regionalize R&D in the major industrialized regions (i.e., East Asia, North America, and Europe) and, increasingly, in developing country regions (e.g., South America, Central Asia), and in each case there is an adaptation of the firm structure to the region and vice versa. The emergence of industrializing regions is in recognition that the tendency is in large part market driven. Firms no longer take for granted that a product made for the USA, Germany, or Japan is necessarily appropriate for, say, Brazil. As reported in an industry trade journal, "the lesson learned in Brazil, whose vehicle industry developed as a mirror image of that of West Germany's, was, according to Michael Basserman, President, Mercedes-Benz of China based in Hong Kong, that a local pattern had to be involved in a new third world market, which suited its unique conditions."[18]

The adaptation of design and manufacture for regional markets suggests a logic for developing country regions. In the auto industry, evidence is beginning to materialize with Brazil and Mercosur, for example. The movement toward a new technological frontier reinforces this trend because firms are interested in sharing the costs of development of new technology. As an illustration, an electric vehicle uses considerable technology from aerospace, and Brazil, among others, has a well developed aeronautics industry. Thus, it could hypothetically enter into the design of products appropriate for the Brazilian market, and involve domestic suppliers. Should this occur, the outcome would be in direct contrast to the concept that industrializing countries are completely dependent upon industrialized nation blocs for core technologies. The opportunity currently exists for industrializing countries to build on their present level of capability for the development of regional products. These trends are indicative of several things. One is that trade initiatives directed at integrating the hemisphere or other equally diverse regions may result in regionalization rather than integration. Second, there appears to be a primary set of regional blocs with developed nations at the core, and an emerging set of secondary regional blocs with advanced industrializing nations at the core, each with a different technological impetus. And third, within the primary blocs, industrializing countries display considerable latitude in developing their technological trajectory.

The Politics of Production

In contrast to the view that states are being held "hostage" by multinationals because of their ability to transfer resources, or that we now live in a "borderless" world where the state is an anachronism, the trends toward flexible production suggest something quite different.[19] That is because firms become rooted in regions where states are participants in entrepreneurial activity. The new convergence of interests comes from the value placed on innovation for shortening the product life cycle and the high costs of research and development. In the effort to reduce these costs, firms have begun to share the burden (and risks) with other firms and with the public sector. Their actions result in the agglomeration of productive and innovative activities within regions, and create positive spillovers.[20] Agglomeration, in turn, creates an innovative environment yielding positive spillovers. The ability to generate innovation then becomes a specialized asset of a locale which is reproduced through local institutions and resources. Through this capacity, state policies have become critical participants in entrepreneurship.

State policies are particularly beneficial to small firms, which, in comparison to large firms, are less able to appropriate innovative functions. Firms that are interconnected through the quasi-market or quasi-(dis)integrated structure and linked to the external provision of functions are more likely than large, integrated firms to benefit from knowledge-based spillovers, such as skilled personnel, or external capital with which to commercialize basic research and development.[21] These policies provide a critical entree for supporting innovative activity by developing countries. In return, innovative activity leads to densely clustered groups of firms with extensive external linkage structures as it simultaneously supports the emergence of regional blocs within which a broad range of design, development, and manufacturing activities can take place.

This has occurred as a result of the relative autonomy of the various steps of design and manufacture – (1) research and development; (2)

component manufacture; (3) assembly; and (4) sales and marketing – from the oligopolistic control of the integrated firm, and their recombination into various quasi-firm structures. The double convergence to which Charles Sabel refers, or the mutually reinforcing tendencies by core firms and suppliers to enter into R&D sharing relationships, is one of the forces behind the new configurations. Another consists of the state policy arrangements that put in motion the sharing of factor inputs. This can take the form of assistance in finance, labor, research and development, technology transfer, and inter-firm network communication, which ultimately depend on the way such critical markets as labor and capital are constructed. In this capacity, state guidance and brokerage are critical.

The new firm structures are more horizontal and the boundaries of the firm are more diffused than under the vertically integrated firm. Their fluidity is evident in the disintegrated nature of the quasi-integrated firms of Japan. The relative autonomy of various aspects of design and manufacture is apparent in the way each can provide a handle for industrialization, with Yugo America being a poignant example. As the firms continue to evolve, their characteristics across regions are beginning to approximate each other, as are the institutional responses for supporting the new competitive structures. Each of these represent dimensions of flexible production, which has become the defining principle of manufacture.

As we take stock of the direction in which the international automobile industry is heading, several prospects are clear: one is that, while we are encumbered with a burden of overcapacity in mature markets, new markets are opening up which will require new investment. This unbalanced development is taking expression as international regional production strategies which reallocate large scale production worldwide and as sub-state regionalized production systems. Thus the emerging era of flexible production is ushering in a new world order that calls into question traditional North–North and North–South distinctions. In this regard, the automobile industry offers a glimpse into the trajectory international economic integration is beginning to take.

Notes

Chapter 1 Flexibility in an Interdependent World Economy

1 James P. Womack, Daniel T. Jones, and Daniel Roos, *The Machine that Changed the World* (New York: Macmillan, 1990).

2 The US Department of Commerce ruled on December 29, 1991, that Japanese auto manufacturers were selling mini-vans in the USA at less than fair value, or lower than the price sold in Japan. However, because the price differences were found to be substantially lower than the 30 per cent originally alleged (i. e., 7.19 per cent for Mazda, 0.95 per cent for Toyota, and 4.23 per cent for other manufacturers), this provided a limited explanation for the disparities in market performance.

3 James Flanigan, "Confronting Japan in the post-postwar era," *Los Angeles Times* (May 5, 1991), D1-2.

4 See Rebecca Morales and Michael Storper (eds), *Prospects for Alternative Fuel Vehicle Use and Production in Southern California: Environmental Quality and Economic Development,* Los Angeles, Lewis Center for Regional Policy Studies, UCLA, Working Paper No. 2 (May 1991).

5 Alfred D. Chandler, *The Visible Hand* (Cambridge, MA: Harvard University Press, 1977).

6 Laura D'Andrea Tyson and John Zysman, "Developmental strategy and production innovation in Japan," in *Politics and Productivity: The Real Story of Why Japan Works*, ed. Chalmers Johnson, Laura D'Andrea Tyson, and John Zysman (New York: Ballinger, 1989), p. 70.

7 Alfred D. Chandler, *Scale and Scope: The Dynamics of Industrial Capitalism* (Cambridge, MA: Harvard University Press), 1990.

8 For a discussion see "Can a keiretsu work in America?" *Harvard Business*

Review (September-October 1990), pp. 180-97.

9 George Stalk, Jr. and Thomas M. Hout, *Competing Against Time: How Time-Based Competition is Reshaping Global Markets* (New York: Free Press, 1990).

10 Patrizio Bianchi and Giuseppe Volpato, *Excess Capacity from Rigidity to Flexibility: The Case of the Automobile Industry*, London Business School Working Paper (1990), p. 6.

11 P. Bianchi and G. Volpato, op. cit. (1990).

12 Michael J. Piore and Charles F. Sabel, *The Second Industrial Divide: Possibilities for Prosperity* (New York: Basic Books, 1984), p. 17. Key differences between the ideas put forth here and the notion of flexible specialization come in the subsequent statement by Piore and Sabel: "This strategy is based on flexible – multi-use – equipment; skilled workers; and the creation, through politics, of an industrial community that restricts the forms of competition to those favoring innovation. For these reasons, the spread of flexible specialization amounts to a revival of craft forms of production that were emarginated at the first industrial divide" (p. 17). The original concept is defined by the use of flexible equipment and skilled workers engaged in craft production. That is not the case here.

13 United Nations Conference on Trade and Development (UNCTAD), *Handbook of International Trade and Development Statistics, Supplement* (Geneva, 1979), tables 6.2 and 6.8.

14 Ibid.; the figures are for 1970 and 1977.

15 United Nations Industrial Development Organization (UNIDO), *Industrial Development and Global Report 1988/89* (New York, 1989), table 1.

16 These figures are from United Nations, *Monthly Bulletin of Statistics*, various issues.

17 United Nations, *Monthly Bulletin of Statistics* (May 1982), special table C.

18 Chad Leechor, Harinder S. Kohli, and Sujin Hur, *Structural Changes in World Industry: A Quantitative Analysis of Recent Developments* (Washington, DC: World Bank, 1983), pp. 39-40.

19 UNIDO, *Industry in the 1980s: Structural Change and Interdependence* (New York, 1985); Peter Dicken, *Global Shift: Industrial Change in a Turbulent World* (Cambridge, MA: Harper & Row, 1986).

20 UNIDO, op. cit., table III.7, p. 44.

21 Yves Doz, "International industries: fragmentation versus globalization," in *Technology and Global Industry: Companies and Nations in the World Economy*, ed. Bruce R. Guile and Harvey Brooks (Washington, DC: National Academy Press, 1987).

22 The Euro-dollar is defined by Dicken, op. cit. (1986), accordingly: "Eurodollars are simply dollars held outside the United States banking system – not only in Europe, although London is the leading centre of the Eurodollar market. Eurodollars comprise a massive pool of credit which has grown extremely rapidly and whose major users are the TNCs [transnational corporations]. An important feature of the Eurodollar market is that it is outside the control of individual national govern-

ments. Hence, the market received a major boost with the tightening of United States financial regulations in 1963" (p. 86).

23 International Trade Administration (ITA), *Foreign Direct Investment in the United States* (Washington, DC: US Government Printing Office, December 1988).

24 Peter Montagnon, "EC's anti-dumping policy is creating new problems," *Los Angeles Times* (March 27, 1989), part IV, p. 10.

25 UNIDO, *World Industry Since 1960* (New York, 1979).

26 UNCTAD, *Trade and Development Report* (New York, 1987), annex table 9.

27 Martin Fransman and Kenneth King (eds) *Technological Capability in the Third World* (London: Macmillan, 1984).

28 Laura D'Andrea Tyson, "Making policy for national competitiveness in a changing world," in *Cooperation and Competition in the Global Economy*, ed. Antonio Furino (Cambridge, MA: Ballinger, 1988), p. 23.

29 Karin Lissakers, *International Debt, the Banks and US Foreign Policy*, staff report prepared for the Subcommittee on Foreign Economic Policy of the Committee on Foreign Relations, US Senate (Washington, DC: US Government Printing Office, 1991); Charles Oman, *New Forms of International Investment in Developing Countries*, Paris: Organization for Economic Co-operation and Development (OECD), 1984).

30 Jeff Frieden, "Third world indebted industrialization: international finance and state capitalism in Mexico, Brazil, Algeria, and South Korea," in *Postimperialism: International Capitalism and Development in the Late Twentieth Century*, ed. David G. Becker, Jeff Frieden, Sayre P. Schatz, and Richard L. Sklar (Boulder, Co: Lynne Rienner, 1987), pp. 131-59.

31 Ibid., pp. 134-5.

32 Tyson, op. cit. (1988), p. 24, with reference to Peter Drucker, "The changed world economy," *Foreign Affairs*, 64, 4.

33 Gordon Bilney, Takujiro Hamada, Uwe Holtz, Boen Wells, and Tony P. Hall, "Stop starving the world's poor to pay debts," *Los Angeles Times* (September 25, 1989), editorial section.

34 Tyson, op. cit. (1988), p. 25, with reference to Paul Krugman, "Comments on economic obstfeld paper," *Brookings Papers on Economic Activity*, 2 (1985).

35 Oman, op. cit. (1984).

36 Oman, op. cit. (1984), p. 72.

37 Office of Technology Assessment (OTA), *Computerized Manufacturing Automation: Employment, Education, and the Workplace* (Washington, DC: US Congress, OTA-CIT-235, April 1984); Robert H. Hayes and Ramchandran Jaikumar, "Manufacturing's crisis: new technologies, obsolete organizations," *Harvard Business Review* (September-October 1988), pp. 77-85.

38 Laura D'Andrea Tyson offers the following typology of knowledge: "[1] knowledge, such as production process knowledge reflected in firm-specific learning curves, that can be internalized within a firm; [2]

knowledge, such as knowledge of product design, that can be reversed-engineered and, once generated, is available internationally; and [3] knowledge that spreads beyond the firm but not very easily beyond national or sometimes even regional boundaries... This third kind of knowledge seems to be the reason behind the development of geographically concentrated 'high-technology centers' where information is embodied in people and transmitted through social and academic networks rather than mediated through the price system." op. cit. (1988), p. 37, with reference to Paul Krugman, "Strategic sectors and international competition," in *Strategic Trade Policy and the New International Economics*, ed. Robert M. Stern (Cambridge, MA: MIT Press, 1987).

39 Raphael Kaplinsky, "Electronics-based automation technologies and the onset of systemofacture: some implications for third world industrialization," *World Development*, 12, 4 (1984); Mytelka, Lynn Krieger, "Knowledge–intensive production and the changing internationalization strategies of multinational firms," in *A Changing International Division of Labor*, ed. James Caporasco (Boulder, CO: Lynne Rienner, 1987).

40 M. Piore and C. Sabel, op. cit. (1984).

41 See, for example, Bennett Harrison and Barry Bluestone, *The Great U-Turn: Corporate Restructuring and the Polarizing of America* (New York: Basic Books, 1988), and Frank Levy, *Dollars and Dreams* (New York: Russell Sage, 1987).

42 Tyson, op. cit. (1988), p. 30, where real weekly wage is measured in 1985 prices.

43 See Dan Luria, "Automation, markets, and scale: can flexible niching modernize US Manufacturing?", *International Review of Applied Economics*, 4, 2, (1990), pp. 127-65, for a discussion of the problem.

44 Rosemarie Philips and Stuart K. Tucker, *US Foreign Policy and Developing Countries: Discourse and Data 1991* (Washington, DC: Overseas Development Council, 1991) [conference report calculated from data in General Agreement on Tariffs and Trade, "International Trade 89-90"].

45 United States International Trade Commission (USITC), *US Global Competitiveness: The US Automotive Parts Industry*, USITC Publication 2037 (December 1987).

46 Gerald T. Bloomfield, "The world automotive industry in transition," in *Restructuring the Global Automobile Industry: National and Regional Impacts*, ed. Christopher M. Law (London: Routledge, 1991).

47 R. Hayes and R. Jaikumar, op. cit. (1988), p. 82.

48 G. Stalk and T. Hout, op. cit. (1990).

49 Kim B. Clark, *High Performance Product Development in the World Auto Industry*, Harvard Business School Working Paper 90-004 (1989).

50 Kim B. Clark, op. cit. (1989); Kim B. Clark, "Project scope and project performance: the effect of parts strategy and supplier involvement on product development," *Management Science*, 35, 10 (1989), pp. 1247-63; Kim B. Clark, W. Bruce Chew, and Takahiro Fujimoto, *Product Development in*

the World Auto Industry: Strategy, Organization, and Performance, paper of the Division of Research, Graduate School of Business Administration, Harvard University (1989); Kim B. Clark and Takahiro Fujimoto, *Lead Time in Automobile Development: Explaining the Japanese Advantage,* paper of the Division of Research, Graduate School of Business Administration, Harvard University (1989); Arnold O. Putnam, "A redesign for engineering," *Harvard Business Review* (May-June 1985), pp. 139-44.

51 This formulation is based on John Zysman, *Governments, Markets, and Growth: Financial Systems and the Politics of Industrial Change* (Ithaca: Cornell University Press, 1983).

52 Robert Wade, *Governing the Market: Economic Theory and the Role of Government in East Asian Industrialization* (Princeton: Princeton University Press, 1990).

53 R. Wade, op. cit. (1990), p. 27.

Chapter 2 Industrial Production, Regional Development, and Public Policy

1 John H. Dunning, *International Production and the Multinational Enterprise* (London: Allen & Unwin, 1981); John H. Dunning, *The Globalization of Firms and the Competitiveness of Countries: Some Implications for the Theory of Industrial Production* (Lund: Crafoord Lectures, 1989); John H. Dunning, *The Governance of Japanese and US M10 Manufacturing Affiliates in the UK: Some Country Specific Differences,* paper of Reading University (May 1990).

2 Alfred D. Chandler, Jr., *The Visible Hand: The Managerial Revolution in American Business,* (Cambridge, MA: Harvard University Press, 1977, pp. 6–7.

3 Ronald Coase, "The nature of the firm," *Economica*, 4 (Nov. 1937), p. 395.

4 Alfred D. Chandler, "The development of modern management structure in the US and UK," in *Management Strategy and Business Development*, ed. L. Hannah (London: Macmillan, 1976).

5 Herbert Simon, *Administrative Behavior* (New York: Macmillan, 1947); Herbert Simon, "Rationality as process and as product of thought," *American Economic Review*, 68 (May 1978), pp. 1-16; Herbert Simon, "On the behavioral and rational foundations of economic dynamics," *Journal of Economic Behavior and Organization*, 5 (1986), pp. 35-56.

6 Oliver Williamson, "The vertical integration of production: market failure considerations," *American Economic Review*, 61 (1971), pp. 112-23; Oliver Williamson, *Markets and Hierarchies: Analysis and Antitrust Implications* (New York: Free Press, 1975); Oliver Williamson, *The Economic Institutions of Capitalism* (New York: Free Press, 1985).

7 Tony McGuinness, "Markets and managerial hierarchies," in *The Economics of the Firm*, ed. Roger Clarke and Tony McGuinness (Oxford: Basil Blackwell, 1987).

8 "A 'rent' is defined by economists as 'a payment to a resource owner above the amount his resources could command in their next best alternative use. An economic rent is a receipt in excess of the opportunity cost of a resource' ... They are 'earned only by the owners of resources that cannot be augmented rapidly and at low cost to meet an increased demand for the goods they are used to produce' ... Land and skills are good examples. In the modern world a technological monopoly can produce rent or technological profits. This fact is central to the debate over what is called strategic trade policy." Robert Gilpin, *The Political Economy of International Relations* (Princeton: Princeton University Press, 1987), p. 187.

9 Kenneth J. Arrow, "Vertical integration and communication," *Bell Journal of Economics*, 6 (1975), pp. 173-83; Oliver Williamson, op. cit., (1975, 1985); Kurt Lundgren, "Vertical integration, transaction costs and 'learning by using'," in *The Firm as a Nexus of Treaties*, ed. Masahiko Aoki, Bo Gustafsson and Oliver E. Williamson (London: Sage, 1990).

10 Alfred Chandler, op. cit., (1977), p. 8.

11 Ibid, p. 11.

12 S. H. Hymer, *The International Operations of National Firms: A Study of Direct Investment* (Cambridge, MA: MIT Press, 1976); Mark Casson, *The Firm and the Market* (Cambridge, MA: MIT Press, 1987).

13 L. Putterman, "Some behavioural perspectives on the dominance of hierarchical over democratic forms of enterprise," *Journal of Economic Behaviour and Organisation*, 3 (1982), pp. 139-60.

14 Masahiko Aoki, "The participatory generation of information rents and the theory of the firm," in *The Firm as a Nexus of Treaties*, ed. Masahiko Aoki, Bo Gustafsson and Oliver E. Williamson (London: Sage, 1990) p. 28.

15 Stephen S. Cohen and John Zysman, *Manufacturing Matters: The Myth of the Post-Industrial Economy* (New York: Basic Books, 1987).

16 Michael Best, *The New Competition: Institutions of Industrial Restructuring* (Cambridge, MA: Harvard University Press, 1990), p. 112.

17 Stephen S. Cohen and John Zysman, op. cit. (1987).

18 Alfred Marshall, *Principles of Economics* (London: Macmillan, 1890); Alfred Marshall, *Industry and Trade* (London: Macmillan, 1919).

19 Giacomo Becattini, "Sectors and/or districts: some remarks on the conceptual foundations of industrial economics," in *Small Firms and Industrial Districts in Italy*, ed. Edward Goodman and Julia Bamford with Peter Saynor (London: Routledge, 1989).

20 Michael Best, op. cit. (1990); Edward Goodman et. al., op. cit., (1989); Patrizio Bianchi, *Industrial Restructuring Within an Italian Perspective*, Working Paper No. 2, Bologna, NOMISMA Laboratorio di Politica Industriale (September 1986).

21 Sebastiano Brusco, "A policy for industrial districts," in Edward Goodman, et. al., op. cit. (1989).

22 Charles F. Sabel, *The Re-emergence of Regional Economies*, Wissenschaftszentrum Berlin für Sozialforschung Discussion Paper, FS I 89-3 (June 1989), p. 5.

23 Alfred D. Chandler, Jr., *Strategy and Structure: Chapters in the History of American Industrial Enterprise* (Cambridge, MA: Harvard University Press, 1962).

24 Maryann P. Feldman and Zoltan J. Acs, *The Geography of Innovation*, working paper, Baltimore, Goucher College and University of Baltimore (February 1992).

25 Annalee Saxenian, *The Origins and Dynamics of Production Networks in Silicon Valley*, paper presented at the International Workshop on Network of Innovators, Montreal (May 1990).

26 Feldman and Acs, op. cit. (1992).

27 Ibid.

28 Zoltan J. Acs and Steven C. Isberg, *Capital Structure, Asset Specificity, and Firm Size: An Empirical Analysis*, working paper, University of Baltimore (October 1991).

29 Adam Smith, *An Inquiry into the Nature and Causes of the Wealth of Nations* (Chicago: University of Chicago Press, 1976 [orig. pubn 1776].

30 David Ricardo, *Principles of Political Economy and Taxation*, in *The Works of David Ricardo* (London: John Murray, 1817).

31 Folker Froebel, Jurgen Heinrichs, and Otto Freye, *The New International Division of Labor* (London: Cambridge University Press, 1980).

32 This model has been criticized for failing to address corporate costs and trade-offs, such as constraints along the production-possibilities curve, or the transitional costs of adjustment that follow from the relocation of factors. It further neglects to account for the evolution of corporations as dynamic entities.

33 Raymond Vernon, "International investment and international trade in the product cycle," *Quarterly Journal of Economics*, 80 (1966), pp. 190-207.

34 Council of Economic Advisors, *Economic Report of the President* (Washington DC, 1985), p. 114.

35 Robert Gilpin, *The Political Economy of International Relations* (Princeton: Princeton University Press, 1987).

36 Sanjaya Lall, *The New Multinationals: The Spread of Third World Enterprises* (New York: John Wiley, 1983); Martin Fransman and Kenneth King (eds), *Technological Capability in the Third World* (London: Macmillan, 1984).

37 Jeff Frieden, "Third world indebted industrialization: international finance and state capitalism in Mexico, Brazil, Algeria, and South Korea," in *Postimperialism: International Capitalism and Development in the Late Twentieth Century*, ed. David G. Becker, Jeff Frieden, Sayre P. Schatz, and Richard L. Sklar (Boulder, CO: Lynne Rienner, 1987).

38 Portions of this and the following sections are based on work by Carlos Quandt as contained in Rebecca Morales and Carlos Quandt, "The new regionalism: developing countries and regional collaborative competition," *International Journal of Urban and Regional Research*, 16, 3 (1992).

39 Jorge M. Katz, "Technological change and development in Latin America," in *Latin American and the New International Economic Order*, ed. R. Ffrench-

Davies and E. Tironi (London: Macmillan, 1982); Alice H. Amsden, *Asia's Next Giant: South Korea and Late Industrialization* (Oxford: Oxford University Press, 1989).

40 Carl Dahlman, Bruce Ross-Larson and Larry Westphal, *Managing Technological Development: Lessons from the Newly Industrializing Countries*, World Bank Staff Working Paper no. 717 (1985).

41 Giovanni Dosi and Luigi Orsengio, "Coordination and transformation: an overview of structures, behaviours and change in evolutionary environments," in *Technical Change and Economic Theory*, ed. G. Dosi, C. Freeman, R. Nelson, G. Silverberg, and L. Soete (London: Pinter, 1988), pp. 95-110.

42 P. Allen, "Evolution and economics," in G. Dosi et. al., op. cit. (1988); G. Dosi, "Technological paradigms and technological trajectories: a suggested interpretation of the determinants and directions of technical change," *Research Policy*, 2, 3 (1982), pp. 147-96; R. Nelson and S. Winter, *An Evolutionary Theory of Economic Change* (Cambridge, MA: Harvard University Press, 1982).

43 G. Dosi, op. cit. (1982).

44 S. Winter, "Schumpeterian competition in alternative regimes," *Journal of Economic Behaviour and Organization*, 5 (1984), pp. 287-320.

45 Christopher Freeman, "Diffusion: the spread of new technology to firms, sectors, and nations," in *Innovation, Technology, and Finance*, ed. A. Heertje (Oxford: Basil Blackwell, 1988).

46 Lynn Krieger Mytelka, "Knowledge-intensive production and the changing internationalization strategies of multinational firms," in *A Changing International Division of Labor*, ed. James Caporasco (Boulder, CO: Lynne Rienner, 1987); William Davidson and Jose de la Torre (eds), *Managing the Global Corporation* (New York: McGraw-Hill, 1989).

47 John A. Hall, "Classical liberalism and the modern state," *Daedalus*, 116, 3 (1987), pp. 95-118.

48 G. Dosi et. al., op. cit. (1989).

49 Giovanni Dosi, Laura D'Andrea Tyson, and John Zysman, "Trade, technologies, and development," in *Politics and Productivity: The Real Story of Why Japan's Development Strategy Works*, ed. Chalmers Johnson, Laura D'Andrea Tyson, and John Zysman (New York: Ballinger, 1989)

50 Ibid.

51 Norma L. Chalmers, *Industrial Relations in Japan: The Peripheral Workforce* (New York: Routledge, 1989).

52 Imai Ken'ichi and Itami Hiroyuki, "Allocation of labor and capital in Japan and the United States," in *Inside the Japanese System: Readings on Contemporary Society and Political Economy*, ed. Daniel I. Okimoto and Thomas P. Rohlen (Stanford: Stanford University Press, 1988).

53 Imai Ken'ichi and Itami Hiroyuki, op. cit., (1988), write: "However, the success of this Japanese type of corporate strategy is premised on several conditions. This first is that changes in demand not be too abrupt, but rather at a rate that permits fine tuning, such as product differentiation and

improvements in an existing product line. The second condition is that the economy continue to grow at a certain speed, creating a stable level of long-run growth for firms. Sustained growth is important because it invigorates the firm's internal labor market and reduces the need for lay-offs. Unless these conditions are fulfilled, the Japanese firm's diversification strategy will run into problems" (pp. 117-18).

54 John Zysman, *Governments, Markets, and Growth: Financial Systems and the Politics of Industrial Change* (Ithaca: Cornell University Press, 1983).

55 For a compelling argument against a state-led model of industrialization in Japan, see Daniel I. Okimoto, *Between MITI and the Market: Japanese Industrial Policy for High Technology* (Stanford: Stanford University Press, 1989).

56 Robert Wade, *Governing the Market: Economic Theory and the Role of Government in East Asian Industrialization* (Princeton: Princeton University Press, 1990).

Chapter 3 Automobile Production and the Industrial Legacy of the USA

1 University of Michigan Transportation Research Institute, *Competitive Survival: Private Initiatives, Public Policy, and the North American Automotive Industry*, Report #92-3 (June 1992) p. 5.

2 Martin Anderson, "Shake-out in Detroit: new technology, new problems," *Technology Review* (August/September 1982), p. 59.

3 David Friedman, "Beyond the age of Ford: the strategic basis of the Japanese success in automobiles," in *American Industry in International Competition: Government Policies and Corporate Strategies*, ed. John Zysman and Laura D'Andrea Tyson (Ithaca: Cornell University Press, 1983).

4 Servet Mutlu, *Interregional and International Mobility of Industrial Capital: The Case of the American Automobile and Electronics Companies* (PhD dissertation, City and Regional Planning, University of California, Berkeley, 1979).

5 Ibid.

6 Mira Wilkins, "Multinational automobile enterprises and regulation: an historical overview," in *Government, Technology, and the Future of the Automobile*, ed. Douglas H. Ginsburg and William J. Abernathy (New York: McGraw-Hill, 1980) pp. 221-58.

7 William J. Abernathy, *The Productivity Dilemma: Roadblock to Innovation in the Automobile Industry* (Baltimore: Johns Hopkins University Press, 1978); Stephen S. Cohen and John Zysman, *Manufacturing Matters: The Myth of the Post-Industrial Economy* (New York: Basic Books, 1987).

8 William J. Abernathy, op. cit. (1978).

9 See Rebecca Morales, "The Los Angeles automobile industry in historical perspective," *Society and Space*, 4 (September 1986), pp. 289-303; also Rebecca Morales, "Place and auto manufacture in the post-Fordist era," in

The Car and the City: The Automobile, the Built Environment, and Daily Urban Life, ed. Martin Wachs and Margaret Crawford (Ann Arbor: University of Michigan Press, 1991).

10 Alan Altshuler, Martin Anderson, Daniel Jones, Daniel Roos, and James Womack, *The Future of the Automobile: The Report of MIT's International Automobile Program* (Cambridge, MA: MIT Press, 1984).

11 William J. Abernathy, op. cit. (1978), p. 37.

12 "No dramatic change seen by auto suppliers," *Iron Age* (December 3, 1979).

13 Akio Okochi and Koichi Shimokawa (eds), *Development of Mass Marketing: The Automobile and Retailing Industries* (Tokyo: University of Tokyo Press, 1981).

14 David Brody, *Workers in Industrial America* (New York: Oxford University Press, 1980).

15 Thomas A. Kochan, Harry C. Katz, and Robert B. McKersie, *The Transformation of American Industrial Relations* (New York: Basic Books, 1986), p. 33.

16 Antonio Gramsci, *Selections from the Prison Notebooks of Antonio Gramsci* (New York: International Publishers, 1971).

17 Ron Landry, "How new-car dealers are gaining hard-parts aftermarket share," *National Petroleum News* (January 1980).

18 The statement made by then GM president Charles E. Wilson in 1952 was that what was good for the country was good for General Motors and vice versa.

19 Davis Dyer, Malcom S. Salter, and Alan M. Webber, *Changing Alliances* (Boston: Harvard Business School Press, 1987), p. 213.

20 See, for example, *Ford Motor Co. v. US*, 405 US 526 (1972).

21 David B. Audretsch, *The Market and the State: Government Policy Towards Business in Europe, Japan and the United States* (New York: Harvester Wheatsheaf, 1989).

22 David B. Audretsch, op. cit. (1989), p. 31.

23 MIT Commission on Industrial Productivity, *Working Papers of the MIT Commission on Industrial Productivity*, 1 & 2 (Cambridge, MA: MIT Press, 1989).

24 Ulrich Juergens, "New technology, work organization and industrial relations in the West German car industry," in *Technology and Labor in the Automotive Industry*, ed. Sung-Jo Park (Frankfurt am Main: Campus, 1991).

25 MIT, op. cit. (1989).

26 *Ward's 1989 Automotive Yearbook* (Detroit: Ward's Communications, 1989), p. 167.

27 United States International Trade Commission (USITC), *US Global Competitiveness: The US Automotive Parts Industry*, USITC Publication 2037 (December 1987).

28 International Trade Administration, *Foreign Direct Investment in the United States* (Washington, DC:, US Government Printing Office, 1988).

29 William J. Abernathy, Kim B. Clark, and Alan J. Kantrow, *Industrial*

Renaissance: Producing a Competitive Future for America (New York: Basic Books, 1983); Michael L. Dertouzos, Richard K. Lester, Robert M. Solow, and the MIT Commission on Industrial Productivity, *Made in America: Regaining the Productive Edge* (Cambridge, MA: MIT Press, 1989).

30 Jon Lowell, "Overcapacity: the outlook's ominous as too many plants spew out too many cars," *Ward's Auto World*, 23, 6 (1987), pp. 28-39.

31 James Flanigan, "Chrysler's red-ink lesson for big blue," *Los Angeles Times* (January 20, 1993).

32 Harry C. Katz and Charles F. Sabel, *Industrial Relations and Industrial Adjustments: The World Car Industry*, paper presented at the Conference on the Future of Industrial Relations, Berkeley, CA (22-3 February 1985).

33 "Here comes GM's Saturn: more than a car, it is GM's hope for reinventing itself," *BusinessWeek* (April 9, 1990), p. 56.

34 General Motors, *1988 Annual Report*, p. 14.

35 Alex Taylor III, "Can GM remodel itself?" *Fortune* (January 13, 1992), p. 26.

36 Judith H. Dobrzynski, "A wake-up call for corporate boards," *Business-Week*, (April 20, 1992), p. 35.

37 See Rebecca Morales, "Work organization, technology, and labor relations in the US automobile industry," *Technology and Labor in the Automotive Industry*, ed. in Sung-Jo Park (Frankfurt, am Main: Campus, 1991).

38 Davis Dyer, Malcom S. Salter, and Alan M. Webber, op. cit. (1987), p. 221.

39 Ibid.

40 David Audretsch, op. cit. (1989), p. 52.

41 Ruth Milkman and Cydney Pullman, *Technological Change in an Auto Assembly Plant: A Case Study of GM-Linden*, Final Report for the Labor Institute, New York (August 1988); Clair Brown and Michael Reich, "When does union–management cooperation work? A look at NUMMI and GM-Van Nuys," in *Can California be Competitive and Caring?* (Los Angeles: UCLA, Institute of Industrial Relations, 1988); Lowell Turner, "Three plants, three futures," *Technology Review*, 92, 1 (1989), pp. 38-45; Mike Parker and Jane Slaughter, *Choosing Sides: Unions and the Team Concept* (Boston: South End Press, 1988).

42 See for example, Harry Katz, *Shifting Gears: Changing Labor Relations in the US Automobile Industry*, (Cambridge, MA: MIT Press, 1985).

43 See, for example, Mike Parker and Jane Slaughter, "Management by stress," *Technology Review* (October 1988), pp. 37-44; or Mike Parker and Jane Slaughter, *Choosing Sides: Unions and the Team Concept* (Boston: South End Press, 1988).

44 Michael J. Piore and Charles F. Sabel, *The Second Industrial Divide: Possibilities for Prosperity* (New York: Basic Books, 1984).

45 Office of Technology Assessment, *Computerized Manufacturing Automation: Employment, Education, and the Workplace* (Washington, DC. US Congress, OTA-CIT-235, April 1984); Robert H. Hayes and Ramchandran Jaikumar, "Manufacturing's crisis: new technologies, obsolete organizations," *Harvard Business Review* (September-October 1988), pp. 77-85.

46 John F. Krafcik and Daniel Roos, "High performance manufacturing: an international study of auto assembly practice," *Automotive Systems Technology: The Future* (Dearborn, MI, September 25-30, 1988), pp. 28-39; John F. Krafcik, "A new diet for US Manufacturers," *Technology Review*, 92, 1 (1989), pp. 28-36.

47 Harley Shaiken, *Work Transformed: Automation and Labor in the Computer Age* (New York: Holt, Rinehart & Winston, 1984).

48 John F. Krafcik and Daniel Roos, op. cit. (1988).

49 For a contending view, see Harry C. Katz, Thomas A. Kochan, and Jeffrey H. Keefe, "Effects of industrial relations on productivity: evidence from the automobile industry," *Brookings Papers on Economic Activity*, 2 (1988).

50 See, for example, Ruth Milkman and Cydney Pullman, *Technological Change in an Auto Assembly Plant: A Case Study of GM-Linden*, Final Report for the Labor Institute, New York (August 1988).

51 Another observation was articulated by labor sociologists Ruth Milkman and Cydney Pullman which they concluded from their study of GM's facility in Linden, New Jersey, that "... like technology itself, organizations such as the team concept or classification mergers are not a panacea for the problems of the auto industry. It seems clear that they have little chance of success unless genuine changes occur in the relationship between management and workers" (Ibid., p. 11).

52 As noted in Audretsch, op. cit., (1985), the nation was so ready for this legislation that, within one year of its passage, ninety cooperative ventures were registered with enforcement agencies (p. 53).

53 Drew Winter, "Suppliers and OEMs find much on which to agree," *Ward's Auto World* (July 1988), p. 67.

54 Drew Winter, "The supplier as extended family," *Ward's Auto World* (July 1988), pp. 59-63.

55 *Ward's Auto World*'s annual supplier survey, as reported in Stephen E. Plumb, "Supplier joint ventures," *Ward's Auto World*, (July 1990), p. 30.

56 Robert B. Cohen, "The new spatial organization of the European and American automotive industries," in *Regional Analysis and the New International Division of Labor*, ed. Frank Moulaert and Patricia E. Salinas (Boston: Kluwer-Nijhoff, 1983).

57 Andrew Mair, Richard Florida, and Martin Kenney, "The new geography of automobile production: Japanese transplants in North America," *Economic Geography*, 64, 4 (1988).

58 Amy K. Glasmier and Richard E. McCluskey, "US auto parts production: an analysis of a changing industry," *Economic Geography*, 63, 2 (1987).

59 Stephen Herzenberg and Harley Shaiken, *Labor Market in the North American Auto Industry*, paper prepared for the Canadian Industrial Relations Research Association Annual Meeting, Victoria, BC (June 2-5, 1990).

60 Ibid.

Chapter 4 European and Japanese Models of Industrialization: A Study of Contrasts

1 Alexander Gershenkron, *Economic Backwardness in Historical Perspective* (Cambridge MA: Harvard University Press, 1962).

2 John Zysman, *Governments, Markets, and Growth: Financial Systems and the Politics of Industrial Change* (Ithaca: Cornell University Press, 1983).

3 Peter A. Hall, *Governing the Economy: The Politics of State Intervention in Britain and France* (New York: Oxford University Press, 1986).

4 Ibid.

5 Wayne Lewchuk, "The motor vehicle industry," in *The Decline of the British Economy*, ed. Bernard Elbaum and William Lazonick (Oxford: Clarendon Press, 1986), p. 141.

6 Ibid.

7 D. Garel Rhys, *The Motor Industry in the European Community* (Portsmouth: Grosvenor Press, 1989).

8 P. Hall, op. cit. (1986).

9 W. Lewchuk, op. cit. (1986).

10 Ibid.

11 W. Lewchuk, op. cit. (1986), p. 136.

12 Martin Adeney, *The Motor Makers: The Turbulent History of Britain's Car Industry* (London: Collins, 1989).

13 D. Garel Rhys, "Motor vehicles," in *Structure of British Industry*, ed. Peter S. Johnson (London: Nichols, 1980).

14 Ash Amin and Ian Smith, "Vertical integration or disintegration? The case of the UK car parts industry," in *Restructuring the Global Automobile Industry: National and Regional Impacts*, ed. Christopher M. Law (London: Routledge, 1991).

15 A. Amin and I. Smith, op. cit. (1991), pp. 177-8.

16 D. Garel Rhys, op. cit. (1980).

17 Yasuo Miyakawa, "The transformation of the Japanese motor vehicle industry and its role in the world: industrial restructuring and technical evolution," in *Restructuring the Global Automobile Industry: National and Regional Impacts*, ed. Christopher M. Law (London: Routledge, 1991).

18 Ibid.

19 A. Amin and I. Smith, op. cit. (1991)

20 A. Amin and I. Smith, op. cit. (1991), p. 180.

21 Stephen Wood, "Developments in the British car industry in the mid-eighties," in *Technology and Labor in the Automotive Industry*, ed. Sung-Jo Park (New York: Campus, 1991).

22 Ibid.

23 Y. Miyakawa, op. cit. (1991).

24 For a discussion of the politics of reciprocal consent, see Richard J. Samuels, "The business of the Japanese state," in *Governments, Industries and*

Markets: Aspects of Government-Industry Relations in the UK, Japan, West Germany and the USA since 1945, ed. Martin Chick (Hants, UK: Edward Elgar, 1990).

25 Konosuke Odaka, Keinosuke Ono, and Fumihiko Adachi, *The Automobile Industry in Japan: A Study of Ancilliary Firm Development* (Tokyo: Kinokuniya, 1988).

26 Ken-Ichi Imai, "Japanese business groups and the structural impediments initiative," in *Japan's Economic Structure: Should It Change?*, ed. Kozo Yamamura (Seattle: Society for Japanese Studies, 1990), p. 170.

27 Christopher Freeman, *Technology Policy and Economic Performance: Lessons from Japan* (London: Pinter, 1987).

28 Y. Miyakawa, op. cit. (1991).

29 Michael A. Cusumano, *The Japanese Automobile Industry: Technology and Management at Nissan and Toyota* (Cambridge, MA: Harvard University Press, 1985).

30 David B. Audretsch, *The Market and the State: Government Policy Towards Business in Europe, Japan and the United States* (New York: Harvester Wheatsheaf, 1989).

31 Michael Gerlach, "*Keiretsu* organization in the Japanese economy: analysis and trade implications," in *Politics and Productivity: How Japan's Development Strategy Works*, ed. Chalmers Johnson, Laura D'Andrea Tyson, and John Zysman (New York: Ballinger, 1989).

32 Ibid.

33 Konosuke Odaka, Keinosuke Ono, and Fumihiko Adachi, *The Automobile Industry in Japan: A Study of Ancillary Firm Development* (Tokyo: Kokusaibunken Insatsusha, distributed by Oxford University Press, 1988).

34 Robert E. Cole, *Work, Mobility, and Participation: A Comparative Study of American and Japanese Industry* (Berkeley: University of California Press, 1979).

35 Hiromichi Mutoh, "The automotive industry," in *Industrial Policy of Japan*, ed. Ryutaro Komiya, Masahiro Okuno, and Kotaro Suzumura, (New York: Academic Press, 1988). He also argues that the foreign exchange difficulties and "Special Procurements" policy of the Korean War worked in favor of the protectionist position.

36 C. Freeman, op. cit., (1987), p. 34, as contained in Fukukawa's 1982 lecture titled "Features of the Industrial Policy of Japan."

37 Michael Best, *The New Competition: Institutions of Industrial Restructuring* (Cambridge, MA: Harvard University Press, 1990).

38 H. Mutoh, op. cit. (1988).

39 Ibid.

40 H. Mutoh, op. cit. (1988), , p. 315.

41 Ibid.

42 H. Mutoh, op. cit. (1988).

43 Ibid.

44 James Abegglen and George Stalk, *Kaisha: The Japanese Corporation* (New

York: Basic Books, 1985); Masahiko Aoki, *The Economic Analysis of the Japanese Firm* (Amsterdam: New Holland, 1984); Rodney Clark, *The Japanese Company* (New Haven: Yale University Press, 1979).

45 MIT Commission on Industrial Productivity, *Working Papers of the MIT Commission on Industrial Productivity* (Cambridge, MA: MIT Press, 1989) Vol. 1, p. 22.

46 Kuniko Fujita and Richard Child Hill, *Toyota's City: Corporation and Community in Japan* (East Lansing: Department of Sociology, Michigan State University, 1987).

47 Masahiko Aoki, "The Japanese firm in transition," in *The Political Economy of Japan, Vol. 1: The Domestic Transformation*, ed. Kozo Yamamura and Yashukichi Yasuba (Stanford: Stanford University Press, 1987), p. 283.

48 M. Aoki, op. cit. (1987).

49 M. Aoki, op. cit. (1987), p. 284.

50 Masayoshi Ikeda, "Production network of big firms and smaller subcontractors in Japan," European Institute of Business Administration (INSEAD), *Euro-Asia Business Review*, 7 (1989).

51 M. Aoki, op. cit. (1987).

52 Ira C. Magaziner and Thomas Hout, *Japanese Industrial Policy* (Berkeley: University of California Press, 1981), pp. 32-3.

53 John McElroy, "Why can't Germany compete?" *Automotive Industries* (August 1992) pp. 22-5.

54 J. McElroy, op. cit. (1992).

55 J. McElroy, op. cit., (1992), p. 22.

56 As just two of many examples, see Peter J. Katzenstein (ed.), *Industry and Politics in West Germany: Toward the Third Republic* (Ithaca: Cornell University Press, 1989); and Peter J. Katzenstein (ed.), *Policy and Politics in West Germany: The Growth of a Semisovereign State* (Philadelphia: Temple University Press, 1987).

57 Marsha A. Chandler, "The state and industrial decline: a survey," in *Industrial Policy*, ed. Andre Blais (Toronto: University of Toronto Press, 1986).

58 Gary B. Herrigel, "Industrial order and the politics of industrial change: mechanical engineering," in P. Katzenstein, op. cit. 1989.

59 Henry Ford is reported to have received the highest form of civilian recognition, the *Schwarzer Adlerorden*, by Adolf Hitler in 1939 for his contribution in modernizing German industry (Wolfgang Streeck, "Successful adjustment to turbulent markets," in P. Katzenstein, op. cit. (1989).

60 Ibid.

61 W. Streeck, ibid. (1989), notes: "In-house value added accounts on average for 40 percent of total production value, as compared to 30 percent in France, 33 percent in Italy, and 35 percent in the United Kingdom" (p. 121).

62 Delbert A. Taebel and James V. Cornehls, *The Political Economy of Urban Transportation* (Port Washington, NY: Kennikat Press, 1977).

63 Ulrich Juergens, *National and Company Specific Differences in Organizing Production Work in the Car Industry*, paper presented at the workshop on "The Organization of Work and Technology: Implications for International Competitiveness," Brussels (May 31-June 1, 1990), pp. 12, 14.

64 W. Streeck, ibid. (1989), p. 128.

65 MIT Commission on Industrial Productivity, *Working Papers of the MIT Commission on Industrial Productivity*, vol. 2 (Cambridge, MA: MIT Press, 1989), p. 45.

66 Philip Glouchevitch, *Juggernaut: The German Way of Business: Why it is Transforming Europe – and the World* (New York: Simon & Schuster, 1992).

67 In 1985, this was as follows: VW: Deutsche Bank, Dresdner Bank; Audi: Bayerische Vereinsbank, Commerzbank; Daimler-Benz: Deutsche Bank, Commerzbank; Ford: Commerzbank; BMW: Dresdner Bank; Porsche: Landesgirokasse, Landessparkasse (W. Streeck, op. cit. (1989), p. 120 fn).

68 W. Streeck, op. cit. (1989), p. 131.

69 Philip Cooke and Kevin Morgan, *Learning Through Networking: Regional Innovation and the Lessons of Baden-Württemberg*, (Cardiff: Regional Industrial Research, Report Number 5, May 1990), pp. 28-9.

70 Charles Sabel, Horst Kern, and Gary Herrigel, "Kooperative Produktion, Neue Formen der Zusammenarbeit zwischen Endfertigern und Zulieferern in der Automobilesindustrie und die Neuordnung der Firm" (Collaborative manufacturing: new supplier relations in the automobile industry and the redefinition of the industrial Corporation), in *Zulieferer im Netz – Zwischen Abhängigkeit und Partnerschaft*, ed. H. G. Mendius and U. Wendeling-Schroeder (Cologne: Bund, 1991), pp. 203-27.

71 Ibid.

Chapter 5 Emerging Nations: Profiles of Interdependent Development

1 Peter F. Drucker, "The changed world economy," *Foreign Affairs* (spring 1986).

2 Manuel Castells and Laura D'Andrea Tyson, "High-technology choices ahead: restructuring interdependence," in *US Policy and the Developing Countries: Growth, Exports, and Jobs in a Changing World Economy, Agenda 1988*, ed. John Sewell and Stuart K. Tucker (New Brunswick, NJ: Transaction Books, 1988).

3 Daniel T. Jones and James P. Womack, "Developing countries and the future of the automobile industry," *World Development*, 13, 3 (1985), p. 393.

4 See, for example, Richard Newfarmer, *Transnational Conglomerates and the Economics of Dependent Development: A Case of the International Electric Oligopoly and Brazil's Electric Industry* (Greenwich, CT: Jai Press, 1980).

5 David G. Becker, Jeff Frieden, Sayre P. Schatz, and Richard L. Sklar, *Postimperialism: International Capitalism and Development in the Late Twentieth*

Century (Boulder CO, Lynne Rienner, 1987), pp. 3-4.

6 F. Froebel, J. Heinrichs, and O. Kreye, *The New International Division of Labor* (Cambridge: Cambridge University Press, 1980).

7 Maria Patricia Fernandez-Kelly, *For We Are Sold I and My People: Women and Industry in Mexico's Frontier* (Albany: State University of New York Press, 1983).

8 Harley Shaiken, *Mexico in the Global Economy: High Technology and Work Organization in Export Industries* (San Diego: Center for US–Mexican Studies, University of California, 1990); Manuel Castells, "High technology, world development, and structural transformation: the trends and the debate," *Alternatives*, 2 (1986), pp. 229-343.

9 D. Becker et. al., op. cit. (1987), p. 6.

10 Motor Vehicle Manufacturers Association of the United States (MVMA), *World Motor Vehicle Data* (Detroit: MVMA, 1992).

11 Kenneth S. Mericle, "The political economy of the Brazilian motor vehicle industry," in *The Political Economy of the Latin American Motor Vehicle Industry*, ed. Rich Kronish and Kenneth S. Mericle (Cambridge, MA: MIT Press, 1984).

12 In 1962, the Mexican auto industry consisted of the following companies: DINA (100 per cent domestic); Fabricas Auto-Mex (33 per cent Chrysler, 67 per cent domestic); Ford (100 per cent foreign); GM (100 per cent foreign); Promexa (100 per cent domestic); VMA (100 per cent domestic); Impulsora Mexicana Automotriz (100 per cent domestic); Reo de Mexico (100 per cent domestic); Representaciones Delta (100 per cent domestic); Nissan (100 per cent foreign).

13 Rich Kronish and Kenneth S. Mericle, "The Latin American motor vehicle industry, 1900-1980," in R. Kronish and K. Mericle (eds) op. cit. (1984).

14 The firms manufacturing motor vehicles in 1965 were as follows: Fabrica Nacional de Motores, Ford, GM, International Harvester, Mercedes-Benz, Scania Vabis, Simca, Toyota, Vemag, VW, Willys Overland.

15 K. Mericle, op. cit. (1984).

16 Chrysler had also re-entered the market.

17 K. Mericle, op. cit. (1984).

18 Rhys Owen Jenkins, "Internationalization of capital and the semi-industrialized countries: the case of the Motor industry," *Review of Radical Political Economics*, 17, 1, 2 (1985) pp. 59-81.

19 Mark Bennett, *Public Policy and Industrial Development: The Case of the Mexican Auto Parts Industry* (Boulder CO: Westview Press, 1986).

20 Sylvia Maxfield, *Governing Capital: International Finance and Mexican Politics* (Ithaca: Cornell University Press, 1990), p. 48.

21 M. Bennett, op. cit. (1986), p. 18.

22 Caren Addis, *A Supplier-Driven Motor Vehicle Industry: Alternative Paths to Brazilian Development*, working paper of the Kellogg Institute, University of Notre Dame (September, 1992), p. 8.

23 C. Addis, op. cit. (1992).

24 M. Bennett, op. cit. (1986), p. 218.

25 My discussions with personnel in one German specialty car maker indicate that this was in fact the case.

26 Rhys Jenkins, *Transnational Corporations and the Latin American Automobile Industry* (London: Macmillan, 1987), p. 212.

27 K. Mericle, op. cit. (1984).

28 Rik Turner, "GM leaders open r&d site on Brazil visit," *Automotive News* (February 8, 1988), p. 2.

29 Harley Shaiken with Stephen Herzenberg, *Automation and Global Production: Automobile Engine Production in Mexico, the United States, and Canada* (San Diego: Center for US–Mexican Studies, UCSD, 1987).

30 Asociacion Mexicana de la Industria Automotriz (AMIA), *La industria automotriz de Mexico en cifras* (Mexico City: AMIA, 1989).

31 Harley Shaiken, *Mexico in the Global Economy: High Technology and Work Organization in Export Industries* (San Diego: Center for US–Mexican Studies, UCSD, 1990), p. 42. He notes that, because of the car's fuel efficiency, it balances out other less efficient models, and is important for helping the company comply with the corporate average fuel economy (CAFE) legislation. However, to be included, at least 75 per cent of the parts by value must come from the USA, since this is the minimum requirement for inclusion in US fuel economy fleet averages. The problem for Mexico is that it reduces their share to a minimum, of which most is sourced from the surrounding industrial park.

32 United States International Trade Commission (USITC), *The Internationalization of the Automobile Industry and its Effects on the US Automobile Industry*, (Washington, DC: USITC Publication 1712, 1985).

33 Motor Vehicle Manufacturers Association of the United States (MVMA), *MVMA Motor Vehicle Facts & Figures '90* (Detroit: MVMA, 1989).

34 Raul Hinojosa and Rebecca Morales, "International restructuring and labor market interdependence: the automobile industry in Mexico and the United States," in *Labor Market Interdependence*, ed. Clark Reynolds, Jorge Bustamante, and Raul Hinojosa (Stanford: Stanford University Press, 1991).

35 Jorge Carrillo, "Transformaciones en la industria maquiladora de exportacion," in *Las maquiladoras: ajuste estructural y desarrollo regional*, ed. Bernardo Gonzalez-Arechiga and Rocio Barajas Escamilla (Tijuana, Baja California, Mexico, El Colegio de la Frontera Norte/ Fundacion Friedrich Ebert, 1989); Bernardo Gonzalez-Arechiga and Jose Carlos Ramirez, "Productividad sin distribusion: cambio tecnologico en la industria maquiladora mexicana," *Frontera Norte*, 1, 1 (1989), pp. 97-124.

36 Stephen Baker, Elizabeth Weiner, and Amy Borrus, "Mexico: a new economic era," *BusinessWeek* (November 12, 1990), pp. 102-12.

37 Auto makers can import 15 to 20 per cent of their cars provided they maintain a trade surplus. Net exports of $2.50 are required for every $1 of finished vehicle imports in 1991. The export requirement drops to $2 in 1992 and 1993, and $1.75 in 1994.

38 Stephen Downer, "Price tag rises for Nissan's plan in Mexico," *Automotive News* (February 4, 1991), p. 39.

39 S. Downer, op. cit. (1991), p. 39.

40 Asociacion Mexicana de la Industria Automotriz (AMIA), *La industria automotriz de Mexico en cifras* (Mexico City: AMIA, 1989).

41 Instituto Nacional de Estadistica Geografia e Informatica, Mexico City, May 1990.

42 H. Shaiken with S. Herzenberg, op. cit (1987).

43 Peter Evans, "Class, state, and dependence in East Asia: lessons for Latin Americanists," in *The Political Economy of New Asian Industrialism*, ed. Frederic C. Deyo (Ithaca: Cornell University Press, 1987), p. 217.

44 Jinjoo Lee, *Two Different Development Paths: The Comparison of Local Firm and Joint Venture in Korean Automobile Assembly*, working paper of the Korea Advanced Institute of Science and Technology, Seoul (October 1987).

45 Chuk Kyo Kim and Chul Heui Lee, "Ancillary firm development in the Korean automobile industry," in *The Motor Vehicle Industry in Asia: A Study of Ancillary Firm Development*, ed. Konosuke Odaka (Singapore: Singapore University Press, for the Council for Asian Manpower Studies, 1983), p. 290.

46 C. K. Kim and C. H. Lee, op. cit. (1983), pp. 291-2.

47 C. K. Kim and C. H. Lee, op. cit. (1983), p. 314.

48 C. K. Kim and C. H. Lee, op. cit. (1983), p. 305.

49 Se-Il Park, *Labor Policy in Korea: Its Features and Problems*, working paper of the College of Law, Seoul National University (August 1987).

50 For a discussion of this, see J. Lee, op. cit. (1987); and Young-Suk Hyun and Jinjoo Lee, "Can Hyundai go it alone?" *Long Range Planning*, 22, 2 (1989).

51 J. Lee, op. cit. (1987).

52 See, for example, Harold Lydall, *Yugoslav Socialism: Theory and Practice* (Oxford: Clarendon Press, 1984); or Rikard Lang, George Macesich, and Dragomir Vojnic (eds), *Essays on the Political Economy of Yugoslavia* (Zagreb: Informator Zagreb, 1982).

53 Laura D'Andrea Tyson, Sherman Robinson, and Leyla Woods, *Conditionality and Adjustment in Socialist Economies: Hungary and Yugoslavia*, University of California at Berkeley, Berkeley Roundtable on the International Economy, October, 1984; Diane Flaherty, "Economic reform and foreign trade in Yugoslavia," *Cambridge Journal of Economics*, 6 (1982), pp. 105-43.

54 Slobodan Smiljanic, "Prospects and chances of the world automobile industry," in *Technology Development of Yugoslavia* (Belgrade: Yugoslav Public, 1989). This material also comes from personal interviews with plant officials.

55 Mica Jovanovic, "'The business of the century': the de-coupling of business and self-management," in *Technology and Labor in the Automotive Industry*, ed. Sung-Jo Park (Frankfurt am Main: Campus, 1991).

56 *Global Motors, Inc.: Managing the Future*, industry brochure.

57 Ibid.

58 Darrell Dawsey, "Trouble for Yugo," *Los Angeles Times* (January 31, 1989), part IV, p. 2.

Chapter 6 Assessing the Prospects for Development under Flexible Production

1 Arnold O. Putnam, "A redesign for engineering," *Harvard Business Review* (May-June 1985).

2 Kim B. Clark, *High Performance Product Development in the World Auto Industry*, Harvard Business School Working Paper, 90-004 (1989).

3 Masahiko Aoki, "Frontiers in corporate globalization," *Japan Echo*, XVII, special issue (1990), pp. 26-32.

4 Ibid.

5 Roger Schreffler, "The future according to Kawamoto," *Automotive Industries* (September 1989), pp. 73-4.

6 K. Clark, op. cit. (1989).

7 "Companies slowly wake to profits of research," *El Financiero International* (November 9, 1992), p. 12.

8 Rebecca Morales and Michael Storper, "*Prospects for Alternative Fuel Vehicle Use and Production in Southern California: Environmental Quality and Economic Development*, Working Paper No. 2, The Lewis Center for Regional Policy Studies, University of California, Los Angeles (May 1991).

9 *Research and Development Consortia Registered Under the National Cooperative Research Act of 1984*, prepared by the Clearinghouse for State and Local Initiatives on Productivity, Technology, and Innovation, Office of Technology Commercialization, Technology Administration, US Dept. of Commerce (December 1992).

10 Ibid, pp. 121, 165, and 167.

11 Ken'Ichi Imai, "Industrial policy and technological innovation," in *Industrial Policy of Japan*, ed. Ryutaro Komiya, Masahiro Okuno, and Kotaro Suzumura (Tokyo: Academic Press, 1988).

12 Ministry of International Trade and Industry and Electric Vehicle Council, *Essentials of the Electric Vehicle Market Expansion Programme in Japan*, (Tokyo: Japan Electric Vehicle Association, 1992), pp. 12-13.

13 Source: correspondence with the Consorzio Bologna Innovazione.

14 *Convergence and Community: The Americas in 1993*, A Report of the Inter-American Dialogue of the Aspen Institute (Washington, DC, 1992).

15 Robert Gilpin, *The New World Political and Economic Order*, paper presented at the Foro Nacional, International Conference on the New International Order, Rio de Janeiro, Brazil (April 13-14, 1992), pp. 28-9.

16 Sylvia Ostry, *The New International Order: The Regionalization Trend*, paper presented at the Foro Nacional, International Conference on the New International Order, Rio de Janeiro, Brazil (April 13-14, 1992).

17 John Zysman, *Technology and Power in a Multi-Polar Global Economy*, BRIE Working Paper (September 1990).

18 "Daimler-Benz to get green light for plant," *Auto Industry*, 10, 111 (1988), p. 3.

19 For a contrary opinion, see Raymond Vernon, *Sovereignty at Bay: The Multinational Spread of US Enterprises* (New York: Basic Books, 1971).

20 Maryann O. Feldman and Zoltan J. Acs, *The Geography of Innovation*, working paper, Department of Economics, University of Baltimore (February 1992).

21 Feldman and Acs, op. cit., (1992); Zoltan J. Acs and David B. Audretsch, "Innovation and firm size: the new learning," *The International Journal of Technology Management*, forthcoming; Zoltan J. Acs and Steven C. Isberg, *Capital Structure, Asset Specificity, and Firm Size: An Empirical Analysis*, working paper, University of Baltimore (October 1991).

Index